CRICKET ALL MY LIFE

GERALD HOWAT

Methuen

First published in Great Britain 2006 by
Methuen Publishing Ltd
11–12 Buckingham Gate
London
SW1E 6LB

10 9 8 7 6 5 4 3 2 1

Copyright © Gerald M.D. Howat 2006

Gerald Howat has asserted his right under the Copyright, Designs and Patents Act 1988 to be identified as the author of this work.

Methuen Publishing Ltd Reg. No. 3543167

A CIP catalogue record for this book is available from the British Library.

ISBN-10: 0413 776247
ISBN-13: 9780413776242

Typeset by SX Composing DTP, Rayleigh, Essex
Printed and bound in Great Britain by MPG Books, Bodmin, Cornwall

This book is sold subject to the condition that it shall not by way of trade or otherwise be lent, resold, hired out, or otherwise circulated without the publishers' prior consent in writing in any form of binding or cover other than that in which it is published and without a similar condition being imposed on the subsequent purchaser.

Contents

Preface and acknowledgements *page* vii
List of illustrations ix
Foreword xi

Part I First Innings

1	A Scottish Upbringing	3
2	At Edinburgh University	17
3	National Service and Caribbean Interlude	23
4	West Country Experience	39
5	Training the Teachers	45

Part II Cricket in Many Guises

6	Cricket in 1791	57
7	W. G. Grace	69
8	Cricket and the Victorian Church	77
9	Cricket and the Victorian Novel	89
10	England v. Australia, 1905	101
11	England v. Australia, Lord's 1930	107
12	A Second Golden Age	113
13	Faded Memories – Essex, 1939	127
14	Cricketers well met	131
15	Three England Captains	139
16	Three Cricket Characters	147
17	Sir Neville Cardus	151
18	E. W. Swanton Remembered	159
19	MCC in Australia, 1903/04	163
20	Letters from Warner & Allen – 1932/33	171
21	The First International, 1844	181
22	Cricket and American Puritanism	185
23	Thomas Hughes' two Rugbys	197
24	Learie Constantine – the first West Indian star	203

| 25 | Bermudan Hero | 207 |
| 26 | Hong Kong Cricket – the Colonial Chapter | 211 |

Part III Second Innings

27	Radley College and Lord Williams's, Thame	221
28	An American University	229
29	Journalist and Author	235
30	In the Press Box	243
31	An English Village	247
32	MCC 1	253
33	MCC 2	257
34	Talking on Cricket – Home and Away	261
35	Post Hoc	265
	Index	269

Preface and acknowledgements

I dedicate this book to two people who strongly urged me to write it. They are David Rayvern Allen, broadcaster and author of the award-winning biography of Jim Swanton (and much else) and Professor Sir Brian Harrison of Oxford University and lately Editor of the *Oxford Dictionary of National Biography*. Without their encouragement my 'last' book really would have been my last!

I may find the composing of a book relatively easy (or, at least, no harder than it ever has been) but the demands of modern technology are taxing. I am grateful to a 'team' in North Moreton, led by Nora Haycock, who included Dean Beedell, Jenny Carpenter, Mandy Claridge, Anne Howat and Jenny Wiseman. David Nobes took responsibility for preparing my photographs and Anne Howat also helped compile the index. Nico Klynsmith of Xacca Solutions (Wallingford) took charge of the technical production of Part II of the book. My thanks are also due to Polly Hancock whose photographic work at Lord's supplied the back cover. I am most grateful to Derek Pringle for writing such a felicitous foreword.

Peter Tummons, managing director of Methuen, my publisher, gave me invaluable help and was always there when I needed him. His colleagues Sam Carter and Alan Little were equally helpful, while Ken Daldry at Lord's helped me in my pursuit of pictures.

The writing of an autobiography, I learnt, caused some emotional strain and there was a point when I was close to wanting to consult my parents, long since dead. I hope I have been not less than considerate to any of the army of relatives, friends, colleagues and acquaintances who have crossed my various paths over nearly eighty years. They span a time from the Great Exhibition of 1851 – when my great-grandmother, whom I just remember, was born – to grandchildren who will stretch out pointers to the twenty-second century.

The arrangement of the book calls for some comment. Part I is my autobiography up till 1968 – the first forty years. Part II is a selection from articles I have written with some original pieces. Part III picks up the autobiography from 1968 to the present day – my second innings.

Chapters 17, 24 and the 'As an entrepreneur' section of chapter 7 are adapted from my Notices in the *Oxford Dictionary of National Biography*, 2004 (with the permission of the Oxford University Press); chapter 7 is adapted from *The MCC Year-Book*, 1998; chapters 8, 20, 22, 26 and the first section of chapter 18 were first published in the *Cricket Society Journal*; chapters 11 and 12 are adapted from *Cricket's Second Golden Age*, 1989; chapter 13 is by permission of the *Essex Guardian* and chapter 25 is adapted from *The Cricketer*, 1995. Photographs 25, 26, 28, 29 and 33 by permission of MCC.

Gerald Howat
North Moreton
September 2006

Illustrations

1. Aged three with my father and two cars.
2. Aged seven – very Scottish.
3. Aged six with my dog.
4. The Lochee Park team, 1943.
5. The Ardvreck team, 1942.
6. Ardvreck School.
7. Trinity College, Glenalmond.
8. Edinburgh University Students' Representative Council.
9. Cricket at Rossie Priory.
10. Kelly College, Tavistock.
11. My father, as Dean of Brechin.
12. My mother.
13. Our marriage in 1951.
14. Tropical cricket.
15. Culham College, Oxfordshire.
16. Michael displays early talent.
17. The Reverend A.H. Winter, Moreton and Middlesex.
18. England v. Australia, Lord's, 1930.
19. W.G. Grace.
20. With Len Hutton.
21. Len Hutton's 364.
22. 50th anniversary of Hutton's 364.
23. J. Darling.
24. F.S. Jackson.
25. L.E.G. Ames.
26. G.O. Allen.
27. With Jack Parsons.
28. W.R. Hammond.
29. E.W. Swanton.
30. In Australia.
31. Jamestown, the 'cradle' of American cricket.

32. Thomas Hughes' 'other' Rugby.
33. Hong Kong pavilion.
34. Learie Constantine.
35. Western Kentucky University.
36. Radley College, Oxfordshire.
37. With David Money.
38. Going out to bat in Kentucky on the Merion ground.
39. Our daughter, Gillian.
40. Our elder son, David, in 1974.
41. Michael gets his Cambridge Blue, at Lord's, in 1977.
42. Our house in North Moreton.
43. The author as an editor, 1973.
44. The church and North Moreton House.
45. With David Rayvern Allen and my wife at Lord's.
46. With Stephen Green, MCC Curator, at Lord's.
47. With Michael on the Kent tour.
48. Moreton CC at home, 1973.
49. Moreton CC in Holland, 1987.
50. Moreton CC, 2002.

Foreword
By Derek Pringle

When most new books on cricket are hastily-cobbled-together accounts of players that have been in the game two minutes, how refreshing to find one with a scope that spans decades and whose subject matter delves well beyond the tawdry obsessions of celebrity culture.

Gerald Howat is no cricketing legend, even within his own family, but the game has been a constant and diverting companion of his for over 60 years. Dealing with cricket's role in Empire building, and busting, to its place in the bucolic idyl of his beloved Moreton, Gerald has played, watched and written about the game with a keen eye and even keener pen.

A schoolmaster by profession, Gerald's own education was at various Scottish schools and Edinburgh University, which provided an ideal template for his writings on the game, if not his playing. That came mostly during his National Service with the RAF, and later in Trinidad, where he accepted a teaching post just as Britain's grip on its colonies was being loosened.

These days the world is a more complex place, though cricket's capacity to absorb the shockwaves of clashing cultures and ideologies, much as in the past, reveals it as a constant in a changing world. As I write, England and Pakistan have just played each other home and away with barely a peep of disquiet from players or fans. Such relations uphold the contention made by Charles Dickens some 170 years earlier: that cricket's most useful property is as 'social cement'.

A wicketkeeper-batsman in the most generous sense (he was still pulling on the gloves well into his seventies), Gerald is better known for his cricket scholarship than his stumpings, at least beyond the Moreton parish boundary. Biographies on those disparate Trinidborn knights, Sir Learie Constantine and Sir Pelham Warner, are among twenty books written over the years, while his journalism for various cricket magazines and the *Daily Telegraph* has tackled varied aspects of the game. Some of his offerings, like the chapter on W.G. Grace, are included here alongside Gerald's treatment of other epochal moments in cricket's 400-year evolution.

Gerald Howat has been indefatigable in his service to Moreton cricket club over forty years, and has held almost every post at the club. Stalwarts exist in other sports, but cricket lends them a bearing that is quite distinct from the mere cut of a blazer. When I made my only appearance there one summer in the mid-1980s, there was never any doubt over who was running the show.

My own connection with Gerald is a slight one. In 1980, I played cricket at Cambridge with his younger son Michael, a genuinely fast bowler albeit one with temperamental radar. That team played nine first-class matches against the counties and failed to prevail in a single one of them. Part of cricket's enduring beauty is that one's enjoyment of it is not result conditional and those times remain a treasured memory.

The memories and incidents contained here summon up an even more distant past and the book is the richer for it. Cricket all your life is a noble and worthy topic to lay upon the page providing you have clocked up the required mileage – something Gerald Howat has most assuredly done.

Part I
First Innings

1
A Scottish Upbringing

We all have a first visual memory. The image may not be genuine but a consequence of looking through the family photograph album. And our childhood memories are sunny ones. The camera, in a pre-digital age, did not lie: it merely made its preferences known.

Among my first memories, when I was two, were those of the airship R 100. My father called me into the garden to see the R 100 on its outward-bound journey to Canada. Records show that it passed over the west of Scotland on the morning of 30 July 1930. When the R 100 returned to Britain it would never fly again. Only three months later, on an ill-conceived flight to India, its sister-ship, the R 101, crashed in France and the whole airship programme of the day was abandoned.

I also recall a less imposing aircraft: a small passenger biplane stationed for a summer or two at the Ayrshire town of Girvan where I lived. My parents made friends with the pilot who, like many an ex-serviceman, was trying to earn a living with the skills he had learned in the First World War. The pilot and his wife lived in a caravan and offered joyrides to the good citizens around. There were brief, if spectacular, flights across the Clyde estuary, over Ailsa Craig, the Isle of Arran and the Mull of Kintyre. In my childhood days Ailsa Craig was a looming presence. This igneous rock, whose micro-granite had once been used to make curling stones, arced in a semi-circle some 1,000 feet above the sea. In those days, a dozen people dwelt there and the boat from Girvan took an hour to get to their jetty.

While I could not quite see the Atlantic from my bedroom window, I can recall the ocean gales buffeting against it, together with happier recollections of days on the long sandy beach which made Girvan an attractive town for tourists long before Scots dreamed of package tours abroad. Girvan could not vie with Scots resorts such as Helensburgh, but its long line of Victorian houses facing seawards still testifies to the modest holiday trade it once enjoyed.

In 1933 it was time to go to school. It was customary for a child of the Manse or Rectory to go to the local elementary school. I, for some reason or other, went to St Joseph's Convent, a Roman Catholic Community which cared for the sick and the poor as well as providing both primary and secondary education. The school won Government recognition and many senior pupils went on to St Andrews University. My father was the local Episcopalian (Anglican) incumbent and I must have been the only Protestant in the school. My recollections of my earliest school years are few but include breaking a window while throwing marbles and being taken to the local cinema to see a moving film for the first time. I was also given as a prize for history a book called *On the Sands*. When we were about to move to Dundee in 1935, I trudged along the seafront and the 150 yards up to our home in tears. I was sad to leave, and even sadder to say goodbye to our dog, Peter, who was too old to make the move. I offered to stay behind with him in Girvan but my parents spurned the suggestion. Peter found a good home with Bob Laing, our old gardener. As a young man, Bob drove a coach-and-four down to Stranraer with passengers bound for the Larne ferry.

It may seem far-fetched to trace a connection between the best-selling novelist Rosamund Pilcher and me. Let me explain. If anyone is to take credit for the course much of my life would follow, let it be Graham Pilcher, a family friend. As a young man he had been in the 1st XI at Clifton and one day he took me, an eight-year-old, to watch him play for Forfarshire on the county ground at Forthill. Forfarshire was the old county name, still borne by the cricketers, of what had become the Scottish county of Angus – in the Mearns on the east coast of Scotland, near Dundee. A year or two later he took me to the North Inch, in Perth, where Forfarshire were playing Perthshire in the County Championship. The latter were unbeaten while Forfarshire were low in the table. The drama, as the Dundee *Courier* reported, unfolded on a sultry afternoon before a crowd of 4,000. Forfarshire had been dismissed for 97, my 'hero' sadly making nought. But Perthshire's batting 'was a nervy, uninspired crawl' and, against all expectations, Forfarshire won by 8 runs. Back at Graham Pilcher's house, I saw for the first time the yellow covers of *Wisden*, which offered me glances of, as yet, an uncomprehended world of cricket. Soon afterwards, war would break out and the cricketers of Brechin, Montrose, Luncarty, Balruddery, Cowdenbeath and Freuchie were called to sterner tasks. Freuchie would also challenge the might of English village cricket and win the national knockout competition at Lord's fifty years later. I asked one of the umpires of that game how they had achieved it. He replied, 'By their fielding and catching'. They had come to Lord's and conquered, with their kilts and pipes. From those visits, in the mid-1930s, I became enslaved to the game of cricket. It would, in due course, take me to Australia, South Africa and the West Indies and would lead me to take the chair in the Committee Room at Lord's, besides playing for the Marylebone Cricket Club (MCC). Friendships would blossom and doors would be opened to me as a writer and cricket journalist.

I was to return to Dundee in 1980 as guest speaker at the centenary of Forfarshire Cricket Club. Afterwards, I spoke to some members of the 1930s side and the toastmaster was kind enough to call me 'the Viv Richards of the whole occasion'!

The story is told, many years later, that I came home one day to tell my family that I had seen two books in an Oxford shop that I had written. 'One was next to a book by Don Bradman and the other next to one by Christopher Hill,' I told them. 'If you had been as great a cricketer as Bradman and as distinguished an historian as Hill you would have been one of the greatest men of our time,' remarked my elder son. 'Unfortunately,' commented his younger brother, 'you batted like Hill and wrote history like Bradman.' The quick riposte was clever, not unkind and I had to own that there was a grain of truth therein.

As for Rosamund Pilcher, I established the connection some sixty years later when Graham was at my mother's funeral. 'I don't think you've met my wife, Rosamund . . .'

So cricket it became. This book is as much an autobiography as a series of snapshots on how the game has touched me over seventy years. Inspired by that introduction to cricket at Forthill, I took up cricket in Dundee. My father was by then the incumbent of a large parish in Lochee, a working-class district of the city. We were often erroneously called 'the English church' and the fact that we were seen playing cricket in the garden on Sundays helped to endorse that impression among God-fearing Presbyterians. These were the days of the Depression, and Dundee was badly hit by its impact. The city could no longer compete against the low production costs of Calcutta, and men were laid off in droves. My father's parishioners included the jute magnates – some of whom had a spell in India (at the source of the raw material) – and the workers in the factories. Many of these were women, and his parish visiting would be to unemployed men in the afternoon and to their wives in the evening. They lived in poor tenement houses with scant accommodation and little privacy, and with an outside 'privy' shared by several families. They would look over from their four- or five-storied homes to the garden where we played our cricket. Yet, in Dundee itself, it was a world of contrasts. For wealth was represented by the jute magnates and those who had been adventurous enough to go out to India for a spell. They came home and bought their houses in the fashionable end of the city.

Lochee boasted the finest and newest tramcars in the city. Resplendent in their livery of green, gold and cream, they made their way up Reform Street through the mean streets of Lochee to the terminus at the end of the town. Yet older, smaller, less well-appointed cars served the fashionable Blackness Road, which carved a way through the city to Downfield in the north. Lochee's new trams had originally been destined for the Blackness route but were too wide to get through some of the narrower streets and so, with some reluctance, the city fathers had let them go to Lochee. New or not so new, all trams were noisy but I enjoyed the comfort and security of their familiar jingles and cacophony as I lay in bed.

Depending on the time of year, another recollection was of a man with a long pole lighting the gaslight outside my window by igniting its taper. It was a scene immortalised by Robert Louis Stephenson's 'The Lamplighter'.

From trams to trains: in those carefree days, so far as rules and regulations were concerned, I was often allowed in the guard's van or the engine of the local train that passed the bottom of our garden on its way from Dundee West to Blairgowrie, and I spent many happy hours in the local signal-box.

The cricket season began in April and, for larger occasions, we would use the nearby Lochee Park. Until 1939 it was fenced in and we had to leave when the 'parkie' ordered us out. When war came, all the railings were commandeered for the war-effort and the 'parkie' – an old man with a limp – was unable to exercise much control. We played, in those long, northern summer evenings of double summertime, until well after ten o'clock.

I had, in the meantime, attended Dundee High School, of which I have scanty but happy memories. A staff all in gowns presented rather an awesome impression to a seven-year-old. Miss Bain, tall with a mass of black hair in a bun, was superficially forbidding but, in fact, quite kind. It was scarcely her fault that for some months I had a recurring dream of her pursuing me over a cliff.

But, in the context of the times (though it was my mother's wish rather than my father's) I was sent away, one May, to a preparatory school as a boarder. I had exchanged the Irish accent bequeathed me by the good sisters of Girvan for a Scots one from Dundee. At Ardvreck I would learn to speak the 'Received Pronunciation' which has been with me ever since. Ardvreck, set in attractive grounds, was in Crieff in Perthshire. Only recently did I discover that my fees were paid by Arthur Cox, a parishioner and doyen of the jute magnates, whose name is on the chimney that still dominates the Dundee skyline.

I know I would rather have gone to the Harris Academy, and I would wistfully watch the bus go past our gate (my holidays were longer) though I suspect one particular girl who went to the Academy was the major reason for my envy.

My prep school, led by David Smythe who had been in the Cambridge XI before 1914, introduced me to a more sophisticated game. We had caps, and wore whites and brown studded boots. Cricket was played every afternoon and our imaginative headmaster would organise internal matches giving us the names of famous players of the day. Once I was Hutton and, on another occasion, Hammond. Little could I know that I would one day write their biographies. Internal matches were a consequence of the scourge of epidemics in those days. A boy had only to get measles for the whole school to be put in quarantine and all contact with other schools, including of course matches, was cancelled. However, one summer during the Second World War, a Kent regiment was posted nearby and the headmaster arranged for us to play them at cricket. Their captain was B. H. Valentine, of Kent and England. After the match, David Smythe asked me to supper with the great man. Smythe knew his boys! Cricket, in that polished atmosphere, continued until the end of July.

As for what I learnt at that school . . . I recall Latin taught by a master who numbered our test-questions from the day he had first joined the staff, so No. 9,466 might be the next question that morning. Greek we learnt from a bishop's daughter not much older than ourselves, whose charms we would compare with those of the art mistress. History was Smythe's own forte. Somehow, he got us through the Common Entrance Examination (to the public schools) on a surfeit of First World War stories, and John Buchan tales on Sunday evenings. One night Smythe woke up the whole school. 'Look at Glasgow burning – fifty miles away – you'll remember the sight all your lives. That is what modern warfare is.'

When I went home I resumed 'command' of the cricket in Lochee park. In retrospect, two things amaze me: that the primitive games I set up in April lasted in the summer without me, and that I would keep in contact by post, sending back team-sheets and other material, running the game by remote control and drawing on the experiences I was acquiring at a higher and more cultured level.

The lesson – and it was one for life – was that I could move easily across the social 'divide'; a divide far more evident in those days than in later decades. In political terms it made me aware of the poverty and desolation of the 1930s.

There is a codicil. Not many years ago, I thought of a reunion of those youngsters I had known in Dundee. A very happy lunch party took place in a city hotel, and those who had been brought up in slender circumstances had all attained a comfortable prosperity. My fears about returning to them with a sense of self-imposed grandeur proved groundless. And their tributes to my father in helping them to personal fulfilment and achievement were manifest and touching. 'He gave us our chance, spotted our potential and got us to St Andrews University,' said a former pupil of Harris Academy, now a gracious lady in her seventies.

One memory of 1939 is a stark one. We had chosen the north coast of Cornwall for our holiday and a man drowned before our eyes in Widemouth Bay. Attempts by my father and others to save him proved fruitless because – although he was brought to shore – he had died of a heart attack. A few days later we beat a hasty retreat from Cornwall with the desire of the homing bird – to get back to Dundee before war broke out.

We stayed with friends for the night of Friday, 1 September at Colwall in Worcestershire. I wandered off after tea, only to come upon the women cricketers of England playing in their annual Festival. Here were the ladies who had played for England against Australia two years earlier, such as Betty Archdale, Myrtle MacLagan and Molly Hide, and some of them found the time to speak to me. I may well have been the only small boy watching. The next day we were on the road to Scotland, passing the many cars returning from Dundee where the annual British Association conference had been cancelled. Pursuing a parallel course to us, that same weekend, was the Yorkshire team travelling home to Leeds. One of the finest county teams of all time had just played together for the last time. Of that XI, Hedley Verity would die of wounds received in action and Bill Bowes would languish in a POW camp. Back in Dundee, on Sunday, 3 September we listened to Neville Chamberlain's fateful announcement.

P. G. Wodehouse wrote that the three essentials for an

autobiography were that 'its compiler should have had an eccentric father, a miserable, misunderstood childhood and a hell of a time at his public school.' Apart from the fact that Wodehouse promptly denied that any of these 'assets' applied to him, a very large proportion of the population – those who did not go to a public school – were, according to his dicta, disqualified.

My father was not eccentric and there will be more about him in a moment. My childhood, despite the incursions of the Second World War, was contented enough and my public school, if not the experience of 'unbroken bliss' which Wodehouse enjoyed, was (in those days) rather a dull institution.

Let me say at once that my father would not have fitted the accepted pattern of many an Anglican parson today. He was always formally dressed in conventional clerical grey. He wore an 'Anthony Eden' hat, was a stickler for punctuality, and worked himself and his curates extremely hard. He had been through the whole of the First World War, was wounded in the Battle of Passchendaele in 1917 and was an unlikely 'recruit' to the band of ordinands whom 'Tubby' Clayton, founder of the Toc H movement, secured for the Church of England. They were, collectively, what we would call 'men's men' and they had faced life at its rawest. Father served at Wigan Parish Church under the Reverend Cuthbert Thicknesse. In the 1990s I would meet, from time to time, Thicknesse's son – a fellow cricket correspondent.

It was difficult to get my father to talk about the war. One day, in the 1990s, I got off a train at Wigan, on an impulse, and made my way to Wigan Parish Church. Outside there stands a vast memorial to the men of the King's Liverpool Regiment killed in the war – my father's comrades. He must have seen those familiar names over and over again in the early 1920s. He never told me. His superior, Thicknesse, became, in due course, a Dean; so too did my father. He was no games player but I found an old newspaper cutting of him batting at Wigan for the clergy. And, in his Dundee days, he would play football for the church against the butchers. He died comparatively young: a combination of four years in the trenches, too much driving and too little walking, and his generation's habit of smoking too many cigarettes. One of his obituaries paid tribute to him as 'an accomplished ecclesiastic, an expert in educational matters and deeply versed in the history and ethos of the church'. He found time to be a journalist, editing a church weekly paper in a businesslike manner. He would be in the office, by Dundee docks, four mornings a week. I was sometimes given 'copy' to be taken to the lino-typists and admired their speed on machines which had a triple set of keys in three different colours. Later on, I might be given some proofreading and, when at Edinburgh University, was twice asked to report a Conference and 'file' my copy.

What my father brought to that drab community, who either trudged long hours in the mills or wasted away unemployed in their poverty-stricken homes, was a sense of colour and light. What his church 'offered' was moderate Anglo-Catholic worship, a robed choir (of both sexes), youth clubs and a Boys' Brigade Annual Camp. 'I want to see you in church *less*,' he said to a young woman fast becoming a religious maniac and finding in St Margaret's church a haven from an over-crowded home lacking comfort and sanitation. Not everything went smoothly. My father had asked one of his curates to take a wedding and a frantic call came though to his office. 'Someone in the congregation has challenged the "any just cause or impediment" bit,' he was told. 'Can you come quickly?' It turned out that the sailor intent on marrying a Lochee girl already had a wife in Portsmouth. Perhaps the documentation had not been checked as thoroughly as it might have been.

After two years at Wigan Parish Church my father sought his Scottish roots and headed north to the Anglican Cathedral in Edinburgh, where he became the precentor in charge of the music. There he met my mother and they were married in the Cathedral. Her background was much more sheltered. While he was at war, she was a girl at the Abbey School, Malvern Wells. If we must talk 'class', he was a peg below her, through his mother's ancestry rather than his father's. His father had been a Victorian actor-manager, a man of some brilliance (so I was led to believe) who was knocked over by a hansom cab and killed when drunk (so I was told). *His* father had been a Presbyterian minister of the deepest dye and a scholar, and he thundered against the playing of cricket on the Sabbath. There is a surviving picture of him and the resemblance to me is striking. What he would have made of my lifetime of cricket on a Sunday afternoon is beyond comprehension. It was on his mother's side that my father's social background would have been perceived as 'lower-middle class'. She, good lady, was the daughter of the landlord of Everton Coffee House – on which slender grounds I support Everton Football Club today. She was left a widow at thirty-one and took a local curate in as a lodger. He meant to stay a few weeks and did so for nearly forty years. Canon Barrett was an Anglo-Catholic priest who was like a grandfather to me. He had a formative influence on both my father and myself and had played cricket with W. G. Grace in Gloucestershire in the 1890s. He batted with the left foot pointed to the bowler, in the fashion of Grace, and he would bowl to me in his vicarage garden. When he was offered a living in Liverpool with a very large vicarage he invited my great-grandmother, my grandmother, her sister and two boys to come and fill it. It was a happy if unusual ménage.

My mother's father was Selwyn Cooke, a clergyman and an intellectual. I found a scrap of correspondence between him and the Archbishop of Canterbury on the finer points of a Greek New Testament passage. It was dialogue gravely entered into at the height (or depth) of the Battle of the Somme in 1916. My mother came of a long line of Edinburgh lawyers, styled 'Writers to the Signet'. The war only touched her in an oblique way. From infected milk, she (and several others) got tubercular hips. She spent a year in bed and was lame for the rest of her life. She wrote a great deal and taught me 'to judge the market you are writing for'. She was a regular contributor to monthly and weekly journals and was the author of two books, one a scholarly biography of Queen Margaret of Scotland. She was a fierce royalist and a firm believer in the virtues of Charles I. When, in my own book on seventeenth-century foreign policy, I mooted the idea that Cromwell was the greatest Englishman of his age, she allegedly never read another word of the book. But she read others I wrote and taught me much about journalism. I admired the determination she brought to her job as literary editor of a London publisher, after she was widowed in 1957 at the age of fifty-one. Both my parents lived on the fringes of the world of journalism and would receive regular requests from the Dundee *Courier* for comments on some event. In particular, my father was friendly with that great Scottish journalist, James Cameron, working at that time for Thomson Publications. I grew up, therefore, in an atmosphere of letters and an awareness of the more immediate demands of journalism.

My childhood did not fit Wodehouse's aphorism. I had left Ardvreck as head boy and a member of the cricket and rugby football teams, and won a bursary to Glenalmond College a few miles east of Crieff. Glenalmond had been founded largely through the efforts of W. E. Gladstone – future prime minister but at that time a young, rising politician. His intention was to create a school for the sons of Episcopalian families and, in the original scheme, to establish a theological college for them as well. The school opened at a time of middle-class expansion when many similar establishments, not least Radley College, were also founded. Charles Wordsworth was the first warden (or headmaster) of Glenalmond. He was related to the poet, though his Cricket Blue from the very first Varsity match was more likely to endear him to the boys.

Glenalmond, during the war, took the Corps very seriously. Originally styled the Officers' Training Corps, it was renamed, in more egalitarian style, the Combined Cadet Force. I knew, at fifteen, how to kill a man with a bayonet. Indeed, my RAF Officer Cadet Training Unit (OCTU) some years later was a much more relaxed affair. Some Old Boy, in fiendish mood, had presented a Cup for drill which we competed for night after night when it would have been far more fun to play cricket. But I have a memory of a very exciting House Final in which I, as the wicketkeeper, went in needing 3 to win. I managed to get 2 of them and so we tied. My house captain was the nicest of seniors who later made his life as a medical professor in America. In the 1990s we met up again when he was over for a reunion of medical graduates which included my wife.

The school strove valiantly and successfully to feed us during these war years and somehow we managed to get to Edinburgh to play matches. Fuel was saved by cycling to the station at Perth, with our cricket kit on our backs. In my last summer, Learie Constantine, the West Indian cricketer, brought H. B. Rowan's XI to play us and there began for me an association which would have a pivotal effect on my later years as a writer. I played some cricket in the holidays at Meigle and Brechin, on one occasion with my old mentor, Graham Pilcher, and on another with my cousin, James Drummond-Hay – the only time I ever saw him in trousers! He habitually wore a kilt which suited well his great height and well-built frame. His brother, Andrew, died of wounds in the war and, as the senior available male relative, I led the funeral mourning in a Highland setting.

I duly took my School Certificate and discovered it was sufficiently distinguished to get me straight into a Scottish University. Various factors came together: I was ready to 'move on', I was conscious that those just a year older than I had gone to the war – and not all had survived. But in making the decision I deprived myself of a year in the Upper VIth and probably a place in the cricket XI. I have warm memories of 'Ben' Gunnery who taught me history in the Lower VIth. He was a stimulating teacher who had spent the previous three or four years serving in the war; he confessed that he had forgotten his history but he knew where to look it up and we benefited greatly from him. Some years later he became a headmaster in India. One tale needs to be told (and possibly two).

In 1973 I was asked to write the Centenary History of the Oxford and Cambridge Schools' Examination Board. I recalled having being told by my Maths master, James Rossiter, when I sat the examination myself, 'You need 72 per cent in your third paper to get the necessary credit.' I did so, with a mark to spare. Finding no record of schools having marked papers before sending them off, I wrote to the warden of my day – long since retired. He replied, 'I daresay it's all right to say so now – we marked the papers ourselves in case they were lost by enemy action.' How 'necessary' my 72 per cent was belongs to the other tale. Without it, I would not have had the necessary matriculation and so would not have met my future wife at Edinburgh.

The qualifications for Edinburgh were one thing; actual

acceptance was quite another. Ex-servicemen and women received 90 per cent of the University places, 8 per cent went to schoolgirls and the final 2 per cent to schoolboys such as myself. As late as October – only days before term began – Edinburgh offered me a place. A major chapter in my life was about to begin.

2
At Edinburgh University

To enter a University, straight from school at the end of the war, was to be propelled into a strangely adult and mature environment. There were colonels and privates, squadron-leaders and aircraftmen sitting cheek by jowl with ex-servicewomen and boys and girls just turned eighteen. One would see some of them in uniform and occasionally spot a DSO or DFC ribbon. The work ethic was strong and hardly anyone fell by the wayside.

One entered the portals of a Scottish University in a manner which had changed little over the centuries, queuing to become a matriculated member and paying in cash to obtain the card of admission to each particular class.

The present generation will boggle at the thought that it cost me just under £20 for a year's study. With my cards correct, I presented myself to the classes in Latin and English taught by Professors Richmond and Renwick respectively. It was the Scottish tradition that the professor taught the first-year students. Large as such classes might be, we sat metaphorically at the feet of great men. In the Latin class, Professor Richmond would invite us over the weekend to turn the leading article in that day's *Scotsman* into Latin prose and present it to him on Tuesday. It was a tough, if fascinating, ordeal.

Edinburgh University, the only post-Reformation foundation of the four historic Universities of Scotland, gave me a great deal. I acquired a wife, a degree, administrative experience and a lot of friends. I met Anne Murdoch at a Church Youth Club and that, effectively, was that. We would be married four years later. I did sufficient work to get a good Second Class Honours degree which was not remote from a First and I was well satisfied. My sense of organising things and people, which had found expression in those days at Dundee not so long ago, was reflected in my election to the Students' Representative Council, subsequently to its Executive Council, and as its press officer and then its assistant secretary. No doubt we took ourselves too seriously, but a lot of good work was done raising money for charity and, in the tentative post-war years, establishing contacts with our fellow-students in what had been occupied Europe. A trip to the Netherlands gave me my only experience of what it was like to go hungry. We had hard brown bread each meal of the day. I also recall the bitter divisions which existed between those who had taken part in the Resistance and so put themselves years back in their careers and those who had just got on with their studies.

Being a member of the SRC brought some 'perks'. We were invited to a Ball in the Scottish Assembly Rooms when the Duke and Duchess of Edinburgh visited the University, and to a Reception to meet the actor, Alastair Sim, who had been elected Rector of the University.

One office which did not come my way was the editorship of the *Student*, partly because Anne voted against me. It was really just as well, as previous post-war incumbents had all failed to graduate, but I was able to keep my literary and journalistic prospects in trim by writing numerous articles, including one to encourage recruitment to the University Air Squadron. I was taken up in a Tiger Moth over the Forth Bridge and 'invited' to experience looping the loop. 'Don't hold on,' said the pilot, 'don't shut your eyes and let the plane take hold of you.' I still recall the sensation when I was momentarily ejected from my seat as the force of gravity took over.

The University Debating Society also claimed my allegiance and I had some interesting trips around the British Isles. I recollect going to speak at University College, Cardiff and finding, to my horror, that I had put my speech in a letterbox in place of the card I had intended to send to someone. It was Celt against Celt for the lively Welsh audience.

I had originally intended to read Law but the prospect of spending all my life in Scotland in the family firm of J. and F. Anderson did not appeal and, after four terms, I switched to History and managed to complete the four-year degree without loss of time. Those who taught me History at Edinburgh were memorable figures. I learnt my Scottish History from Gordon Donaldson, historiographer-royal for Scotland, whose expertise lay in palaeography and who was a fierce publicist of Scottish affairs. A lecture which began with the terse utterance, 'Spottiswoode asserts . . .' was not for the faint-hearted. I kept in touch with him right up until his death in 1993. Richard Pares was the most distinguished of all the long line of Regius professors of History at Edinburgh. He had spent the Second World War as a temporary civil servant making recommendations to Government on priorities in industrial production. When the war was over the Prime Minister, Clement Attlee, urged him to enter Parliament and offered him a place in his administration, but a crippling form of paralysis was already showing its symptoms and he accepted the Chair at Edinburgh instead. Three personal memories come to mind. I had put together rather carelessly an essay on George III (to the leading expert in the field, as Pares was) and received the stinging (and deserved) rebuke: 'This is not only bad but impertinent.' Secondly, an invitation from me to speak at our History Department dinner brought the reply from him, 'I am much flattered by your invitation and I should like to accept,' and he did so. Thirdly, I wrote in *The Times* when he died in 1958, 'He made a tremendous impact on the immediate post-war generation of undergraduates by the brilliance and depth of his teaching and by the importance he attached to tutorial work. He was always concerned that his pupils should comprehend the actions and reactions of the varying social groups in a given century.' One of my contemporaries at Edinburgh, (Sir) Kenneth Scott, wrote: 'This bland and brilliant Oxford don has no wish to go South again and is content to remain in this beautiful city [Edinburgh].' In the end, circumstances forced Pares south and my last sight of him was giving the Ford lectures in Oxford from a wheelchair.

Finally, there was E. W. M. Balfour-Melville who taught Constitutional History and gave me a First therein. His cousin, Leslie, had been one of Scotland's greatest cricketers. A shy bachelor, no woman was ever encouraged to join his specialist research class on the relations between England and Scotland up to 1707 until a red-head among our number breached that male bastion.

Cricket played comparatively little part in my University life. For leisure I ran with the University Hares and Hounds, paying a rare visit to Glasgow where I had been born. I think three factors militated against cricket. It took up a lot of time, it was expensive (travelling to matches) and certainly a part of me had had enough after a daily diet of organised games over eight years at school. I did make 76 runs at Fettes College, in what proved to be my best ever score. I would always keep wicket far better than I batted. There were, however, matches for the Scottish Wayfarers – an old boys' club for the Scottish public schools – and a tour to Perthshire including a match on the lovely ground at Rossie Priory, and one to the south of England which lingers in the memory – not so much for the cricket (though I opened the batting against Eton College and hit two fours) as for the transport we used. I was pillion on a motorbike on the four-day journey there and back. On the return we camped somewhere near Nottingham. When I awoke in the morning, I saw a Dundee bus. My friends ridiculed the idea and I was only vindicated when I got back to Dundee and was informed that some new buses had, indeed, come up from London.

Finally, Edinburgh gave me a host of friends. It was John Hart, future Rugby International and Commonwealth Games hurdler, who suggested that 'we' tried to get Commissions in the Education Branch of the RAF. National Service loomed large for those two per cent who were men from school. John Hart successfully pioneered the route for the rest of us. After an interview at the Air Ministry buildings in Kingsway, London, he was accepted in 1949 and in the following year I followed him. David Millar would do so in 1951 and so a steady round of Edinburgh Arts graduates would present themselves as RAF Officers.

During the long vacation of 1948 I went up to London for the Second Test between England and Australia, seeing (in the proverbial, if rather meaningless, phrase) every ball bowled. Certainly, I saw Don Bradman make 38 and 89, and it was the first time I saw Len Hutton. The Australians also played Surrey at the Oval. Surrey were dismissed before tea and Bradman and Hassett came together. Their partnership for the second wicket would reach 231 on the following morning, each man making a hundred. But I was denied seeing Bradman make his century before stumps were drawn on the first evening. Anne Murdoch, by now my fiancée, was taking me to meet her father (a widower) for the first time and his housekeeper was a stickler for punctuality – we could not be late. It was a story I related to Sir Donald himself when he accorded me an interview in 1985 at Adelaide. The great man appreciated the tale.

On 7 July 1950 I graduated and twelve days later substituted cap and gown for the lowly rank of Aircraftman Second Class and the parade ground at Padgate. My Scottish upbringing was over and square-bashing had begun.

Something of the background to my selection as an officer may be of interest some fifty years later. I was summoned to a 'Wosbe' (War Office Selection Board). 'Wosbe' was no picnic but, in the 1950s, class and social attitudes were still strong. I have no doubt that the combined factors of a spell in the school cadet force, a university degree, a 'good' school and an educated voice all eased my path. One thing I was on course to fail was the Intelligence Test. 'Got a degree?' asked the NCO conducting it. I replied that I was about to get one. 'Just as well,' was his comment. 'Graduates don't need to do this test. You weren't going to pass it, were you?'

Padgate, where I reported for initial training, was first base for all national servicemen entering the RAF. My fiancée saw me off from Euston. It was hardly going to 'the front', taking the train to Lancashire, but there were plenty of tears from girlfriends as we steamed out. At Padgate, transport took us to the billet, we had a meal and then (surprisingly) I recall some of us had a makeshift game of cricket. Again, my background helped me to adjust. Boarding school was not so very far behind me and we bedded down for the night in the Nissen hut. Next day came the issue of kit and, as I recall, some idleness, not to say boredom. Boredom, for many, would be the essence of their national service. I was lucky to be one of the 9,000 commissioned in the RAF out of 300,000 national servicemen recruited in the Air Force, under the legislation which governed the programme from 1947 to the discharge of the last man in 1963.

3
National Service and Caribbean Interlude

'Don't you salute your CO in the morning?' was the gruff question as I went to breakfast in the Mess as a very-newly commissioned pilot officer. The CO noted my appearance rather than my name and said no more. Between then – in October – and my graduating from Edinburgh in July a great deal had happened.

I had spent a week at the basic training ground at Padgate and then made a tedious journey in full kit, including greatcoat, via Manchester to Grantham in Lincolnshire. There was a Test match going on at Old Trafford and the mild temptation to go AWOL.

The Officer Cadet Training Unit (OCTU) at RAF Spitalgate, near Grantham, was divided into two parts. For the first half we lived the life of airmen and went through a rather tougher version of the Padgate programme. The physical aspects were still less demanding than they had been in the Corps at Glenalmond five years earlier. For the second half we lived in the Officers' Mess. We had a room between two (my colleague was a regular NCO who had been selected for a commission) and we learnt how to behave at Mess Nights. At dinner we would wear, somewhat incongruously, a formal black bowtie with our battledress. The Services were keen to revive pre-war customs and we were taught who to introduce to whom – a Naval captain's wife would be informed first of the name of a Wing Commander's wife whom she was meeting. If the ladies' husbands were of equal rank, the senior service would take precedence. The RAF was the junior service of the three.

My diary becomes the custodian of my time. To my great surprise, it told me we had a weekend's leave, after only one week of our OCTU. I went to London and saw Clyde Walcott make a century for the West Indies against Surrey at the Oval and I went to a show with Anne.

I must have sent for my kit because back at RAF Spitalgate there was some cricket to play in the unit. To my great surprise I find that my batting average was 34.37 and I kept wicket for our Course team in fixtures against the Course above us. We were all on parade for Battle of Britain Day in Lincoln Cathedral and we were the first Course in which all cadets were successful. I did a 'deal' with a very senior Warrant Officer who was being commissioned. I helped him prepare his obligatory lectures on current affairs and he helped me with my drill. National Service Officers were entitled to wear Warrant Officers' overcoats and he gave me his – which remains, to this day, the only overcoat I have ever possessed.

John Hart, who had led the 'flight' of Edinburgh graduates into the RAF, was my guest at our final dining-out night and Anne returned from working in a psychiatric hospital in the Isle of Man for the passing-out ceremony.

Then came a month as an Officer under Instruction at Wellsbourne Mountford, near Stratford-upon-Avon, and my encounter with the Group Captain before breakfast. We all had to do a turn as Orderly Officer and mine fell on the second Sunday there. Early in the morning I heard the sound of a plane in trouble; a civilian aircraft was attempting an emergency landing. I grabbed my fistful of 'OCTU' Notes and went into action, including calling out the fire tender. Later that day I was 'up' before the Commanding Officer again. 'I seem to see a lot of you, young man,' he said. 'Well done!' I like to think it may have played a part in my being excused all the passing-out examinations on the Course. I had gone for a weekend to my godmother's at Moreton-in-the Marsh and been taken ill. Perhaps her husband's rank as Lord Lieutenant of the County had something to with it, for he phoned the CO and said I was far too ill to go back to work. I was awarded an *aegrotat* Pass and duly awaited my posting to a unit.

'Got just the posting for you, sir,' said the Orderly Room NCO, 'Titchfield, little village in Hampshire, historic place for cricket. You'll like it there.' And if ever a posting were made in heaven, this was it.

After a week's leave at home in Scotland, I reported to the adjutant to learn my duties. 'You'll be Education Officer with responsibility for the units here at Titchfield and at Southampton Docks, Salisbury, Bournemouth and Portsmouth. There'll be a bit of travelling. I hope you've got a car.' Anne and I had bought a Ford 8 for which we paid £75 each and this would be my faithful steed. I found that I was responsible for the intellectual guidance of officers doing Staff College examinations, teaching airmen working for Education Tests, giving current affairs lectures and the supervision and arrangements of civilian evening classes for all ranks to attend. I learned, some years later, that I had been specially selected for the posting – but whether on grounds of cricket or administrative ability I never discovered.

Such a free-ranging 'brief' enabled me to co-ordinate my summer programme with Hampshire's home fixtures at its three county grounds. Memories include seeing the bowling of Derek Shackleton and Vic Cannings, who took over two hundred wickets between them that season. The match at the United Services' ground at Portsmouth produced a thrilling finish, with Hampshire reaching their winning target of 175 against Lancashire in the last moments of extra time. That day ended, I recall, with dinner on an aircraft carrier with Graeme Rowan-Thomson, a Lieutenant, RN, who would be my best man a few months later.

RAF Titchfield had various lodger units including RAF (Middle East) Base Accounts and the Air Ministry Constabulary Training Courses. Men who had achieved wartime commissions found themselves again reduced to the ranks while they trained there. We were also the regional headquarters for the RAF Police, one of whose number, Harry Taswell, would play a lot of cricket with me, go on to be a Wing Commander, remain a friend over the years and be of some assistance to me in over a court martial at Titchfield. Another cricketer of those days was John Curtiss who would become an Air Marshal and play a key role in the Falklands War.

The court martial came about when a civilian steward came to me in my role as Mess secretary to confide that his civilian staff were being threatened with dismissal if they disclosed that a senior officer was disposing of stock from the officers' mess. In due course my own reporting of the facts led to a court martial. By that time I was far away in Trinidad, an officer on the reserve, and my evidence was given to a retired Air-Vice Marshal who lived in the colony.

On another occasion I was required to act as prisoner's friend to an officer (of equal rank) accused of fraud. The court martial was in London and after the trial we went our separate ways. I changed into civilian clothes in the cells and spent the rest of the day at Lord's.

A copy of the Part II Orders for the Day outlines a long programme for a cricket match for the King's Birthday in 1951. By then I had been appointed sports officer as well. A few extracts from it give the flavour of the occasion:

1015 hrs   Leading Aircraftmen draw equipment from Stores.
1100 hrs   Opposition arrive.
1300 hrs   Lunches in Officers' and NCOs' Messes, Corporals' Club and Airmen's Mess.
1600 hrs   NAAFI Manageress supervises crockery and teas to the ground.

It was village cricket, 'service-style'. On my faded copy someone had written 'casual evening meal for airmen'. It was a long and happy day and, I have to add, I was the right man in the right job to organise it.

About forty years later I reported the match at Lord's between the Combined Services and the Public Schools. 'Remember to call all the Generals "sir",' said my wife as I left. But my seniority in age produced the reverse result while there was a relaxed attitude to rank among the players themselves.

One night in the Mess I overhead the local GP lamenting the lack of assistance in his practice. 'No time for sailing,' he murmured to my CO. This was no time, either, for hesitation and next morning I confessed I had overheard the conversation. 'My fiancée hopes to qualify next month, sir, and she'll be looking for a job.' I was dispatched to Netley, a few miles to the south on the Solent, and sought Dr Turner in his surgery. 'Ring her up tonight. She can work for me.' Brushing aside the prospect of her failing her finals at Edinburgh, I informed Anne of the news.

So it was that a month later we were married on 7 August 1951 at Battersea Parish Church by my father, and began married life in a flat made out of a billiard room in Fountains Park – itself built of stones from the dissolved Abbey at Netley. My wife is entirely Scottish. Her father had been a major in the First World War in the Black Watch while her paternal grandfather (born in 1836, a Hanoverian), in the tradition of many Scots, had made his way to India and Australia where he built railways. Further back direct ancestors had been successive lord provosts (mayors) of Glasgow in the burgeoning eighteenth century. Her mother, May Wilson, came of more humble stock – the daughter of a factor on an estate on the Scottish borders and of his wife, who had come, as a housemaid, from the Highlands. Yet some of their children, including Anne's mother, secured entrance to Edinburgh University. It was not such an unusual achievement in the Scottish Universities of the late nineteenth and early twentieth centuries, but was virtually unthinkable, especially for women, for their English counterparts. Anne would, in due course, follow both her parents as a graduate of Edinburgh University.

So, only days after graduation, Anne began working in the practice and Dr Turner went off sailing. 'If anyone sniffles, put them to bed till I get back,' was his parting shot. These were the days of polio scares and so it was quite feasible that he would return to find a large proportion of the villagers bed-bound. Today's young doctors serve a more regulated apprenticeship, with house-jobs, internships and GP training.

Titchfield did not boast any aircraft and one went to nearby Hamble to fly. I would go regularly in a Tiger Moth, a biplane of great versatility. I had, as we saw in the last chapter, first experienced one in a 'publicity stunt' at Edinburgh University. Here was more routine flying, though my pilot would let me have the controls when safely airborne. But it was not for me to put the plane into a spin or loop the loop. I have vivid memories of flying over Salisbury Cathedral, seeing the Queen Mary setting sail for America and of those rocks at the west end of the Isle of Wight which are pivotal landmarks.

King George VI died on 6 February 1952 and I was sent into Fareham to corner the market in black crepe. Later, the Station paraded for a Memorial Service at Titchfield Parish Church. My second, and last, summer at Titchfield provided plenty of cricket against sides such as RAF Calshot, HMS *Collingwood*, the Movements Unit at Southampton and the newly-established Basic Air Navigation School (BANS) at Hamble. I went to BANS on Saturday mornings to give lectures to National Servicemen a few years younger than me (who had not gone to University first) who were being encouraged to train as navigators and would be commissioned for their final six months in the Service. The hope was that they would sign on for short-service commissions, it having cost the RAF £800 a man to train them. This sum was very roughly equivalent to a Flight Lieutenant's pay for two years.

In those days TV was still a rarity, and I was delighted to see it for the first time when posted to RAF Ringway in Manchester for a week of examining candidates for the Education Tests. I saw Freddie Trueman reduce India to four wickets for no runs at Headingley in his first Test and Len Hutton's first game as England captain. Nearer home there were matches to be seen occasionally at Lord's and on the Hampshire circuit. But life was less carefree. I had a wife and RAF Titchfield had, as we have seen, expanded considerably in numbers. There was also the future to consider.

I applied for a teaching job with Trinidad Leaseholds Ltd and was summoned for an interview at their London office. The personnel officer was a retired Wing Commander and – since I was in uniform – this must have contributed to my success because I learned that there had been over three hundred applicants. My wife being a doctor was an added bonus: the firm got two, if not for the price of one, at least two whom they were able to employ.

With the assurance of a three-year contract with Trinidad Leaseholds and the prospect (or so it seemed) of endless cricket when I arrived, the closing days at Titchfield passed pleasantly enough. To my great surprise, I was made acting adjutant for my last month, issuing Station Orders under my signature for the CO. Indeed, I outstayed my National Service 'welcome' by a few days captaining a local RAF XI to victory by eight wickets during my 'demob' leave. In the few days which remained to us in England, Anne and I visited both our homes, saw Surrey win the championship and spent a day at Lord's, where the Indian Vijay Manjrekar made a century which *Wisden* described as 'one of the best batting displays of the tour'. On Saturday, 30 August 1952 we embarked at Hull on a 10,000 ton oil tanker for Trinidad.

The RAF had taught me how to handle men and given me a structured pattern of life. My father, the veteran of the First World War, could never quite reconcile the personal conflict between his relief that I saw no action and his contempt that I had had it all so easy. He was, of course, quite right.

The transition from the Services to an oil firm was a painless one. The war had not long ended and the great majority of the senior staff of the oil firm had served in it. One could make a broad generalisation: for senior staff, read officers; for junior staff, NCOs; and for Other Ranks, oil company employees. It will serve as a rough benchmark. In more realistic terms, senior staff were expatriates from the United Kingdom and (principally) Canada while junior staff tended to be local Trinidadians, many of them white Creoles. The 7,000 employees were from the indigenous population of Africans, (East) Indians and Chinese in the multi-racial (and happy) community of which the island was composed.

But first we had to get there. We boarded the tanker at Hull, from which I was promptly evicted for having too much money on me. I had exceeded the paltry amount the British Government allowed one to take out of the country. I disembarked, went back into Hull, paid three pounds (or thereabouts) into my Post Office account and returned to the ship. No one greeted me and no one asked any questions. I could have taken ten times the amount overseas.

With one exception, all the passengers on the tanker were bound for Regent School, Trinidad. The exception was a middle-aged lady of white Creole origins, returning from leave. She answered our eager questions readily enough, but gave little away about herself. A surprise awaited us at the school when she turned out to be the headmaster's secretary.

There were eight of the rest of us including wives. I was the 'baby', without any teaching experience (as the headmaster caustically observed when I met him). Douglas Harvey was ten years my senior and had been on the staff of Christ's Hospital in Sussex. I was to learn later that his move to Trinidad was a calculated one. After serving one contract at the school he switched to the personnel department, eventually reaching a very high position indeed within the oil firm and retiring as director-general of the Petroleum Association with an OBE. He and his wife remained friends of ours until their respective deaths towards the end of the twentieth century. His wife, Pat, was a gifted junior school teacher. Then there were the Steads. Jeff was a Physical Education and Maths teacher from East Anglia who came out to run the boarding house at Regent School. He was a cheerful fellow who stoically faced the throat cancer and virtual loss of speech which affected his later years. One of the single ladies found it difficult to believe that most of us had never heard of the Dragon School, in Oxford, where she had worked. She never settled and returned home within a year – but not before ensuring that Dr Garbett, the Archbishop of York, would visit Regent School. Her brother was his chaplain. The other was a gorgeous blonde to whom the males gave a few weeks before one of the many bachelors would marry her. Not so: she remains single to this day, living in quiet retirement in Dorset after a career as a headmistress in Venezuela. Perhaps unusually – but then we were thrown together for a fortnight on the tanker – we remained friends with almost all our group over the next fifty years. Douglas Harvey had seen my luggage (thirty-two cases, he recalled) before he saw me and guessed I was an 'old colonial' returning to the Empire. He was quickly disillusioned. But it was, nevertheless, to the Empire we were going.

My welcome at the nets at Guayacara Park, Pointe a Pierre, Trinidad, a fortnight after leaving Hull, was rather more spectacular and daunting than I had expected. A huge crowd had gathered and it was with some relief that I realised that they had come to see Sonny Ramadhin bowl rather than me bat. Ramadhin, a right-arm spinner, had been the hero of the three victories against England two years earlier when he had taken 26 wickets in the Tests and 135 on the tour. He was employed, as was I, by the oil firm, Trinidad Leaseholds Ltd. Ramadhin was a storekeeper and TLL had a long tradition of looking out for cricketers of talent. As far back as the 1920s Learie Constantine had been taken on as a clerk by TLL at the suggestion of Joe Small, the Trinidad player and another employee of the company. TLL was the first oil company to provide a secondary school for the children of its six hundred senior staff, and I was one of a dozen or so who were employed to take on education from the two primary schools – forty miles apart – which had hitherto catered for the educational needs of the community.

My arrival coincided with that of the Indian tourists and, for the first time ever, there would be three consecutive touring teams visiting the West Indies – India, England and Australia. I was lucky enough to see something of their cricket during my time in Trinidad.

There was plenty of cricket to play, too. As a member of TLL, there were organised league matches after work in the two and a half hours until the light failed. If one chose hockey, a full match could be played while cricketers would take two evenings for a game.

On Saturdays and Sundays there were representative matches. Cricket started early so that a game could be completed before the sudden switch from day to night – 10 degrees from the Equator meant that there was scarcely any twilight. One of the joys of such cricket matches was the prospect of playing against first-class players who most of the time represented their clubs. Few first-class opportunities came their way. I recall, for example, playing against Andy Ganteaume who, a few years earlier, had made a century against

England in his first Test match and was never picked again. Then there were games keeping wicket to J. E. D. Sealy, a Test cricketer between 1929 and 1939 and who still commanded some pace in the 1950s. To meet the Stollmeyers and Gerry Gomez, of the recent West Indian XIs, on the beautiful Test ground at Queen's Park, Port of Spain, was another experience.

Learie Constantine had joined TLL as a company lawyer and I resumed the association which had begun during in my schooldays in Scotland. I would come to know him well. He played occasionally for TLL. We did some cricket broadcasts together and he was my legal adviser in a curious incident to which reference is made later in this chapter. On our eventual departure from Trinidad, Constantine gave a drinks party at which my wife and I were the only white guests. Though our friendship was assured, I did not then contemplate that some years later I would be his biographer.

Cricket was never far away in those Caribbean years. Besides playing, there were the Test matches to watch at Port of Spain. These were the beginning of the halcyon days of West Indies cricket. After their success in England in 1950 they were never again – as they had been in 1947/48 by England – underestimated by their opponents. The 1952/53 (strictly, just 1953 as they arrived in January) Indians played two Test matches at Port of Spain. Both sides were strong in batting and, combined with the matting wicket (which had never produced a definite result in a Test Match since it was first laid in 1934), drawn games were inevitable.

Nevertheless, huge crowds attended to see the majesty of the three Ws: Worrell, Weekes and Walcott, and the artistry of the 'twins' Ramadhin and Valentine. Nor were they alone – a team of all the talents included the Stollmeyers, Gomez and Bruce Pairaudeau.

A year later came MCC, in a tour described in *The Times* as 'the second most controversial tour in cricket history'. We should examine why.

My time in Trinidad coincided with three interacting forces of nationalism, federation and economic advancement, all gathering strength in the mid 1950s. They found their spokesman in Dr Eric Williams, who became Prime Minister of Trinidad. Men such as he provided a middle-class leadership able to secure the grassroots support which the idea of federation lacked. Nationalism would win the day, while economic advancement would gain support from those who felt that the island was insufficiently supported by the proceeds of the sugar crop, in comparison to the royalties accruing from the oil companies. It was into this cauldron of hopes, grievances and fears that Len Hutton, the first professional captain of England in the twentieth century, took his side to the West Indies in 1954.

Hutton, briefed in advance by the Secretary of State for the colonies and by Constantine himself, had no doubts in his own mind that the cricketers were being used as an instrument with which to inflame the dying embers of colonial rule. 'His was,' wrote the editor of *Wisden*, 'the most thankless task a captain had ever undertaken, subjected to the impact of deep political and racial feeling.'

Such feelings showed themselves in the extravagant loyalty displayed by spectators and umpires gave decisions against local players at their peril. The selection of George Headley of Jamaica, once a player of great distinction dubbed the 'black Bradman', but then well past his prime, called for careful treatment by Hutton. Headley's fare back to Jamaica had been raised by local subscription, so fervent were his supporters that he should play in the Test side again. Hutton would say to me, when I wrote his biography, 'we deliberately treated him as gently as we dared without making it obvious.' Hutton recognised that Headley's dismissal for nought would have caused a riot.

Yet nationalism rather than colonialism dominated. 'Even charity could find no justification for his inclusion,' commented the *Trinidad Guardian* on the selection of the Jamaican Headley. Nationalism went even further in British Guiana, where the governor of the colony offered Hutton the First Battalion of the Argyll and Sutherland Highlanders as guardians if he needed them. However, it was the local umpire, Badge Menzies, who really needed police protection.

I was constantly aware of the situation. In particular, I recall arriving rather late on the second day of the Test at Port of Spain. I sat with a friend in the unreserved seats, the only whites in the 'popular' stand. The West Indies were ruthlessly advancing to almost 700, with centuries from all three Ws. At one point they were 517 for three. Starved of so much Test cricket in past years, the public seemed content to see batsmen amass runs. Disconsolate bowlers found salvation only in the occasional 'bouncer'. My friend and I enjoyed, with fixed smiles, endless teasing through a long, hot day.

Yet it cannot have been too bad. I wrote in an article for the British press at the time:

Cricket is everyone's delight in Trinidad.
Picture the Oval at Port of Spain; the crowd is indifferent as to whether it sits on benches or is astride the branches of the widespreading samaan trees. A fellow shouting, 'Somebo'y call me?' touts peanuts and drinks, the latter being 'iced' until honesty and the heat compel him to style them 'cool'. Everton Weekes is batting and my neighour turns to me: 'Sir Everton, boy. He make two hundred now'. And so indeed he does! Presently Mr Weekes is caught and all around is a rustle of dollar bills and a jingle of British coppers. The Minister of Education has allowed the future Ramadhins and Valentines to cast aside their much-thumbed 'Caribbean Readers' and their lunchtime bats of coconut branches and to sit in the schoolboys' stands.

Far into the future lay the appointment of managers with an authority along football lines. Hutton, on that tour in the 1950s, had to carry a burden which belatedly won almost universal praise after his return. Nor was the burden created solely by West Indian pressures. There were arrogant English voices hostile to a professional captain and to his defensive tactics. But once home, the *Yorkshire Post* wrote: 'it was a personal triumph, and honour will not be withheld where it is most emphatically due.' Alec Bannister wrote in the *Daily Mail*, 'I cannot see a serious competitor arising for the leadership of the tour to Australia.' And to Australia Hutton would go, but the West Indies tour had taken a toll from which, in cricketing terms, he would never really recover.

It was at this time that I had a personal experience of the mood of nationalism which pervaded Trinidad at the time. We had taken some local leave and gone to Tobago. At the airport a complete stranger spoke to me, addressing me as the son of the Dean of *Dublin*. I came back to Trinidad from what had seemed an innocent vacation to be greeted at Piarco Airport with the news that I was 'in trouble' and was required to see the General Manager of TLL the next morning.

Any doubts about the reason for such a summons were dispelled by a leading article in the Trinidad *Clarion* entitled 'Bishop Wilson's Cloth'. The Bishop of Trinidad, it declared, had dismissed the headmaster of the Bishop's High School, Tobago and wished to appoint me in his stead. The places I had been were cited as evidence that I was involved and had met the requisite people and the leader concluded: 'Let there be no mistake about it. This is the sort of incident from which gradually flows a Nationalism . . .'

My 'offence' was twofold: to have supplicated for a job without seeking TLL approval (this was no concern of the *Clarion*) and to have secured the appointment over the existing local (and black) holder of the headmastership who had been summarily dismissed.

Learie Constantine, as TLL's lawyer and as a personal friend, could not have been more helpful. He secured a total withdrawal of all the paper had said and to that extent I was vindicated. But, on the analogy that there was no smoke without fire, my denial of any intent to apply for the vacant post was never completely accepted by the personnel department of TLL.

When I recalled that I had been addressed as the son of the Dean of *Dublin* I was able to identify the source of the story. My father was, at the time, the Dean of *Brechin* – close, but not close enough.

I met Eric Williams, the Prime Minister, on two occasions. On the first, he kept me waiting for half-an-hour and then greeted me with the cryptic, 'I like to keep whites waiting,' but it did not happen again. He wanted me to do some research in the island of Tobago and my family spent an idyllic month there. I realized, with hindsight, that the oil company for which I worked wished to be on good terms with the government at a time of tension. I was a very humble cog in the wheel and my work in Tobago – pleasing to the

Prime Minister – eventually secured me a Fellowship of the Royal Historical Society. We borrowed a house owned by Bridget D'Oyly Carte. The time spent in the unspoilt community of Tobago, long before the days of package holidays, remains a nice, if distant and almost unbelievable, memory. When we asked what time church was, the gentle reply came: 'When de bell ring.'

On another occasion we went to Barbados and enjoyed the fresh atmosphere after the humidity of Trinidad. We were taken to Kensington Oval and had a walk to the 'middle'. No Test match was on, but one still sensed the immense enthusiasm for cricket – not to mention for England itself. 'Carry on England, Barbados is behind you' is the reputed cry from the colony in 1914. Much of Barbados looked English, even down to the Anglican Theological College at Codrington and the very English conduct of the Book of Common Prayer in the churches. Trinidad matched it when Dr Garbett, during his visit, preached in the Anglican Cathedral. The diocesan bishop called on us one day at our bungalow in Pointe a Pierre, resplendent in a large car with a chauffeur. Soon afterwards, we were in his party at the Governor's Ball in Port of Spain. I have a splendid memory of my wife walking up to receive a raffle prize in that grand setting. There was still an Empire!

Trinidad was a cosmopolitan society. Of the original American Indians, none remained, but there was the community of white creoles who went back several generations. Three centuries of slavery had brought the Africans. From India, after the end of slavery, there had come (from 1845 to 1917) Indians on fixed contracts to work on the sugar estates. Few were ever able to go back and I met an old man in the 1950s who had been among the last to come from India in 1917. Finally, there were the Chinese, as ever a hard-working and prosperous group. The Legislative Council of Trinidad, in its composition, reflected all the racial groups. There was no obvious colour-bar – more one created by wealth. But I recall the surprise, not to say embarrassment, evident when a white creole family produced a child who was distinctly black. The obvious conclusions were discounted and the family admitted to a black strain two or three generations back. Trinidad also had a fair proportion of

Roman Catholics, stemming from its Spanish background. I used the Anglican Book of Common Prayer to illustrate my points in teaching about the English Reformation. There was a cry from some parents that I was introducing Protestant literature into the classroom and the 'protest' went to the personnel officer of the Company. Relations between him and the headmaster were strained and the latter resented something which he regarded as an internal school-matter being taken out of his hands. Of the internecine quarrel I heard no more. The incident, however, illustrates the role of parent-power in the school, especially among parents who held senior posts in the Company. There was another example: a member of staff had gone on leave and I had taken over her School Certificate Latin class. When she came back, she reasonably enough resumed teaching it. A howl from protesting parents indicated their view that I was qualified to teach Latin and that she was not, nor had she (apparently) taught the pupils very well. I took over the class and got them their Certificate passes. Perhaps an explanation is called for. In the colonies candidates sat the Cambridge Overseas School Certificate which required (like the old School Certificate in England) a collective pass. Individual passes in each subject, as in the General Certificate of Education recently introduced for English schools, did not apply. An incident less to my credit was the writing of a school report upon a pupil who had been absent the entire term on long leave in England. It took some time to live it down with my colleagues.

As for the cricket, I had enjoyed watching as many Test matches in three years as Trinidad had hosted in the previous twenty. I had played with the 'stars' and I never ceased to appreciate going on the field in, say, January and February, and sparing a thought for those back at home in the throes of winter. And, as it turned out, my Caribbean links would continue and I would, some fifteen years later, write the biography of Baron Constantine of Nelson.

4
West Country Experience

We had crossed the Atlantic in ideal conditions – its waters as calm as a millpond and the sun beating down on us throughout. The England to which we returned was almost as hot as the Trinidad we had left. The safest place for our eighteen-month-old son, David, was in the ship's swimming pool and he made great friends with our steward. Within twenty-four hours of landing at Harwich I had boarded a night train at King's Cross for Dundee, greeted my parents and looked at my post.

A letter invited me to present myself at Kelly College, Tavistock, in Devon for an interview as head of the History department. That night I boarded another train going in the reverse direction and crossed London to get a West Country connection to Tavistock.

Kelly College had been founded in 1877 as a minor public school by Admiral Benedictus Marwood Kelly, who had joined the Royal Navy in 1798, during the Napoleonic Wars. He later commanded HMS *Pheasant*, engaged in the task of capturing slave-trading ships, and became an admiral on the Reserve list in 1863. He had no children by either marriage and in his retirement lived a life of stark simplicity so that money might be found to create a school. The purpose was to establish an institution for the 'education of lineal descendants of the Kelly Family, sons of officers in the Royal Navy and other gentlemen'. The Duke of Bedford presented a site of 20 acres and building began in the 1870s. Kelly has always been admired for the beauty of its architecture and its setting. Fine buildings of grey stone are set into a hill while a grassy slope descends into a leat bank. In the further distance lie the granite-covered slopes of Cox Tor.

Not for nothing, wrote Philip Landon, a chairman of governors, could we claim 'to have one of the loveliest schools in England'.

To this vista I arrived, somewhat bleary-eyed after two nights and an afternoon in trains. I applauded the view which greeted me and – with the passage of the years – have seen nothing to change the judgement of Landon. It was perhaps fitting that the headmaster who greeted me had a strong naval lineage. Rupert Westall had entered Osborne, on the Isle of Wight, as a naval cadet, served as a midshipman at Jutland at the age of sixteen and left the Navy with the rank of Lieutenant-Commander in 1922. Many knew him as 'the commander'. He was fond of telling the younger boys in his schools that he had never experienced schooldays himself. Twelve years later he was headmaster of West Buckland School before taking over Kelly just before the Second World War began. He would remain there until his retirement in 1959.

Westall was in some ways a liberal and in others a conservative. His approach to the boys was well ahead of his time and he believed everyone had something to contribute. He gave himself to them unsparingly and devotedly, requiring in return total loyalty. It was a virtue he prized above all others. Towards his staff he could be remote. A report returned to my pigeon-hole, without comment, on the last Sunday night of term left me in no doubt that my contribution needed rewriting, but no hint was given whether my judgement or my grammar was at fault. Common-room meetings could be monologues and certainly lacked the to-and-fro of their modern counterparts. Praise from him had to be earned and might come in the form of a note penned in his beautiful hand. No typewriter sullied his desk nor secretary disturbed his isolation. His school ran efficiently on a shoestring. His attitude towards parents – his customers – could be dictatorial and almost rude. They were not encouraged to come to Kelly very often. Towards the end of his time a disciplinary incident was not entirely to his credit. 'Do you want me to run the school as if it were Her Majesty's Quarter-Deck?' he peremptorily asked his staff, and he sought to punish the whole school when he could not find the offender. Parents who came to take their charges out were marooned in the Bedford Hotel until the culprit came forward. The miscreant, however, did not confess. A senior parent – a Major-General of Marines – was selected as their spokesman and tackled the head in his study. He returned, crestfallen, and parents drove back through Devon lanes in the 1950s without having seen their offspring.

Perhaps I saw the best of Westall, in his more mellow years. I was almost the last appointment he made but he must be judged by the canon of those times and not ours. I learnt more from him about schoolmastering than from any other mentor. Westall attracted able pupils and the Upper VIth that I took over illustrated this. It was, indeed, the first time I had ever met an Upper VIth – as pupil or master – and perhaps the day was saved by their abilities. Two of them, at least, would have some bearing on my own later career. They included Richard Orchard, the winner of an Open Scholarship in History to Exeter College, Oxford. When I later presented myself as a graduate student at that same college, the Rector commented on my former pupil and promptly accepted me. Another became the highly successful crime novelist Gerald Seymour, whose chance meeting with John Arlott and me eased the passage of my first cricket book. Seymour's brother, Philip, became a university professor, and Nicholas Bomford, headmaster of Harrow. I would never teach such an able group again. Westall took a bit of a chance in appointing me, though I did not make too much of my lack of VIth form experience. Certainly, I had to learn my European History, teaching one century which I had never studied as an undergraduate and keeping, in the old phrase, a lesson or two ahead of the pupils.

We now had three children, Gillian and Michael both being born in Tavistock. With a young family, a lot of academic reading to be done and the busy life of a master in a small public school to lead, there was not much time for cricket. I remember annual appearances in the Staff matches, and turning out for the XI always raised against the school by a certain Commander Murray. The staff only totalled sixteen men so it was not particularly competitive to get into the staff XI. Curiously, Westall did not encourage his staff to play sport in case they were injured and could not teach. The main recreational activity of the school was athletics, and Kelly would easily eclipse all the Devon Public and Grammar Schools in the annual inter-school sports. Boys were frequently selected for the National Schools' Athletic Association Championships. Cricket very much took second place, with matches broken off to allow an athletic run to take place. Hockey came a close second, and so jealously was the 1st XI hockey field guarded that in one wet term not a single match was played on it. It had been my hockey, I daresay, which had been as influential as my historical knowledge in getting me the post. I had played the game up to four times a week in Trinidad, appeared for Trinidad Leaseholds 1st XI and been selected for an island trial at Port of Spain. What I lacked – and quickly had to learn – was knowledge of how to umpire and coach the game. Kelly had high standards and would win a large number of its matches. Kelly would also be responsible for a team raised from all the Devon schools to play the county and, one year, I felt justice demanded that our boys commanded eight of the eleven places.

The administrative skill bequeathed by a combination of the RAF and my work in Trinidad enabled me to run the hockey throughout the school and to ensure that sides always turned up.

A third facet of my endeavours at Kelly was to be adjutant of the Combined Cadet Force. In an over-enthusiastic display of authority, in my opening weeks, I had punished someone for a modest misdemeanour by requiring him to change from mufti to Corps uniform and back three times.

'That's no way to get boys to like the Corps,' said 'Tug' Wilson, the CO, 'you'd better join the Corps yourself.' So, obliquely, I added a Territorial commission, in the rank of Captain in the Royal Marines, to the one I already held on the Reserve of Officers in the Royal Air Force. Among my adventures was having the Corps out on some exercise when a Dartmoor mist came down, and getting all the boys safely back to base.

Finally, I was appointed VIth form master, which included

handling University entrance. I was summoned one evening to bring a boy of my choice to meet the chairman of governors after dinner. After a few minutes' conversation, he remarked to the boy, 'We look forward to seeing you at Trinity [Oxford] in the autumn.' That life could be so simple! Kelly was a happy school helped by its environment and by the quality of the staff. I remember, for example, Robert Edwards, an Old Kelleian, who had been President of Athletics at Cambridge, taught English with flair and played a major role in Kelly's high reputation for athletics. In such a small school one fulfilled many roles. I ran the Current Affairs Discussion Society and introduced the idea of visiting speakers. With some surprise I look back on the names of a few of those I invited to come down to the far West (long before motorways) to talk to the boys. They included our local MP (perhaps understandably), the Bishop of Southwark, Mervyn Stockwood (but then he *was* an old Kelleian) and always an admiral or two (Westall kept up his naval connections). I also ran the Kelly Press, a rather primitive institution which would produce cards and programmes. On one occasion I spotted a misprint not long before the school play began. Hurriedly we printed the remainder correctly and ensured that the headmaster and all those near him got the 'proper' version.

Kelly in the 1950s drew upon a steady clientele of West Country parents who would not have dreamed of sending their sons eastwards. A fair proportion of fathers were in the Services (not necessarily the Navy) and a tidy number of boys would make their way overseas to work in the colonies. Kelly had expanded from ninety boys on the roll when Westall came in 1939 to well over two hundred when he left twenty years later. Oxford and Cambridge places were secured and Blues won at those Universities. It is only marginally fanciful to suggest that the 1950s were the 'Golden Age' of Kelly College. Today, fifty years later, it flourishes under a different philosophy, with a wide age-range of boys and girls, and among its headmasters of a later age was Chris Hirst (who had been a colleague of mine at Radley), whose distinguished leadership led to his being appointed headmaster of Sedbergh. But depending on your geographical view of things, Tavistock in the 1950s was still seen as something of a backwater and it was a self-contained community.

With no West Country associations, I was never going to stay long there. I knew I wanted to write and I felt that Oxford (or thereabouts) beckoned if I wished both the environment and the leisure to pursue a 'second' career. When a post was advertised that included both a lectureship at a teacher-training college and also a research studentship at Oxford University, I applied for it at once and was successful.

Kelly left happy memories, not least of the hours spent on the beach at Widemouth, near Bude. It was a beach which had the foreboding memory of the tragedy I had witnessed there fifteen years or so earlier, but that gave way to the pleasure of my young building sandcastles and paddling. We kept our links by buying a cottage at Brentor, which for a dozen years or so provided a holiday home and a chance to retain our West Country links.

5
Training the Teachers

Kelly College had been established, *inter alia*, to educate 'the sons of gentlemen'. Culham College had looked to a lower social stratum in the structured fabric of nineteenth-century society. It was founded by Samuel Wilberforce, that redoubtable Oxford bishop who serves as the prototype for the reforms introduced into the Church of England. He founded Cuddesdon College to train clergy and Culham College, nearby, to train schoolmasters who 'would go out to serve the elementary schools within the Diocese of Oxford and beyond'.

Teaching there was a link with my grandfather, Selwyn Cooke, who had been chaplain at Cuddesdon. Indeed, the very desk at which I write these words had adorned, in its time, our respective studies at Cuddesdon and Culham.

In the language of the day, Culham men were trained to serve and to teach those 'in the station to which they had been born'. There was no encouragement towards social mobility, though individuals would challenge this. An early entrant to Culham went on to take a doctorate in music at Oxford University, and at least one of those nineteenth-century students became a bishop.

In essence, the teacher training colleges of the south of England provided, for some, the only way in which a man of limited means might obtain any form of higher education. Oxford and Cambridge and, to a lesser extent, London were all distant dreams. The great age of municipal universities belonged to the Midlands and the North of England. Thus not all who came to Culham in the nineteenth century necessarily entered the teaching profession.

Through various vicissitudes the College survived the years, and when I took up my appointment in 1960 it was not so very different from its original foundation. But within a year or two of my arrival, all would change. I came to a place of fewer than two hundred men, entirely residential, and built around an attractive neo-Gothic quadrangle. Culham enjoyed a high reputation for games and many an Oxford College would be vanquished. The most celebrated games player attracted to the College was John Snow, the England fast bowler. He read history. The story is told that I gave him rather a poor mark for an essay and that I was due to face him in a cricket match. Legend has it that I preferred to be run out! Snow asked my advice on whether he should accept a teaching appointment or an invitation to play professional cricket – I recommended the latter and Snow had a successful playing career, and after retirement ran a business arranging overseas tours.

The aim, as it had always been, was to equip its students both with the academic knowledge of their subject and the techniques of how to teach it. Francis Venables, the principal, gave me my appointment. In many ways he was a man similar to Westall of Kelly. He was a Victorian who had served in the First World War and he had been a headmaster. But there were differences: Westall never wore his religion on his sleeve, while Venables very much did so. Woe betide the man who missed College Chapel. I only knew him for one year and it was as well that his retirement was due. The small, inward-looking College was his ideal and he had long held out against the powers-that-be who had urged him to take more students. He would have been unable to resist as change beckoned.

In 1963 the Robbins Report on higher education was published. It recommended that Teacher Training Colleges be called Colleges of Education and that their links with Universities be closer. The Report proposed the introduction of a four-year course leading to a Bachelor of Education degree and a professional qualification. The effect on Culham was five-fold. Numbers of students trebled, women were admitted, the college became day as well as residential, a building programme was launched and a degree course was initiated.

The new principal was entirely in tune with these changes. John

Barnett had served in the Second World War and had been an Italian POW. Culham had, curiously, two Japanese POWs on the staff. 'Don't ever mention it to them,' he once said, 'but I quite enjoyed being a POW. The Italians were easygoing, we had enough to eat and I got on with my studies.' John Barnett was a man for the future. Halfway through his principalship he spent a term as a Ford Foundation Scholar in the United States and came back full of ideas. These were the years, in the late 1960s, of student troubles and it may well be that this vision and capacity to anticipate student demands was his greatest quality as principal. Culham moved with ease and harmony into a more democratic framework.

One of the Japanese POWs was the College Chaplain, Henry Babb. He bore the scars lightly but his annual address to the men on 11 November never deviated: 'War is not a giant rugger match,' he would say, 'It is awful and gruesome.' Henry Babb was a tall, well-built man and a boon companion of the vice-principal, Len Naylor, who would tell me of years teaching in Liverpool in the Depression – 'I got a First in History but was lucky to get a job at £100 a year.' Naylor was an outstanding scholar in the Whig tradition and had contributed to the writing of the *History of Parliament*. This bachelor surprised us all by getting married after he had retired. He and his fiancée had waited till an old mother had died and they would know a few happy years together. I owe a lot to Naylor: he schooled me in research techniques, requiring of me the same discipline (and more) which he asked of his students. I recall one who had not supplied footnotes to his 10,000 word dissertation; Naylor sent him back to the north of England to pursue his sources. Probably the dissertation was the most demanding and satisfying piece of work the history students did. Certainly, my Oxford research degree owed a lot to his guidance.

I played my part in the exciting challenge of these years. For three of them I was 'seconded' from my duties as an historian to run a new Foundation Studies Course. Once a week the entire body of first-year students gathered together for a varied programme to introduce them to aspects of the wider world. Teacher training could still be criticised for being mono-technique in its policy. My recollection is of some of the interesting people we would 'put up' in our house for the night who had come to Culham to speak. There was James Blades, the percussionist, and Joan Goossens, one of a celebrated family of musicians. Out of it came a book, *Essays to a Young Teacher*, whose chapters give a flavour of what we endeavoured to offer: 'Education and Social Change', 'The psychosomatic relationship in childhood', 'Music in remedial education', 'The impact of Science on Civilisation', 'Young People and the Trade Unions'. We were well served by Oxford dons and others who would contribute to the dialogue.

Presently, I returned to the history department and I have a clear recollection of how my activities on one particular day highlighted both the challenge and even friction within my job. I spent the morning with a don at Christ Church discussing the work for the Oxford 'Further Subjects' degree paper in seventeenth-century history, which my students would sit with Oxford undergraduates and for which I would teach. One of them, incidentally, got a straight *alpha* in his paper. I spent the afternoon with a headmaster discussing a student's problems in dealing with a low-level class in an Oxfordshire secondary school. I wryly reflected that the two worlds in which I myself was expected to show some expertise and competence were poles apart to the two men with whom I had spent the day. Culham College lecturers and their pupils had to cope with the tensions created by the twin goals of pure scholarship and applied performance.

One consequence of the expansion of Culham was the need for more space. The College became a tenant of Nuneham Mansion, in Nuneham Courtenay. This had been the home of the Harcourt family till sold to the University of Oxford. The RAF had been a tenant during the War and Culham took over some years later. My own History department moved there, together with the musicians and mathematicians. We tried to ensure that students who studied any of these three subjects did not live in Nuneham as well. It did not always work, and I had to take steps to stop a young lady quitting her room at ten to nine just in time, and somewhat dishevelled, for my lecture at 9 o'clock.

Nuneham was a Palladian house built in the 1760s by the Earl Harcourt. It satisfied all the dictates of an Italianate villa and its landscape was the work of 'Capability' Brown. Its romantic garden, designed by William Mason, claimed to be the first in England created during the late eighteenth-century Romantic movement. Drama was lent to the garden by the well in which the unfortunate Earl Harcourt (who had built the house) drowned in 1777 whilst trying to save his dog. As Oliver Goldsmith dryly observed: 'the dog it was that lived.' One of my teaching colleagues was Mavis Batey. Slightly my senior, during the war she had worked at Bletchley Park, the secret cipher centre, a fact that only emerged in a TV programme many years later.

When the great pleasure parks of the eighteenth century were laid out, local villagers were often evicted to create a sense of isolation. The village of Nuneham Courtenay, on the main road to Oxford, still has the lines of 'model' houses to which the residents were compulsorily moved – all except Barbara Wyatt, who refused to go and whose place in history is ensured by Oliver Goldsmith's *Deserted Village*.

But dark clouds loomed and the sun was setting on the old College at Culham. Fresh questions were being asked in Parliament about the nature of teacher training. The delicate relationship between universities, polytechnics and colleges of education (as the three 'arms' of higher education) became a major area of discussion. By 1973 the writing was on the wall for Culham, which was particularly vulnerable as one of 26 Church of England Colleges and as the most expensive to run. The government of the day also wished to bring the European Jet Energy project to Culham Laboratory and use the College as a school, at a time when it looked as if Italy would secure the proposed project.

Years after Culham had closed, I was asked to write the second edition of the College *History*. I wanted to get as close as I could to the facts which led to the order for closure coming so swiftly and at the very point when the College was likely to be accepted for the new Council of National Academic Awards (CNNA) degree – a more suitable experiment than the Oxford B.Ed. had proved to be.

I went to see two senior civil servants in London. They were courtesy itself, while obeying the thirty-year rule on State Papers. 'We'll look at what you've written and see what you might change,' one of the two ladies said. In the end Culham's vulnerability proved the College's undoing, and in August 1976 the Department of Education and Science made the formal announcement of the College's closure. In the last resort, the reason was political, as became abundantly clear when the site of the College became that of the European School. That some Colleges had to go was accepted: the national birth rate was declining and there was the prospect of 'sustained unemployment for young teachers'. But for the losers, such as Culham, there was inevitable sadness.

On coming to Culham both our own professional and domestic pattern had changed very considerably. Kelly had been a demanding job, with every member of a small staff wearing many hats. At Culham I was able to lead a very different life. I became an awarder, and subsequently senior awarder, for the Oxford and Cambridge Schools' Examination Board and would hold the appointment for 25 years. We would meet for a week in August, alternating between colleges in Oxford and Cambridge, and arbitrate on the fate of the young. Bureaucracy was unknown and computer technology a dark secret. Beautifully composed coloured charts would guide our decisions. My recollection is that we made very, very few mistakes or errors of judgement. I was also appointed a University of Oxford examiner in the History of Education and acted as supervisor in that field to postgraduates pursuing a Bachelor of Letters degree. More pertinently came an invitation from the publishers, Thomas Nelson, to act as General Editor for the proposed *Dictionary of World History*, no less. They saw the project as taking five or six years and it was not a decision to be taken lightly.

In fact, it marked the parting of the ways in my professional career. One or two major headmasterships had been mentioned and, aged just under forty, I had to determine what would be the pattern of the twenty years of service which I still had to offer. To accept Nelson's invitation was the recognition that writing would be a major part of my life and that I would have a diversity of opportunity not available if I accepted a post with serious responsibility. When I agreed to do the *Dictionary of World History* the die was cast, though events would not quite turn out as I had planned.

Culham, whose future was not in doubt when I began my work on the *Dictionary*, gave me six months' leave of absence which influenced my decision. My first task was to establish a working-structure and I proposed an Advisory Board of distinguished academics. A. J. P. Taylor agreed to be the Advisory Editor and his advisory panel included Max Beloff, Asa Briggs, G. R. Elton, R. W. Southern and Sir Ronald Syme from either Oxford or Cambridge. From overseas I recruited J. A. la Nauze from the Australian National University in Canberra and Don Fehrenbacher from Stanford University, California. The 'tier' who did the major editorial work were my Executive Editorial Board. Their ranks included Fred Alexander from the University of Western Australia, Basil Davidson, Visiting Professor at the University of Ghana, E. B. Fryde of the University College of Wales, Betty Kemp and Wilfrid Knapp of Oxford, with R. B. Smith and M. E. Yapp both of the London School of Oriental and African Studies.

Their task was to secure contributors, and a list of over three hundred was compiled. I also established an administrative staff of eight. If the phrase 'people, places and things' may be said to define all the needs of history, so it represented how the contents would be made up. The requirements were worldwide. There would be 20,000 entries in a total of two million words.

One reviewer picked out the entry on 'Cricket' for comment, remarking on a last paragraph in which the contributor had written: 'No game has produced a greater response from artists, poets and men of letters, while some distinguished players have later held high office in Church and State throughout the Commonwealth.' The reader need not exert himself greatly to guess the authorship! In the alphabetical order of things it was preceded by 'Crichel Down 1950–54' (a British political crisis which raised issues of ministerial responsibility) and followed by 'Crime of 1873' (a popular cry in the United States by advocates of bimetallism).

There were, inevitably, some crises, especially when the publishers suddenly became concerned at escalating costs and threatened to end the project in mid-stream. I recall a meeting between Taylor, myself and the celebrated lawyer, Lord Goodman, which effectively put an end to Nelson's threats. Goodman, while conducting our business, simultaneously dealt on the phone with two other clients. Our case fitted his overall concern with equity and justice. He commented that Nelson had entered into a contract with a large number of professional people and could not now reject them. Another crisis was when the publishing house lost the entire manuscript of the letter 'S'. I kept some local children happy over Christmas with extra pocket money from Nelson while they dug out all the entries beginning with 'S' from the assorted submissions of three hundred contributors.

One of my pleasant recollections was the friendship I struck up with the writer Nicolas Bentley, who was on the staff at Nelson and acted as Literary Adviser to the enterprise. We would meet at Henley-on-Thames, roughly halfway between his home and mine, and over a pub lunch discuss the issues of the moment. I look at his cartoon of myself as I write these words. Indeed, he was a man of many parts, declaring he would like to be a fireman and a clown as well as a cartoonist and a writer. He achieved all his ambitions.

I delivered the finished manuscript to Nelson five years to the day from their letter of invitation. In those pre-computer days, we (or rather, they) agonised on how to do the index. In the end, it was done manually by Brenda Hall and the work took her eighteen months.

The *Dictionary* was well received and I was delighted, when visiting a school in Western Australia, to see a copy on the library shelves. In 2003 a Chinese firm wrote asking permission to produce an edition but in the end Zhu Jiang's proposal came to nothing. A more positive reaction had come, soon after the original publication, from Mitchell Beazley who invited me to join their staff for a year and to edit their illustrated biographical dictionary, *Who Did What*. Several of my own editors also contributed. James Mitchell, before he left Nelson to found the firm of Mitchell Beazley, had been a director at Thomas Nelson. He was a young man of immense energy and enthusiasm who pioneered much of the later publishing of part-works and whose *The Moon Flight Atlas*, *Atlas of the Universe* and *World Atlas of Wine* all became international bestsellers. The firm would win a Queen's award for success in exporting. For a year I went to London as a conventional 'commuter', although there were not the demands which my younger neighbours now have. 'Be in the office by 9.30,' I was told, 'and we usually finish about 5.' Nevertheless, the publishing work got done and it was an interesting year for me away from the academic and scholastic world. James Mitchell died young and, since this is an autobiography, I must relate an incident that nearly brought the same fate to me. A neighbour in North Moreton served in the RAF and regularly flew to Malta. 'Like a trip one weekend?' he asked. 'You're still on the Reserve of Officers, aren't you?' I thought I was and looked out my kit, but on the Friday afternoon he came round. 'Sorry. The CO looked you up and you're no longer on the Reserve. Nothing doing.' Two days later, on the Sunday morning, there came a knock at the door. Michael, aged six, had put on my RAF hat and tunic and answered to a Group Captain similarly attired, plus his trousers! 'Is your father in?' he asked. I came downstairs to be told that the entire crew had been killed in a crash in bad weather conditions in Malta. There was no more to be said. But it was in a sombre mood that I played the organ for my friend's funeral at All Saints', North Moreton, six days later. This autobiography would have ended at Part I.

Culham, as I have said, gave me the leisure to write and in my years there I managed to produce *Stuart and Cromwellian Foreign Policy* and *From Chatham to Churchill*, two textbooks for schools well received in their time but rather 'dated' nowadays. I also edited a series of books which Pergamon Press produced in Oxford and to which my wife and I contributed *The Story of Health*, which rather accidentally ended up a textbook for nurses.

While working on the *Dictionary* the future of Culham became uncertain. Towards the end of my year working with Mitchell Beazley I accepted an invitation from Dennis Silk, the Warden of Radley College, to join his staff as head of history. It was not a future I planned and I suspected that my opportunities for writing would be extremely limited. But, with the closure of Culham, there were distinct advantages. We would remain in Oxfordshire, though we had to let the house which we had bought in North Moreton. Nor would our children's education be affected. I would thus become the only person (and shall so remain) to have taught at Culham and Radley, two nineteenth-century foundations facing each other astride the River Thames. I left Culham with some sadness after thirteen years there and they were good enough to make me a Principal Lecturer-Emeritus after my departure.

Anne and I had lived in rented accommodation for the first nine years of our marriage and, when we went to Culham, the time had come to purchase – wisely, as it happened, with the inflationary age around the corner. My wife chose Old School House, North Moreton, which had been the village schoolmaster's house until 1938. She consulted me over the phone and I asked the essential question: 'Is the lawn 22 yards long?' She replied that it was and the purchase took place. A few years later, my younger son – spending an unadventurous 'gap' six months working in a local bank – spent the spring bowling ferociously to me on that 22 yards. The exercise was enough to win him a freshman's Blue at Cambridge as a fast bowler. Today, almost fifty years later, the 'wicket' is used for more sedate batting practice.

I will describe our life in North Moreton, my close links with the village and its cricket, and the writing on cricket which those years produced in later parts of this book. Culham, in man's span of things, marked a natural halfway point and the end of the first innings.

Part II

Cricket in many guises

6
Cricket in 1791

Hambledon cricket enjoyed the pre-eminence, but not the monopoly, of cricket in the second half of the eighteenth century. Its story is faithfully recorded in the minutes and accounts lodged in the Hampshire Record Office in Winchester. And it has its historians in F. S. Ashley-Cooper and R. D. Knight. Elsewhere, cricket flourished in Norfolk, Kent, Sussex, London and the Midlands. Newspapers in the British Museum and in county record offices, cricket libraries such as those at Lord's and Trent Bridge, and Haygarth's Scores and Biographies *will all reward the patient researcher. I chose to ask who the cricketers were in 1791: a year of transition as Hambledon gave way to MCC and the rural world of the eighteenth century conceded place to the Napoleonic era and an urban, bustling nineteenth century.*

The 1791 season began at Lord's with a three-day match between the Marylebone Cricket Club and Middlesex in conditions which, according to the Annual Register, were cloudy though the temperature reached 57°F. Middlesex were dismissed for 110, Thomas Lord himself making 21 against the club. Before close of play MCC had lost several wickets cheaply, including that of the Earl of Winchilsea. He and Lord were firm friends – the social difference between the two of little consequence – and both were at the forefront of the establishment of Lord's ground and of MCC itself. But by playing cricket that day Winchilsea absented himself from a meeting of the Hambledon Club some sixty miles away in Hampshire. A further three of MCC's XI were also gentlemen members of Hambledon and were also absent, while two of the Hambledon players were being employed for the MCC match on a day when Hambledon had no fixture. As for the match itself, Middlesex won a low-scoring game by 30 runs.

Symbolically, Monday, 16 May represented rather more than just a clash of commitments for a few cricketers who could not be in two places at once. Of more consequence is the recognition that one club was laying the foundations of its distinguished future, and the other was sinking into obscurity. Winchilsea had been president of Hambledon twice, in 1787 and 1789, but had not played for them for the past two years and would not do so again. Lord Harris and F. S. Ashley-Cooper, in *Lord's and the MCC* (1920), described him as, more than any other man, 'the founder of the MCC'. Of the other three Hambledon members, one of them, the 21-year-old Edward Bligh, had only been elected in the previous year and his cricketing future too would lie with MCC and with *three* counties, principally Kent, although his elder brother, the Earl of Darnley, would be President of Hambledon in 1793. The two Hambledon players at Lord's that Monday were the professionals William Beldham and Richard Purchase. The 25-year-old Beldham was at the beginning of a career which would last until 1821 and he would live to be the only Hambledon player captured by photography.

The meeting of the Hambledon Club that Monday was rather a sad one. Nine members sent in their letters of resignation. They included the 27-year-old Edward Hale, whose family owned Windmill Down, the club ground. None of them, however, was a future MCC player and only two (Hale and George Boult) were playing members of Hambledon. Their resignations simply endorse the fact that the great days of the club were over. As a social institution Hambledon CC had less appeal to its gentlemen members while its players – be they members themselves, such as Winchilsea, or the professionals, such as Beldham – were now attracted to Thomas Lord's new ground at St Marylebone. There were still fifty-two members on the books in 1791 but a quarter of them (including Bligh) had not paid their subscriptions. The club would still function for a few more years and it would meet on eighteen more occasions in 1791, with a further final meeting proposed on 'a Moonlight night'.

That the new MCC was exerting its influence even behind 'the closed doors' of a Hambledon meeting may be deduced from the entry on 16 July 1791 in the Club Minutes:

> The Umpire said: 'I really think the Ball hit the Ground, but I cannot be positive'. It was unanimously agreed by the following Members of the Marylebone Club to be decisive [and nine names followed].

So here were nine Hambledon members speaking as MCC members. A three-day match on Windmill Down between England and Hampshire had just ended and some doubtful decision must have been discussed.

In September, at the final meeting of the season, the Honourable Captain Hugh Conway, who had only been a member since May, was elected President for 1792. Since fewer than ten members had attended at each of the July and August meetings the choice cannot have been a wide one. At least he stayed with the club to the end, was not an MCC man and became an admiral. He was a friend and exact contemporary of Admiral Nelson, and (though it came to nothing) sponsored him as a parliamentary candidate in 1795.

Some three weeks after the MCC–Middlesex match at Lord's, Hambledon itself played there against XXII of Middlesex. The Hambledon XI had many of those immortalised in John Nyren's *The Cricketers of my Time* (1833) – John Small (father and son), Beldham, Purchase, the Walkers ('those anointed clod-stumpers'), John Wells and David Harris. It was an all-professional side, the best which could be mustered by the members who had a thousand guineas on the game. Nine of them were placed by Nyren in his XI of the most eminent players in the Hambledon Club in its glory, of whom he wrote: 'No eleven in England could have any chance with these men; and I think they might have beaten any two-and-twenty.' But on this last appearance at Lord's of the Hambledon CC so styled – against XXII – they lost by three wickets in a low-scoring game. There we may leave, for the moment, the Hambledon of 1791 – the gentlemen players seeing where the new powerhouse of cricket lay and the professionals such as Beldham seeing equally perceptively from where their livelihood would come – and turn to the burgeoning fortunes of MCC.

On the morning of Thursday, 2 June the spectators at Lord's had scarcely settled down when the Earl of Darnley, opening for Kent against MCC with his fellow nobleman, the Earl of Thanet, was bowled by a stripling of eighteen. Thus the bowler Lord Frederick Beauclerk announced his arrival. He would exercise an influence and authority at Lord's for some sixty years – as great an autocrat as Lord Harris and as long a tenant as Sir Pelham Warner. When Beauclerk died in 1850, the two-year-old WG was making his first infant forays with bat and ball. MCC won the match by an innings and 113 runs, their last pair, Beldham and William Fenner, the two professionals, each making a fifty and between them accounting for (caught or bowled) thirteen of the Kent wickets. MCC needed a win – they had lost to Middlesex twice in their only two preceding matches of 1791.

In the season as a whole, MCC played eleven matches. They had beaten Kent at Lord's but lost to them there in a combined side with Hambledon. This game in August was styled 'MCC with five of the Hambledon Club against Kent'. It represents the last time that the name of Hambledon appeared at Lord's. The fusion of the two clubs into one XI for this match serves to indicate the pragmatic change which was taking place probably with no hard feelings on the part of the participants. Hornchurch beat MCC at Lord's but lost on their own ground in Essex; Andover were beaten at Perriam Downs, near Luggershall in Wiltshire and Nottingham at King's Meadow, Nottingham – as were XXII of Nottingham. MCC lost both games against Middlesex at Lord's and they beat the Old Etonians and Leicestershire at Burley in Rutland.

The two matches at Nottingham were warmly welcomed in an area where the game had been established for some twenty years, making 1791 'memorable . . . in the local annals of the game' as written by John Sutton in his *Nottingham Cricket Matches* (1853). Colonel Charles Churchill was stationed in the town with his regiment and was so struck by the enthusiasm for cricket that he issued a challenge to MCC. Winchilsea and his friends arrived 'attended by a gay coterie and a retinue of servants'. They stayed for a week in two local hostelries and played on the Upper Meadow, 'which was staked and corded for the occasion'. Booths were erected and some 10,000 spectators came to watch in 'remarkably fine' weather. The match, Sutton wrote, 'witnessed the introduction of a new style of play [and] old science had to contend with new science'. John Blackner, writing in 1815, had taken the same view: 'the system of playing adopted by the MCC was one with which the Nottingham men were not then acquainted.'

MCC won the first game by ten wickets, a single bye in the 2nd innings being sufficient. A second game against XXII of Nottingham was quickly arranged, which MCC won by 21 runs and in which Churchill himself played. As an example of the unreliability of the scores of those days, Captain Markham's score for MCC is variously given as 5, 33 and 35, being confused with that of Louch, who made either 33 or 1! Off the field, the visitors clearly enjoyed themselves: every spare hour was spent in 'cocking', 'milling' or some kind of 'gentlemanly amusement', some of which involved them in rather childish horseplay on a wet afternoon. In 1792, MCC entertained Nottingham at Burley, but thereafter the two sides did not meet for over fifty years.

There was a week's cricket in June at Burley which was near Oakham, a few miles over the border from Leicestershire. This was Winchilsea's country seat, where cricket was played in front of the magnificent Baroque mansion. In a three-day game England (alias MCC and Hambledon) beat Hampshire (also, alias MCC and Hambledon) by 54 runs. Immediately afterwards fourteen of the players took part as Old Etonians against MCC; each side having four 'lent' men. Winchilsea, for his old school, made a career-best 76. The week ended when Leicestershire met MCC for the first time, losing by an innings. Cricket had taken root in the county both as a game for the gentry, under Winchilsea's influence, and for craftsmen and artisans engaged in hosiery piece-work. At East Leake Meadow, in the same year, Beeston beat Mountsorrel by an innings and 39 runs; the only local match in Leicestershire in 1791 of which a record survives.

There were two other matches at Lord's. 'The Gentlemen of Eaton' played their Westminster counterparts, losing the match and 500 guineas, though *Scores and Biographies* lists the Etonians' opponents as the 'Gentlemen of England with Grange'. Thomas Lord assisted Eton and Grange was a Middlesex player: presumably both teams were one short. At the very end of September, XXII of Hertfordshire, Essex and Middlesex beat Kent, despite the assistance of Harris and Beldham, by an innings and 101 runs. The highest MCC innings of 1791 was 240 and the highest individual score was 89 by the Hon. H. Fitzroy. Beldham was the mainstay of the professional batting with three half-centuries and two forties.

Hampshire, as an entity, played and lost four matches. Hambledon players were invariably in the side. At the Vine, Sevenoaks there was an exciting game against England. After both sides had been dismissed for under 50, England were set 117 to win and lost five wickets for under a dozen runs before scrambling home by a single wicket. The two sides met again, for a thousand guineas, on the historic Windmill Down ground in mid-July, probably the match involving the umpiring controversy mentioned in the Hambledon Minutes. We may be confused about whether it was Hampshire or Hambledon playing. The contemporary *Hampshire Chronicle* of 25 July spoke of the 'Hambledon Club informally dressed in sky-blue coats, with black velvet collars and the letters C.C. (Cricketing Club) engraved on their buttons'. This time, England won by 60 runs. The trilogy of matches was completed on Perriam Downs, ten days later in late July, when England completed a hat-trick of victories against Hampshire. With a massive total of 275 runs, they won by an innings and 68 runs. Beldham's 91 was the highest score recorded in major cricket in 1791 so far that summer, to be eclipsed the same week at Burley by Colonel Lennox's 103 in a game between Winchilsea's XI and Bligh's XI. This game took place the day after the third England–Hampshire game had ended in Wiltshire, so four of the gentlemen players, one of them Lennox, must have had to make a north-easterly journey of some ninety miles by carriage.

They took their sport hardly! Since the initials of fifteen of the players are not given, one may assume that Winchilsea simply dragooned sufficient of his estate employees to give him and his friends a game.

The Holt, at Wreckesham (near Farnham) in Surrey, was the scene of a three-day match for 1,000 guineas between Surrey and Hampshire. Once again, Hambledon men could be found on both sides, not least Beldham, who played for Surrey on a ground which he himself had prepared that year at the request of another enthusiastic nobleman (but non-player) Lord Stowell. Surrey, in their only appearance of the summer as a county side, won by 17 runs.

A late-September match at Windmill Down between Sussex, west of Arundel (with Winchilsea, Small and Purchase) against 'the Town of Hambledon' ended Winchilsea's busy summer and brought a Sussex victory by 11 runs. It had taken place on the three days following the last meeting of Hambledon Club members that year and since Richard Nyren, the secretary and 'General', was paid for his purchase of ten bottles of claret, four of port and one of sherry, the season ended on a high note. Cricket in Sussex had benefited that year from the opening by the Prince of Wales of a ground to the north of Brighton, later railed in and known as Ireland's Gardens. Middlesex played a match there against Brighton (or Sussex) at the very end of the summer, in which John Hammond scored 50 on debut. He became one of the great cricketers of the immediate post-Hambledon generation.

'County' cricket further north than Nottinghamshire had yet to develop. The *Sheffield Register* had no reports of any cricket in Yorkshire at all in 1791 and Lancashire was more than half a century away from having a county side.

Cricket as played by patrons and their social and economic dependants thus emerges as an important and well-documented aspect of the game in 1791, though few patrons could claim that their schools had been the inspiration. Eton and Harrow were the exceptions where Winchilsea and the Duke of Dorset (whose playing days were over by 1791) had respectively first played. On 22 July Eton met the town of Maidenhead in a two-innings match.

Eton's opening batsman was Keate who would return as a formidable headmaster. The *Morning Chronicle,* a 'national' paper, reported the match with the full score-sheet. Papers such as this, as well as the numerous weekly provincial newspapers, were beginning to provide coverage to games which might interest their reading public. They would give advanced notice of a match, an indication of the betting and hospitality arrangements and (though less frequently) a report on the result. Disputes were good 'copy' for the journalists though references to them should not distort our image of the game. Nevertheless, money was often involved and patrons, players and spectators alike had more than a sporting interest in events. Cricket was being played across a broad band from Norfolk in the east to Hampshire in the south-west, together with the Midlands and the north. A few examples taken from various local papers give something of the flavour of cricket in 1791 at grassroots level.

We read of the postponement of Farnham's match in Hampshire against XXII of Odiham on Tuesday, 7 June owing to the Hambledon Club being engaged 'in a grand match in Marylebone fields'. This was the match against Middlesex mentioned above: it endorses the view that there was a limited number of cricketers to go around. In Sussex, an invitation game in Chiddingly was proposed for Wednesday, 29 June for 'such persons who may choose that manly exercise and assemble together on the sport by 10 o'clock; two persons to make their choice, each alternately, in order to render the success of the game as equal as possible.' On Friday, 15 July play began at Tomsett's Green near Forest Row 'between two players at 4 a.m. and ended in a tie'.

The *Maidstone Journal* reported in detail the events at Marden on Saturday, 30 July. Play ended with Burwash needing 70 to win with eight wickets in hand:

> and the umpires declining to decide the game according to the agreement of both parties previous to beginning, the gentlemen of Marden with great civility offered to let the Burwash gentlemen off by putting 1s into their pockets and spending another out of the 2s

6d for which they played: but the gentlemen of Burwash were so ungrateful as not to accept the proposal, unreasonably demanding of Marden to spend something with them!

On Thursday, 15 September the married of Thorpe-le-Socken in Essex played the bachelors. The two-innings match between Twyford and Wargrave on Friday, 30 September at Shiplake in Berkshire, was won by Twyford by 'five notches' and, unusually, reported in the *World* with the full scores. The match is typical of the time in embracing noblemen, Esquires, those styled with a 'Mr', initialled players and the un-initialled. It is also typical in that the noblemen went in first. A report in the *Cheltenham Chronicle* indicates how seriously the laws were being taken at all levels, the paper noting on 16 September that 'a capital player of the Chelmsford side was taken ill and according to the rule of the game they were not permitted to take in another.'

Mapledurham inserted an advertisement in the *Reading Mercury* on Thursday, 9 June offering to play at Goring (two days later) 'against any side that will play'. There is no report of how many sides (if any) turned up – a rather more casual occasion than the match between Brighton and Mr Bean's Club on 29 August, which, said the *Morning Chronicle*, 'has taken up the attention of many these two days past. The bets are in favour of the former. Booths have been kept up and everything resembles a wake.'

The key source for our knowledge of the matches played by MCC, and for other major fixtures, is Samuel Britcher (1743–1803). In 1791 he published a list of the principal matches of the preceding year and a second publication in 1792 covered twenty-six matches in the year 1791. He was the pioneer of those who took cricket scoring on from the recording of notches to the setting down of a written record which could stand examination, especially at a time when huge wagers depended on a result, and when the press was taking an interest in the game.

Britcher was clerk of the parish of Linton in Kent – a centre of the game – and he had a daughter who married a Marylebone man. He was especially well known to Linton's Sir Horace Mann – another of the great patrons – and his family links, after the marriage in 1783, would have brought him up to London. As Winchilsea saw in Lord the man to run the ground for MCC, so Mann saw in Britcher someone to keep its records. Thus Britcher found himself scoring for MCC and, in due course, launching his annual publication of scores which continued, under his name, until 1806.

Britcher's publication for the 1791 season included a few other matches not involving MCC members such as, for example, East Malling v. Banning at East Malling and Waltham v. Hornchurch at Waltham Abbey, where presumably he or a friend was present to obtain the scores. Closely following him is the record printed by William Epps (1765–1833), a printer in Kent, which was published in 1799. Epps' work, beginning in 1771, ends in 1790 because, as he said in his preface, the 'regular annual publication by Mr. Britcher . . . obviates the necessity of continuing this publication.'

In 1823, Henry Bentley (1782–1857) published his record of the matches between 1786 and 1822, twenty-two of which related to 1791, and all included in Britcher's book. Bentley copied his from MCC scorebooks at Lord's which were subsequently destroyed in a fire in 1825. Bentley was a player for some thirty years, a professional umpire for MCC and a talented flautist.

From 1862 onwards came the celebrated *Scores and Biographies*, in which the lifelong researches of Arthur Haygarth (1826–1903) appeared under the imprint of Frederick Lillywhite in fifteen volumes covering the years 1746 to 1878. While drawing on the sources already mentioned, Haygarth also cited well over a hundred books, newspapers and periodicals which he consulted in an exercise first begun when a schoolboy at Harrow.

Hambledon itself has its own coterie of chroniclers and historians. To the works of John Nyren, John Mitford and James Pycroft must be added the research of the antiquarian and scholar F. S. Ashley-Cooper (1877–1932) whom Irving Rosenwater called the 'Herodotus of Cricket'. Ashley-Cooper's *Chronicle* is the printed source for the surviving 'Minutes and Accounts' of the Club. Among nineteenth-century books touching on events in the late eighteenth century is John Sutton's account (1853) of Nottingham matches. Periodicals such as the *Sporting Magazine* and (marginally) the *Gentleman's Magazine* offer occasional evidence. More fruitful are contemporary local newspapers in local county archives or at British Library Newspapers at Colindale, Hendon. Many of these furrows were ploughed in the 1920s and 1930s by the surgeon George Buckley (1885–1962).

The evidence of sources such as these leaves us in no doubt that cricket was a well-established sport in 1791. According to the *Hampshire Chronicle* of 8 August, 'cricket and archery [were] the prevailing amusements relieved by occasional visits to the Fleet at Spithead.' It competed, however, with 'driving' at Brighton, with 'wiving' at Harrogate and with dancing at Margate, wrote the *London Recorder* on 25 September.

The weekend habit was still half a century away, and games were played irrespective of the day of the week. Depending on your circumstances you might or might not have viewed the eighteenth century as a 'leisured age'. Those who toiled did so irrespective of whether the day were Monday or Saturday, many a self-employed craftsman was his own master as to when he took a day off and generously awarded one to his apprentices. The nobility and gentry were entirely the arbiters of their own timetable except for the demands of Court, Army and the Bench. The professional cricketers were often their employees, working as bailiffs, huntsmen or servants when not required to play cricket, though a new type of professional was emerging in the growing urbanisation of London. He would stay in some lodging house in Oxford Street and seek summer employment as a cricketer. There need be no surprise, therefore, that many a match began on a Monday and lasted the two days following. Cricket on Sunday did take place, though not frequently. The eighteenth century, with its latitudinarian approach to religion, stood apart from seventeenth-century Puritan injunctions and nineteenth-century Sabbatarian disapproval.

As to how many people played cricket in 1791, one can only offer the crudest of estimates. The population of Britain and Ireland, ten years before the first census of 1801, was about 17 million. From the number of matches reported there must have been at least 800 different performers, a figure which may be multiplied several times to take account of the numerous ordinary games which attracted neither the public, publicity, nor punters.

Cricket, at its apex, was a sport for some 30 men of substance and leisure, drawing upon a further 60 who were paid to play. These young noblemen and their friends assumed a leadership natural to their generation. Their leisure might be devoted to cricket and its concomitant association with gambling, but the game was also a means of establishing a relationship with the tenantry who served on their family estates. If they were not politicians themselves, they were close to the corridors of power. Winchilsea was a Lord of the Bedchamber (and would become a Knight of the Garter), and his father had been Lord President of the Council. Lennox became Governor General of Canada, his uncle was Secretary of State and his cousin was Charles James Fox, the Leader of the Opposition to William Pitt. Thanet's uncle was the cricketing Duke of Dorset who had been British Ambassador in Paris. Hambledon's last president, Lord John Russell, was the father of a Victorian prime minister (and the great-grandfather of Bertrand Russell). Even Sir Horace Mann, on whose time and purse cricket made so many demands, was a Member of Parliament.

1791 may be seen as a watershed. By then, the war clouds were gathering. The French Revolution was ending a social and cultural epoch in England, while politicians were increasingly alarmed at radical influences. At the same time, the philanthropists were calling into question a society which condoned slavery, upheld a savage penal code and betted heavily. But the old order gave way reluctantly: in June 1815, the month of Waterloo, Lord Frederick Beauclerk was still playing for MCC against Middlesex at Lord's and odds were being offered on the result while Lennox, now a Duke, would find time to play a match or two in Canada during his gubernatorial tour of duty.

7
W. G. Grace

His first century in first-class cricket
William Gilbert Grace, eighteen years old by a whisker and already sporting a trimmed black beard, had begun to get used to Isambard Kingdom Brunel's Great Western Railway. It had first borne him from Temple Meads, Bristol to Paddington Station two years earlier to play at the Oval for South Wales against Surrey and in 1865 he had come up from the West Country to play at both Lord's and the Oval for the Gentlemen against the Players. Now, on 30 July 1866, he was playing for an England XI. These were the twilight days of the travelling professional 'circuses' which frequently played against odds. Grace himself would become associated with the United South of England XI and draw his expenses – as an amateur.

The side to meet Surrey in a three-day match contained Southern professionals together with amateurs such as Grace himself. In 'unfavourable weather' England chose to bat. E. M. Grace, senior to WG by seven years and whose fame would be eclipsed by his brother in matches such as this, went for 9 runs. At 90 for three, WG came in. His innings, recorded *Scores and Biographies*, was 'steadily played as well as finely hit', with three chances. He was 137 not out overnight and on the following day was left undefeated for 224, having hit two 5s, eight 4s and done a staggering amount of actual running. There were, in those days, no sixes. The applause for his batting, it was said, could be heard a mile or so away at Mr Spurgeon's Tabernacle.

One of his partners had been James Lillywhite – who would

become, in 1877, England's first Test match captain. Lillywhite's *Annual* conceded that Surrey's 'weakness in bowling was painfully apparent'. England made 521, the fourth highest total in any class of cricket in the country. Surrey were dismissed for 99 and 126, England's bowling being 'so good [that] young Mr. Lillywhite was never put on at all.' Nor, for that matter, was WG.

Having caught out Julius Caesar, he featured no more on the score-sheet. Indeed, he had other fish to fry, for his captain, V. E. Walker, gave him leave of absence to run at the Crystal Palace where he won the 440-yards hurdles. This was unusual on his captain's part, but not unique. In a far more crucial match over fifty years later, with Middlesex's bid for the Championship hanging on the result, 'Plum' Warner let Hendren and Durston go off to play football for Brentford while Surrey were batting and his own men were in the field.

W. G. Grace had made the highest score ever at the Oval and the record stood until 1871, when he beat it himself. Twenty years or so later he wrote in the *English Illustrated Magazine* that 'at the Oval you get some of the best wickets in the world'. There, too, he would play his last innings in first-class cricket forty-two years later. It would again be for England (albeit for the Gentlemen thereof) against Surrey. The weather was not just 'unfavourable'; it snowed!

As an entrepreneur

In 1867 Grace, at the age of nineteen, followed in the family tradition by embarking on a course at Bristol medical school. The death of his father four years later reduced his financial resources, although marriage to his cousin, Agnes Day, in 1873 brought a settlement. The honeymoon was spent touring Australia and the *Melbourne Age* hailed him as 'a cricketing phenomena [sic]'. More pertinently, he was paid the staggering sum of £1,500 plus expenses on condition he played in every match.

He eventually completed his medical studies at St Bartholomew's Hospital, London and qualified in 1879 as MRCS (London) and LRCP (Edinburgh). Thereafter, he worked for twenty years both as a parish doctor for the Bristol Poor Union and in his own, largely working-class, practice.

It was also in 1879 that MCC presented him with a cheque for £1,500 from a national testimonial the club had itself instigated. He was given the money 'as he was old enough to take care of himself', noted *Wisden*.

His approach to medicine, still more of an art than a science in his time, was a practical and commonsense one. To a chimney sweep asking for a tonic, he offered, instead, a few rounds of boxing against himself.

A second visit to Australia came in 1891/92, organised by the Earl of Sheffield, for which Grace was paid £3,000 plus expenses and the cost of a locum tenens. Such tours were seen as financial enterprises and no eyebrows would have been raised at his negotiating terms.

A few years later, Grace's relationship with Gloucestershire ended abruptly. The dispute arose initially over the question of who should select the sides. Then money became an issue. Grace was known to have accepted an invitation from the Crystal Palace Company to manage the London County Cricket Club at a salary of £600. His resignation from Gloucestershire followed, though good relations were restored in 1903.

Grace was a quintessential Victorian in his commitment to work and play, and in his entrepreneurial approach to moneymaking, his self-assurance, his competitiveness and his paternal authoritarianism. In his person he symbolised the cricket's progress from the loosely organised game of his youth to the formalism of Test matches and the County Championship, with cricket linked to empire and commonwealth. He pioneered technical advances which have set the pattern for the twentieth and twenty-first centuries. His presence attracted supporters in huge numbers and could double the entrance fees charged to grounds. There remains the enigma to a later generation that the most famous amateur of his day was the best-paid professional.

MCC and Lord's

'I think of him, at the end of the third afternoon, carrying his bag in haste for the train to London,' wrote Neville Cardus. 'He would have said that his home in first-class cricket was Lord's,' declared Lord Harris. 'When a man is tired of London, he is tired of life,' pronounced Samuel Johnson. Grace, 'the great enjoyer of life' (Cardus again), never tired of life nor of London. Lord's was for him as the coffee shops were for Johnson. As the cognoscenti of the eighteenth century listened to Johnson's aphorisms, so the masses of the nineteenth century watched Grace's mastery of bat and ball. Two men of girth from the shires had come to Town.

William Gilbert Grace was born in 1848, the year of revolutions, though none disturbed England. But as has been often said, he revolutionised the game of cricket. He had first played at Lord's aged sixteen, scoring a fifty for the South Wales Club against MCC – 'my brother and I were only separated from Wales by the Severn.'

His first wicket was that of one A. Infelix ('O unhappy man') a week later. He made 34 and 47 for the club against I Zingari. Among his opponents in that second match was R. A. Fitzgerald, MCC Secretary, who must have noticed the promising youngster. *Lillywhite's Annual* thought he would be 'a good bat'.

Five years later, in 1869, Fitzgerald would second Thomas Burgoyne, the Treasurer, in nominating Grace for membership of MCC. Fitzgerald had come to office at a time when fortunes were at a low ebb, MCC's membership small and the club facing calls for a 'Cricket Parliament' to replace it as the game's arbitrator. Fitzgerald must have seen in Grace, whose reputation was now established, the harbinger of better days for MCC. Within the context of the times, the son of a West Country doctor was an unlikely candidate. But Fitzgerald judged well. The newly elected member obliged with a century on his MCC debut against Oxford University, made three more in the season and averaged 60.33 for the club. Grace made nine appearances for MCC in the year of his election and played in six other first-class matches (one at Lord's). Not for a year or so would Gloucestershire County Cricket Club – very much a family affair – start officially. In 1875, for example, he played in all Gloucestershire's matches together with five for MCC and seven at Lord's. Over the major years of his career there was some conflict of interest. He was, after all, Gloucestershire's captain.

Twenty years on, in his 'Indian Summer' of 1895, he played in all eighteen of Gloucestershire's matches while also appearing for MCC. In his whole career Grace batted for MCC on 224 occasions, for Gloucestershire 618 and at Lord's 364. In all he would make thirty-eight centuries involving MCC and/or Lord's – nineteen were for MCC. In the famous 'eight days' in August 1876, his 344 for MCC in the Canterbury Cricket Week was the first triple-century in first-class cricket. But the nearest he got to Lord's in that feverish spell of run-making was in the cab which took him from Charing Cross to Paddington on Sunday, bound for the train to Bristol. His 177 on Monday for Gloucestershire was followed by 318 at Cheltenham later in the week and his aggregate for those eight days was 839 runs. He had also bowled 181 four-ball overs.

MCC and Lord's were also the beneficiaries in 1895 when between 9 May and 30 May he scored a thousand runs (including his 100th hundred) in the month, 330 of them at Lord's. A century against Kent later in 1895 was his final one for MCC, while that for the South against the North in 1900 was his final hundred at Lord's; 'the veteran was in wonderful form [and] his cricket was faultless,' commented *Wisden*. And the 'Veteran' could still take five for 29 for MCC against the Australians in 1902. On his 56th birthday in 1904 (though not at Lord's) he scored 166 for his other club, London County, against MCC, while he bowed out of first-class cricket at Lord's in the same year with 27 for MCC against the visiting South Africans. For MCC he had made 7,780 runs and totalled 12,690 runs at Lord's.

Grace's impact on the Gentlemen v. Players match was both immediate and lasting. As Sir Pelham Warner wrote, 'the advent of one player completely turned the tables.' The Gentlemen, until his appearance, had only won seven times in twenty-seven matches. That changed with the Lord's match in 1865, though ironically it was E. M. who made the larger contribution – through his bowling. Between 1868 and 1876 WG made six centuries. The following figures show the disparity between his own score and that of the next highest batsman: 1868, 134 (28); 1870, 109 (22); 1872, 112 (48); 1873, 183 (41); 1875, 152 (70); and 1876, 169 (103). Of the 1868 innings, made on a difficult wicket, Frederick Gale in *Bell's Life* wrote: 'Had I been a batsman I should have liked to have worn a life-guardsman's cuirass and a tin stomach-warmer.' In the 1875 match he also took twelve wickets for 125 and, as a batsman, 'got runs from balls which other batsmen would have thought themselves clever to have simply stopped.'

In the following year he drove a ball 'passed the little chestnut tree for seven. Ah! That seven was a hit. The ring of it tingles in this compiler's ears,' recorded *Wisden* lyrically.

Not until 1895 did Grace make another century in this fixture at Lord's and it would be his last. In 1898 MCC changed the date so that the match would coincide with his 50th birthday. Warner, three years off his own first appearance in the match, ranked it 'among the best of these classic contests' between the Gentlemen and the Players. An injured Grace (batting at no. 9) put on 78 for the 10th wicket with C. J. Kortright in a vain bid to save the match; Grace was left 31 not out. The final Lord's match was in 1899. Grace was run out for 78 when well set for his hundred, 'his partner forgetful of his age and weight'. His side, however, won by an innings and 59 runs. At Lord's, in this fixture, he had scored 2,398 runs (40.64) and taken 108 wickets (17.25).

Grace had been playing for a dozen years when Test cricket between England and Australia began. Not until 1884 did Lord's host a Test match, and Grace made the first of his five Test appearances there. Only in these Lord's Tests was he seen at less than his very best, averaging 30.57 without making a century. Nevertheless, he captained England to victory twice at Lord's, each time scoring a half-century himself. His 75 not out was the top score in the match in 1890. *Wisden* commented: 'he hit magnificently and his innings was entirely worthy of his reputation.' Grace's loyalty to MCC and to Lord's was absolute. It had been expressed both as a player and as unifying force when relations between MCC and the emerging county clubs could be tense. In his autobiography, *Cricket* (1891), he would assert his defence of MCC's authority 'as the chief bulwark of our national game'. He was a participant in MCC's Centenary Celebrations in 1887, speaking to the toast to Medicine at the banquet and playing a part in the two matches, MCC v. England and MCC v. XVIII Veterans. Shortly afterwards, the Club commissioned a portrait of him by the artist Archibald Stuart-Wortley.

MCC elected him a lifetime member in 1899 and a later generation might ask why Grace never became President of MCC. He neither achieved that office, a trusteeship nor Committee membership. At the very least, his residence in London from 1898 for the remaining seventeen years of his life would have made such positions feasible. The *Pall Mall Gazette* had hoped for a knighthood while *Punch* satirically settled for its own variation – 'Companion of the Bat'. In truth, Grace was a generation too early for the sportsman's share in an honours list. Sir Francis Lacey, later Secretary of MCC, in 1926 became the first to receive a knighthood for services to sport. As for MCC, the presidency was never even remotely possible for someone who was no scion of the aristocracy, and could lay no claim to a public school upbringing or an Oxbridge education. What Grace did was pave the way for the Victorian middle classes – men of the professions and commerce – to enter the ranks of MCC.

By the season of 1914, many of this class were now members and, indeed, the year was the apogee of cricket's Golden Age. As the cricketers played in that warm summer, Greek tragedy unfolded. Five days before the fateful assassination of the Archduke at Sarajevo, MCC held a dinner to mark the centenary of the foundation of the present Lord's ground. Grace, 'to an overwhelming reception', replied to one of the toasts. Six weeks later he was there again to pay a final visit, fifty years after his first. It was a sombre occasion. In Sir Edward Grey's famous phrase, the lamps were 'going out all over Europe'. The Great War had broken out the week before and the Oval had been commandeered. Lord's agreed to stage Jack Hobbs' benefit match between Surrey and Kent. MCC waived the rule forbidding collecting boxes, and they were taken round the ground on behalf of Hobbs. Grace himself would also be taking round collecting boxes for Belgian refugees at a charity match in London on Whit Monday in 1915.

Five months later Grace was dead. He was not quite the victim of a Zeppelin raid, as German propaganda proclaimed, but horrified at the unfamiliar concept of total war. Men and women of Grace's generation knew only the distant war in the Crimea as a memory of their young days, or those slightly younger than themselves embarking for South Africa in the Boer War. Grace's memorial at Lord's would be a biography organised by the MCC Committee in 1919 and the Grace Gates, erected in 1923, to 'The Great Cricketer'.

8
Cricket and the Victorian Church

This chapter, and the one on 'Cricket and the Victorian Novel' which follows, take a philosophical look at the influence of cricket upon a generation which took both its church-going and its novel-reading seriously. The Victorian age was a period, as Sir Neville Cardus observed, when WG was the one 'GOM' (Grand Old Man) and Mr Gladstone the other. In the originals, which were written nine years apart, there was some overlap. I have avoided this as much as possible but James Pycroft and Thomas Hughes must still command a place in both.

In the first year of Queen Victoria's reign a Kent vicar denounced his parishioners as sinners if they watched the county play Sussex. Happily, this condemnation was untypical of the relationship between the church, or, at least the Church of England, and cricket in Victorian times. Possibly his grudge was against Sussex rather than cricket, for the Victorian clergy were generally closely associated with the game, and none more than James Pycroft (1813–95). Pycroft was responsible for reviving the match between Oxford and Cambridge Universities in 1836, after a lapse of seven years. Curiously, the identity of Oxford's captain at Lord's that year remains a mystery, but as Pycroft had not only organised the fixture but also opened the batting, we might hazard an optimistic guess. After leaving Oxford he played for the famous Lansdowne Club in

Bath and was ordained as an Anglican priest in 1841, soon becoming perpetual curate (the title was a technical one, giving him the freehold) of St Mary's, Barnstaple in Devon where he remained until 1856. The rest of his long life was devoted to writing and to his love of cricket.

In 1835, while still an undergraduate, Pycroft published *The Principles of Scientific Batting, or Plain Rules, founded on the practice of the First Professionals and Amateurs, for the Noble Game of Cricket*. To maintain his anonymity, the authorship was ascribed to 'a Gentleman'. It is a forty-four page booklet with thin brown covers and was sold at one shilling and sixpence. Pycroft listed a formal set of rules for batting. In repeating one of them he wrote, in tutorial rather than undergraduate fashion:

> I have told you once – pardon me if it has gone out of your head – that you should, on the delivery of the ball, throw back the point of the bat towards the top of the wicket; this will enable you to meet the ball by the play of the wrist, and adds very much to your power of hitting.

Pycroft also had some advice on abstemiousness:

> If you are a man carrying up and down between the stumps a wadding of meat pie, lobster, duck and seasoning, salad, with mustard and vinegar, gooseberry tart and custard and cheese with bottled porter or cider to set all working and fomenting, then let me advise solid meat with a moderate amount of vegetables and a hard crust with jelly; drink soda water or weak wine and water. Ale and porter render the eye dull.

Pycroft's great cricket work was his *The Cricket Field*, or *The History and Science of Cricket*. It was again anonymous, dedicated to the members of North Devon Cricket Club and carrying the initials 'JP'. The original edition was a slim green volume with a red spine. There were to be nine editions between 1851 and 1887, besides an American one (to coincide with the game's rising popularity there) published in Boston in 1859. The book is both informative and historical. Its technical chapters deal with how to play the game, while its historical ones seek 'to save from oblivion the records of cricket'. Pycroft is a major source of our knowledge of the game in the eighteenth and nineteenth centuries. With the heavy hand of the Victorian moralist, he wrote a section entitled 'A Dark Chapter in the History of Cricket' in which he looked at betting. But the historian triumphed over the moralist, and Pycroft let himself get caught up in the excitement.

Pycroft saw cricket as 'a standing panegyric on the English character', demanding 'not only physical and intellectual but moral qualifications also'. How typically Victorian! The appeal to the Victorian mind of pursuits which combined tests of mental agility with examinations of one's manly fibre was important. Cricket, intellectually, called for 'judgment, decision and the organ of concentrativeness' and 'cricket and scholarship very generally go together'. The moral demands on the cricketer he thought considerable:

> Of what avail is the head to plan and hand to execute, if a sulky temper paralyses exertions, and throws a damp over the field; or if impatience dethrones judgment, and the man hits across at good balls, because loose balls are long in coming; or, again, if a contentious and imperious disposition leaves the cricketer all 'alone with his glory', voted the pest of every eleven? The pest of the cricket-field is the man who bores you about his average – his wickets – his catches; and looks blue even at the success of his own party. If unsuccessful in batting or fielding, he gives up all – the wretch concentrated all in self. No! Give me the man who forgets himself in the game, and, missing a ball, does not stop to exculpate himself by dumb show, but rattles way after it – who does not blame his partner when he is run out – who plays like play and not like a painful operation.

Cricket was an expression of a man's good fellowship. In an age when the Victorian parson joined with the doctor in counselling his flock, no flotilla of psychiatrists and social workers moved in to help those in trouble and despair. Pycroft had a remedy at hand:

> Who does not feel his daily burthen lightened, while enjoying the joyous spirits and good fellowship of the cricket-field, those sunny

hours when 'the valleys laugh and sing' and between the greensward beneath and the blue skies above, you hear a hum of happy myriads enjoying their brief span too! How generous and social is our enjoyment! Every happy moment – the ball springing from the bat, the sharp catch sounding in the palm, the long reach or sudden spring and quick return, the exulting throw, with balls and wicket flying – these all are joys enhanced by sympathy, purely reflected from each other's eyes. In the cricket-field, the sport is in the free and open air and light of heaven. No incongruity of tastes no rude collision interferes.

His literary output went far beyond the bounds of cricket. There were textbooks in Latin and Greek, reminiscences in *Oxford Memories,* cautionary tales in *The Advantages and Temptations of a University Education* and several novels, one of which, *Elkerton Rectory,* makes some reference to cricket. Pycroft, born before the Battle of Waterloo, ended his days at Brighton, serving on the Sussex committee and almost seeing out the old century: he died in 1895. E. V. Lucas remembered seeing a 'tall, erect, clerical figure, clad always in black, with a cape and a silk hat, pure white hair and a fringe of white whisker walking round the ground'.

Towards the end of Pycroft's life there appeared a contribution to clerical thought upon cricket from Henry Hutchinson Montgomery, throwing light upon Montgomery's view of the game as a vehicle of social good will. H. H. Montgomery (1847–1932) – he always used the initials – had opened the batting for Harrow in 1865 with the future Lancashire and England captain A. N. Hornby. He had played at Cambridge, without getting a Blue, and was mentioned in *Scores and Biographies* by Haygarth as a fine, free hitter. 'Had he been able to participate in the great matches of the day he would most likely have highly distinguished himself.'

Montgomery was ordained to a curacy in Southwark to begin a period of fifteen years' work in London, mainly south of the Thames. From 1879 to 1889 he was Vicar of St Mark's, Kennington before spending the rest of the century as Bishop of Tasmania. In 1901 he returned to England as Secretary of the Society for the Propagation of the Gospel. He lived to a great age, and so saw his son, the future Field Marshal Viscount Montgomery, well established in his own distinguished career.

Just before he left for Tasmania, Montgomery gave instructions for his collected contributions to his parish magazine at St Mark's to be published as *A History of Kennington*. Some 25,000 words, a quarter of the book, were devoted to cricket. Montgomery aimed to give his parishioners something of the history of cricket. He undertook considerable research, knew his way about Pycroft, and made material about the game's origins available to a new reader. He described the early history of the Oval and of the Surrey club, and included score-sheets from as early as 1773, when Surrey played their first recorded match. He did not often moralise in his cricket essays, but when he did so, it was with effect:

> Cricket is the greatest outdoor game in the world. He who plays it in the right spirit learns endurance, is taught to keep his temper under trying circumstances, gives up his own selfish interests for the sake of the general good, and practices himself in undergoing a hard day's work, when eye and hand and foot are hard put to it, to overcome rivals in healthy combat. And if a man is called to be captain of an eleven he learns in his youth how to manage men, to be quick in resolution, warm in commendation, a judge of character, and a tower of strength in the moment of discouragement. Need we add a word more to prove that cricket must even be the great English game? It is more than a game: it is an education. I am ready to own that had it not been for a long apprenticeship to this sport I should have not learnt some of the most priceless lessons of life – lessons which are indispensable for all, however high they may rise in Church or State. Some learn them in the study, some in the tented field. Since success in after life depends upon *character,* English gentlemen must win their character by nobleness displayed in all their pursuits. Long may cricket continue to be the nursery for healthful, unselfish, openhanded, and generous-hearted young men.

But the real clue to Montgomery's love of the game, and his recognition of the part it played in the life of his parishioners, comes in another passage: 'It has been one of the privileges accorded to the Vicar of Kennington, in past days, to witness, from a window in the

Vicarage, many a vast, good-humoured, happy crowd impartially cheering failures and successes.'

By and large, the Victorians did not waste time. They firmly believed in the Protestant ethic of work equating with virtue. Victorian history is full of the evidence of all classes working hard, albeit the masters from choice and the servants from necessity. Victorian clergymen were no exception. They were busy about their parishes – preaching, teaching, advising and organising. What, then, is the explanation we can offer for their playing cricket?

In answer we first turn to Pycroft, whose admiration of cricket's intellectual and moral qualities has been noted. He was in the vanguard of a large group of Oxford and Cambridge cricketers destined to become clergymen. Charles Wordsworth was more distinguished a player than Pycroft. He was one of the intellectual giants of his day, and during his Oxford career achieved a First in Greats, played in the 1827 Varsity match and rowed in the first boat race two years later. In *Reminiscences of Oxford* H. Tuckwell summed him up as 'the best scholar, cricketer, oar, skater, racquet-player, dancer, pugilist of his day'. Wordsworth became a clergyman and a schoolmaster. He taught at Winchester – 'no master ever did more to promote all that was noble and manly among boys,' recalled one of his pupils. Subsequently, he became Warden of Trinity College, Glenalmond and Bishop of the Scottish diocese of St Andrews – comparative obscurity for a man who, in the words of a contemporary, 'might have been anything he pleased'.

If intellectuals such as he could justify time spent on cricket, so might lesser men. Wordsworth and (in his small way) Pycroft were pioneers of an important cult, that of muscular Christianity, embracing the pursuit of Christian ideals through manly endeavour on the sports field. Its impact on nineteenth-century Oxford and Cambridge was considerable. Men absorbing the religious fervour at the universities, particularly Oxford, were also caught up in the mood of athleticism. The equation of cricket and the church takes shape. The Victorian historian F. W. Maitland, a Cambridge man, remarked: 'The Lord delighteth in a pair of sturdy legs.' Muscular Christianity also found a firm home in the public schools, although it appealed far less to that great prototype of Victorian headmasters, Thomas Arnold of Rugby, than it did to one of his pupils, Thomas Hughes, who immortalised the Rugby of his day in *Tom Brown's Schooldays*. Arnold himself deplored what he called 'the brutality of the soul' in 'cultivated athleticism'.

But the public school headmasters of the generation after Arnold became firm advocates of the moral value of games. Many of them had been distinguished performers themselves. H. M. Butler, headmaster of Harrow who nearly gained a Blue himself, told his common room in 1868 that he equated the school's moral improvement with its admiration for physical achievement. Even E. C. Wickham, the Master of Wellington, who was a non-games player with only a slight interest in cricket and none in any other sport, believed firmly he must have a staff of men capable of beating the boys at cricket. E. W. Benson, Master of Wellington and later Archbishop of Canterbury, George Cotton, Headmaster of Marlborough and later Bishop of Calcutta, and Frederick Temple, Headmaster of Rugby and later Archbishop of Canterbury, all encouraged the cult in their schools.

The clerical cricketers of Victorian England came from this background of public school and university. As undergraduates they had absorbed the trinity of cricket, rugby and rowing, but it was cricket that survived. A man got too old for rugby and too remote from a river. Cricket remained: no wonder he played it with a clear conscience and with the hope of improving his flock; and so countless parsons up and down the land played cricket with their parishioners.

One such parson, Charles Kingsley, exuded muscular Christianity in his own approach to life (though he called the phrase itself a 'clever expression, spoken in jest'). He has told us that in his parish:

> The young men used to take their bats and stumps to church and deposit them in the belfry till after service was over, after which the adjournment to the field took place. They were dressed in their best with their sweethearts to look on.
> It was gala evening when the weather was warm and bright, and

they were on their good behaviour, and I do not remember any riotous conduct or drunkenness arising out of it all.

Kingsley hints at two important aspects of the parson and his cricket – benevolent paternalism and the fear of alcohol. Paternalism meant simply a fatherly concern for what was best for the children; a shepherd's concern for the flock. Cricket provided a wholesome use of the very limited leisure time Victorian working men and women had to enjoy. Kingsley's own paternalism became linked to Christian Socialism, which attacked the bitter injustices in society, especially in the cities and more particularly among London's poor. There is something of this in H. H. Montgomery's concern that cricket should be watched (a consolation prize for not playing) by his Kennington parishioners. The same spirit took the missions from the public schools to the poor with the aim of giving young men from deprived backgrounds opportunities for sport. Thomas Hughes taught boxing at a Working Men's College in London, which took up less space and cost less money than cricket. The fear of alcohol and its effects upon the poor led many a Victorian parson to associate himself with the Temperance Movement. Cricket was one way of giving men an alternative interest – and the game lasted a long time. One cleric founded a village club with the declared intention of reducing drunkenness and noting, after a season or two, the benefits of his idea.

Victorians were regular chapel and churchgoers. The customs of the times expected it, and indeed a Warwickshire incumbent forbade absentees from his morning service to play cricket in the afternoon. Whether anyone paid heed to the parson's sermon is another matter, though one thought that the clergy should play in the village cricket side in the hope of winning admiring congregations:

> for so shall he find that the fine hit to leg wicket which opened the mouth of the rustic spectators on Saturday, will leave them a little open on Sunday morning; and that he whom the parson has taught to twist the ball will be the more ready to listen to his dissuasives from tortuous conduct.

Aged three with my father and two cars.

Aged six with my dog.

Aged seven - very Scottish.

The Lochee Park team, 1943.

The Ardvreck team, 1942.

Ardvreck School.

Trinity College, Glenalmond.

Edinburgh University Students' Representative Council – the Executive Committee. Author seated extreme left; Anne Murdoch, second from right, standing.

Cricket at Rossie Priory.

Kelly College, Tavistock.

My father, as Dean of Brechin.

My mother.

Our marriage in 1951.

Tropical cricket.

Culham College, Oxfordshire.

Michael displays early talent.

The Reverend A.H. Winter, Moreton and Middlesex.

England v. Australia, Lord's, 1930.

W.G. Grace.

The author with Len Hutton.

Len Hutton's 364: Congratulations by Bradman, Tuesday 23 August 1938.

Fifty years on. Hutton with his biographer, the Oval, Tuesday 23 August 1988.

Captains and 'twins' in 1905: J. Darling (left) and F.S. Jackson (right).

L.E.G. Ames.

G.O. Allen.

No doubt there were clergymen who played too much cricket and incurred Episcopal displeasure. Two incumbents got round it by playing under assumed names and another retired from the first-class scene at his bishop's request after making a century. Victorian bishops and archdeacons were active figures about their dioceses, helped by the railways and by the major revival of activity in the Church of England; errant clerical cricketers would have been marked down, but, on the whole, dignitaries looked indulgently. A great parish like St Mary's, Southsea fielded an entire eleven of curates which can only have been to the general value of their work in the neighbourhood.

Who were the cricketing clergymen of Victorian times? Oxbridge Blues accounted for 209 of their number. Of 338 Oxford Blues awarded in the period, 105 went to men who went on to holy orders. At Cambridge, 357 Blues translated to 104 clerics. One man in three became ordained: a powerful advertisement for 'muscular Christianity' at work in the ancient universities. Fifty-nine men (not necessarily all having won Blues) played first-class cricket for county sides and a few were picked for the annual encounters between Gentlemen and Players. Countless others achieved lesser fame as good school and college cricketers, minor county performers and country house guests. Nearly all played much of their cricket at lower levels and for village sides. In these days of grouped parishes, it is difficult to imagine every village with an incumbent, and this in the days when what today would pass for suburbia was then still a village. The Victorian country parsons were enjoying their 'golden age'.

We cannot linger on their ecclesiastical achievements. Some became rural deans. Others aspired to canonries, prebendal stalls and archdeaconries. There were perpetual curates like Pycroft and bishops like Montgomery. Seven of the 209 Blues became bishops.

But it is as cricketers rather than as clergymen that we must contemplate their achievements. The record of the great majority must remain nestled in Victorian scorebooks, faded newspapers and treasured scrapbooks which survived salvage drives and turned-out attics. Only those who played the first-class game may be easily tracked down in *Wisden*. A few must be testimony to the many.

W. Rashleigh hit the first century by a freshman in sharing in an Oxford first-wicket partnership of 243 versus Cambridge in 1886. He later played for Kent, scoring 163 out of a total of 201 against Middlesex in 1896. A. P. Wickham, while Vicar of Martlock, kept wicket for Somerset in the 1890s wearing brown pads. Against Gloucestershire at Bristol in 1895, he conceded only 4 byes in a total of 474, of which W. G. Grace made 288. A. H. Winter, who later played for Middlesex, was in 1867 the first University wicketkeeper to dispense with a long-stop. In 1881 W. Peake bowled so fast for Oxford against the Gentlemen of England on the Christ Church college ground at Oxford that the game was abandoned after lunch. Three men had been injured on the 'hastily-prepared wicket' and a fresh start was made in the Parks later in the day. The Australian brothers P. S. and E. F. Waddy both played for New South Wales. E. F. topped the inter-State batting averages in competition with Trumper and Noble and was nominated in the final twelve for a Test match. Augustus Orlebar, Vicar of Wilington in Bedfordshire for fifty-four years, was the original of Tom Brown in *Tom Brown's Schooldays* and had played in the famous match between Rugby School and MCC on which Thomas Hughes based his book. Far different from the rural obscurity of Orlebar was the life of C. T. Studd – possibly the most unusual personality of them all. He was the youngest of three brothers who captained Cambridge in successive years from 1882–84. As an undergraduate at Cambridge in 1882, Studd made a hundred against an Australian attack including Spofforth, Garrett and Giffen. In the same summer he played for the Gentlemen and for England. He toured Australia in 1882/83, returning to captain the University in the summer. He played sometimes for Middlesex until leaving for the Chinese mission field. The rest of his life was devoted to his work in China, South America, India and the Belgian Congo. On furlough from China, he played occasional games clad in Chinese costume and wearing a pigtail.

Walter Fellows bowled 30 wides in the Westminster innings against Rugby in 1852: as many runs as his school made in their two innings put together. Four years later, as an Oxford Blue, he drove a ball 175 yards from hit to pitch on the Christ Church ground.

J. R. Napier, while serving as an incumbent in Lancashire, had two particularly good matches for the county in 1888. A fast bowler, he took seven for 102 against the Australians at Old Trafford in May and made the top score in Lancashire's second innings, helping the county to a 23-run win against the tourists. A month later he took four for 0 in the 'Roses' match at Bramall Lane, Sheffield. It was not uncommon in the nineteenth century for schoolmasters to play in the boys' XI. F. W. Wright and F. K. Hilton were two clerical schoolmasters who clearly monopolised play at the expense of the boys. Wright, a former Lancashire player, made 307 not out against his own pupils at Eastbourne, while Hilton shared in a partnership of 333 with another master for the Ardingly side.

Finally one may note Henry Manning, Cardinal-Archbishop of Westminster, who had been an Anglican archdeacon before entering the Roman church. He had played in the first Harrow v. Winchester match and retained an interest in the game all his life. *Wisden* devoted half his obituary to an explanation of why it was included at all! Indeed, the monopoly of Anglican cricketers calls for comment. Both Roman Catholics and Nonconformists had followed different traditions since the break-up of mediaeval Christendom. Catholic priests were trained abroad for the most part, while many of them came from Ireland. Their education, therefore, was neither at the public schools nor at Oxford and Cambridge. The Catholic priesthood, both by lack of association and by philosophical difference, was no part of the concept of 'muscular Christianity'.

Nonconformists, so styled because of the refusal in 1662 of some two thousand clergy to conform to the Anglican Book of Common Prayer, were banned from admission to the Universities of Oxford and Cambridge. By the time Queen Victoria came to the throne, nonconformity, over nearly two hundred years, had created its own distinctive ethos in English society. Many of its ministers had been educated at Dissenting Academies and at Scottish (and sometimes Dutch) universities. Neither by educational background nor by inclination would those who ministered in chapels be identified with cricket, especially when the game was played on a Sunday. An archdeacon, who announced that he had instituted cricket between the morning and afternoon service, looked after the match himself and found it the best way he knew of 'binding the people together,' incurred the wrath of one particular Presbyterian minister:

> The advocacy of Sunday cricket clubs by an archdeacon – does any man in his senses doubt that the handwriting on the wall has gone out against the Church of England already? The shepherds in place of leading their flocks to green pastures are leading them only to the barren heath, the stinking morass and the river of death.

This was strong stuff. The passage was contained in a paper by Dr Hugh Howat, my great-grandfather, which he delivered on several occasions to nonconformist audiences in the north of England in 1869.

One further point may be made: in the world of the Industrial Revolution, many nonconformist ministers laboured in the heart of the new cities where grass was sparse and leisure limited. Nevertheless, the name of that great historian of Yorkshire county cricket, the nonconformist minister R. S. Holmes, cannot be ignored.

But let Anglicanism have the last extravagant word:

> Put your whole soul into the game, and make it your very life. Hit clean and hard at every loose ball. 'Steal a run' whenever you safely can, for the least bit of work that helps anyone nearer to God is blessed work, and gladdens the Captain's heart. Be alert and ready, and you will keep up your end. Lay on hard and you will run up a grand score. And when 'time' is called you will 'bring out your bat', your conscience will say 'Well done', and those you have cheered and helped will say, 'A good man! Thank God for such an innings'. Aye, when on the resurrection morning you come out of the pavilion robed like your glorious Captain-King, your joy will be as full as you hear the captain and 'the innumerable company of angels' greet you with the words, 'Well played, Sir!'

All the clerical cricketing clichés which ever were can never match that priceless piece of Victorian rhetoric, from Thomas Waugh's *The Cricket Field of the Christian Life*. Montgomery might have smiled and Pycroft would have understood.

9
Cricket and the Victorian Novel

Cricket and the novel in Victorian times share much common ground. Both were turning their back on a Regency past, be it Lord Frederick Beauclerk or Sir Walter Scott; both were making an appeal to an expanding urban middle class – a receptive audience in summer or winter; both were ready to embrace the virtues of patriotism, moral fervour and self-endeavour; both found markets in the British Empire and both prospered because transport, literacy and communications sponsored their cause.

It is therefore not inappropriate that the accession of Queen Victoria should coincide with the publication of Charles Dickens' *Pickwick Papers* (1837) with its classic description of Mr Pickwick and his friends meeting Alfred Jingle on the day when Dingley Dell play All-Muggleton: 'Capital fun – lots of beer-hogsheads; rounds of beef-bullock, mustard-cartloads; glorious day-down with you; make yourself at home – glad to see you – very'. The Pickwickians settled down to watch play and we may share with them the opening moments of the match:

> All-Muggleton had the first innings; with intense interest as Mr Dumkins and Mr Fodder, two of the most renowned members of that most distinguished club, walked bat in hand to their respective wickets. 'Play!' suddenly cried the bowler. The ball flew from his hand straight and swift towards the centre stump of the wicket. The

wary Dumkins was on the alert; it fell upon the tip of his bat, and bounded far away over the heads of the scouts, who had just stooped low enough to let it fly over them.

Later in the Blue Lion, Mr Jingle, who had shown himself as something of an authority on the game, tells Mr Pickwick about his cricketing experiences in the West Indies.

> Warm – red hot – scorching – glowing. Played a match once – single wicket – friend the Colonel – Sir Thomas Blazo – who should get the greatest number of runs – Won the toss – first innings – seven o'clock am – six natives to look out – went in; kept in – heat intense – natives all fainted – taken away – fresh half-dozen ordered – fainted also – Blazo bowling – supported by two natives – couldn't bowl me out.

This is Dickens at his lightest: the cricket of good fellowship under eternal blue skies. In contrast is the pathos of the child in *The Old Curiosity Shop* (1841) dying with his bat at his bedside and, in a pamphlet called *Sunday under Three Heads* (1836), the social reforming Dickens attacked the Sabbatarian view which forbade sport on the one day of leisure the poor had. He portrays the happy scene he saw one Sunday evening of a very animated game of cricket, in which the boys and young men of the place were engaged. When a clergyman approached he trembled for an angry interruption of the sport, and was almost on the point of crying out to warn the cricketers when he realised that the good man had established the whole thing, that it was his field they played in, and that it was he who had purchased stumps, bats, ball and all. Dickens creates the same sort of setting in *Martin Chuzzlewit* (1844). Tom Pinch on his coach-ride up to London on a summer's evening passes churches in quiet nooks and the village green where 'cricket players linger yet and every little indentation made in the fresh grass sheds out its perfume on the night.' Cricket was very much a part of Dickens' life. There is a well-known picture of him bowling the first ball at Gad's Hill, his home in Kent. Once a match began he often did his duty as scorer. Not long before his death in 1870 he wrote:

Cricket really places a thousand joys within the reach of those who, without their powers with the bat and ball, would find existence a very humdrum and monotonous affair. It acts as the social cement of classes. More valuable acquaintances, more permanent and faithful friendships, have been made in the cricket field than in any other social rendezvous of the United Kingdom.

To George Meredith, a novelist more remembered today for his name than his works, Cricket was something more detached. He did not move in cricketing circles and had struggled, as a lawyer turned journalist, for some forty years before he won any recognition as a novelist. Often unsure of where he stood in society, especially when his financial circumstances were at a low ebb, he viewed Victorian England as somewhat feudal in its attitudes. Cricket had its part in breaking down barriers, as he wrote in *Evan Harrington* (1861):

> the sons of first-rate families are in the two elevens mingled with the yeomen, and whoever can do best the business. Fallowfield and Beckley, without regard to rank, have drawn upon their muscle and science. One of the bold men of Beckley at the wickets is Nick Frim, son of the gamekeeper at Bickley Court: the other is young Tom Copping, son of Squire Copping, of Dox Hall in the parish of Beckley.

Meredith, unusually for his generation, was no male chauvinist and was well aware that Victorian men could be condescending to their womenfolk. In *Diana of the Crossways* (1885), Diana envies the masculinity and prowess of Tom Redworth (her eventual husband), as she watches him play. 'I think the chief advantage men have over us is in their amusements,' she tells her friend Emma. She sees Tom as a man who might play cricket with his sons but lock up his daughters in the nursery. Emma, already married, seems to have things better organised as her husband has already given up playing, with the remark: 'My stumps are down. I'm married.'

Meredith extols the virtues of being British – he is writing in the late-nineteenth century period of splendid isolation from events in Europe. Sir George Lowton, the MP in *Evan Harrington,* conducts a running commentary on the batting of the estate team interspersed with his views on national pride. When his team wins, Meredith remarks: 'Success does not turn the heads of these Britons, as it would of frivolous foreigners.'

In the *Adventures of Harry Richmond* (1871), the cab driver supports Surrey, chiefly because they had a gentleman bowler who had done things in the way of tumbling wickets to tickle the ears of cricketers. 'Gentlemen-batters were common,' he told his passenger, 'gentlemen-bowlers were quite another dish.' Touching his hat, the driver asks why 'don't more gentlemen take to cricket? 'stead of horses.'

> Now there's my notion of happiness; cricket in cricket season! It comprises -count lot's o' running; and that's good: just enough o' taking it easy; that's good: a appetite for your dinner, and your ale or your port, as may be the case; good, number three. Add on a tired pipe after dark, and a sound sleep to follow, and you say good morning to the doctor and the parson; for you're in health body and soul, and ne'er a parson'll make a better Christian o' ye, that I'll swear.

He bids his passenger farewell with the remark that 'it was a nice joke to see a foreigner playing at it: Hadn't stomach for it.' The passenger is, indeed, borne along with a boisterousness which is typical of Meredith's style of writing. There was, wrote his biographer Siegfried Sassoon, an 'irrepressible energy'.

Meredith was a man for out of doors. A contemporary described him scouring the countryside 'for uncommon types: of cricketers and prize-fighters'. He had played a little cricket as a boy, boxed, climbed and sailed. He accepted the physical and moral challenges which sport involved – training and self-discipline. Cricket demanded that you kept your end up: 'the two last men of an eleven are twins; they hold one life between them, so that he who dies extinguishes the other.' It was the same when mountaineers shared a rope. And, for good measure, it was good for social order – 'Give some of your lean London straws a strip of clean grass and a bit o' liberty,' Squire Uploft tells Sir George.

Anthony Trollope had been deprived of cricketing opportunities in his boyhood. 'Of the cricket-ground or racquet-court I was allowed to know nothing. And yet I longed for these things with an infinite longing.' The explanation lay in his poverty. He was a Harrow dayboy walking long distances to school 'in disordered clothes' with a father always in debt and demanding constant hard work from his son. If he played cricket during his three years at Winchester as a boarder, he does not tell us so. Later, when he was an author earning £2,000 a year, he rode to hounds.

Trollope's contribution to the literature of cricket is small, although compelling and at variance from his normal style. No Victorian novelist surpasses his ability to deal with professional people and his characters are never larger-than-life figures, never out of proportion. Yet in a book he wrote at the end of his life, and which he did not even mention in his autobiography, he breaks all his own rules of characterisation. Although chapter five appeared in *Blackwood's Magazine* in 1881 under the title 'The Cricket Match', the book as a whole was published posthumously as *The Fixed Period* (1882). It is a social satire on colonialism and the expansion of Britain, suggesting that he had read Samuel Butler's *Erewhon* published a few years earlier.

To the imaginary island of Britannula (the Empire of the South Pacific) sails a community of people pledged to end their lives when they reach the age of sixty-seven. Just before the first of them surrender to euthanasia, Trollope arranges for a British gunboat to take over the island. Having done so, the expeditionary force challenges the colonists to a cricket match. The game takes place at Gladstonopolis and is set in the year 1980. The two teams embark on a month's intensive training so that 'each man should be in the best possible condition', though the visiting opening bat, Sir Kennington Oval, also finds time to fancy a local girl, the fair Eva, whose conduct gains her some notoriety.

When the match begins, Sir Kennington opens with Sir Lords Longstop. Trollope does not pause to explain why these two knights should have been part of an expeditionary force. At any rate, their team is now masquerading as England and England's opening pair are suitably equipped with india-rubber guards and a 'machine upon the head' by which brain and features are protected. But the head-gear of a future age is not worn against mere fast bowling. The batsmen face a steam-bowler ridden to its place by an attendant engineer. Fifteen minutes is spent setting the machine's sights before Sir Kennington is dismissed first ball, smoke rising from the stumps. A gun is fired to announce the fall of a wicket and Trollope supplies the equivalent of the modern cacophony of noise – 'kettle-drums, trumpets, fifes and clarinets'.

Despite this setback, England amass over a thousand runs. In their second innings, Sir Kennington makes over three hundred and the colonials are set 1,500 to win. Jack Neverbend, their captain, scores with such prolific speed that he passes his personal thousand dispatching every ball into infinite space in a ground so huge that spectators can see little without field-glasses.

On the last morning, Britannula still need 560 with three wickets left. Despite all England's efforts, the runs keep coming and off the last ball of the last over Neverbend hits a skier – knowing that he can run the single required for victory before the ball descends to be caught. The wicketkeeper makes the catch but the run counts – a clear abrogation of Law XXVI as it stood: 'A ball being caught no run shall be reckoned'.

That Trollope chose to bring a cricket match into his novel reminds us that, despite the absurdities, he was a realist with an awareness of contemporary events.

He visited Australia in the 1870s and when he came to write *The Fixed Period* England and Australia had met each other four times. When they played at the Oval for the first time in September 1880 there was, according to *Wisden*, unprecedented worldwide interest. W. G. Grace's 152 may have inspired Sir Kennington Oval's triple century, and W. L. Murdoch's 152 not out Jack Neverbend's fictional 1,275. Even the catch taken by G. F. Grace off a skier so high that the batsmen had started their third run before the ball came to rest may have contributed to the poetic licence in the description of Britannula's winning hit. Lord Harris and the Hon. Alfred Lyttelton played for England at the Oval, mirrored by the two knights at Gladstonopolis. Never before had either ground seen such huge crowds. And Trollope had anticipated something of the fierceness and political conflict which would surround the game in later years. There is a telling sentence at the end: 'They regarded it as though a great national combat had been fought, and the Britannulists looked upon themselves as though they had been victorious against England.'

Dickens, Meredith and Trollope are, of course, major Victorian novelists. Cricket gets a whisper of a mention in Thackeray's novel *The Newsomes* (1885). We turn to two very different writers in James Pycroft and Thomas Hughes, each of whom has sustained a reputation in a rather more oblique way. Pycroft, who in *Cricket Field* had set out to do for cricket what Isaac Walton did for Rod and Line, used cricket in his novel *Elkerton Rectory* (1860). Henry Austin forms a cricket club in his parish to encourage sympathy between man and man, however wide their ranks might be asunder. Men are taught 'to bowl in the fast underhand fashion and instead of vying with each other in smoking and drinking, were subjected to the improving influence of their rector'. When winter came and the public house was regaining its old customers, he formed a Poor Men's Club. Pycroft is demonstrating Victorian paternalism, so essential in any understanding of the role of squire and parson in a village. As a novelist Pycroft has striking similarities with Trollope – gentle but not unkind mocking; romance, some of it unrequited; hard work rewarded. His books were well reviewed at the time but he must remain among the forgotten Victorian novelists. When I ordered *Elkerton Rectory* in the Bodleian Library, Oxford, its pages remained to be cut after more than a century.

Unlike Pycroft, Hughes was a significant public figure in Victorian society. He was a Member of Parliament, barrister, county court judge and social reformer. His one novel of importance, *Tom Brown's Schooldays* (1857), immortalises the cult of muscular Christianity. Hughes had been in the Rugby School XI of 1841, won an Oxford Cricket Blue a year later, and stroked the Oxford crew in 1843. In the closing minutes of the fictional match between

MCC and Rugby, on Tom's last day at school, he and a master exchange views:

> 'The discipline and reliance on one another which it teaches is so valuable, I think,' went on the master, 'it ought to be such an unselfish game, it merges the individual in the eleven; he doesn't play that he may win, but that his side may.' 'That's very true,' said Tom, 'and that's why football and cricket, now one comes to think of it, are such much better games than fives or hare-and-hounds, or any others where the object is to come in first or to win for oneself, and not that one's side may win.
>
> 'And then the Captain of the eleven! What a post is his in our School-world! Almost as hard as the Doctor's; requiring skill and gentleness and firmness, and I know not what other rare qualities.'

As to the match itself, Hughes' narrative follows, more or less, the pattern of the real one at Rugby in which he himself had played sixteen years earlier. The MCC won on first innings' scores. Tom Brown went in first to 'give his men pluck and scored 25 in beautiful style'. Tom Hughes scored 29. Old Benjamin Aislabie, MCC Secretary, captained MCC in both matches, by his age a link with cricketers of the Beauclerk era.

The 'Doctor' – Thomas Arnold – was not entirely in sympathy with the cult of muscular Christianity, and perhaps Hughes is a little aware of the fact, for he dispatches him on his annual holiday to the Lakes the day before the match. Before he goes, Arnold counsels the boys not to bring spiritous liquors into the Close. The next morning, and this is a passage conveying a gamut of Victorian attitudes, the eleven went down in a body before breakfast for a plunge in the cold bath. From their different perspectives, Pycroft and Hughes were pursuing similar paths. They espoused patriotism, a manly if simplistic faith, self-discipline and the moral and physical beauties of athleticism. Many a cricket-playing country parson and many a writer of schoolboy tales embraced the same convictions. Pluck and team spirit on one plane and muscular Christianity on another would endure for the rest of the century.

Helen Mathers, in her semi-autobiographical *Comin' Thro' the*

Rye (1875), is the sole Victorian lady novelist to talk about cricket. Helen Adair, the heroine, is hard at work in the schoolroom toiling at seam, gusset and band when the door opens:

> 'Cricket!' says a voice like a trumpet. In thirty seconds the room is cleared and we are all pulling on knickerbockers and blouses! Yes knickerbockers!
>
> Soon wickets are pitched and the ball is flying from hand to hand; we are all waiting for Mr. Russell, the man who introduced the game at Charteris, or rather made it an institution for it has flourished for many years, and many a pretty young mother makes an excellent long stop or fielder to her sons, thanks to the training she received at school.

Helen awaits her first ball but unfortunately for the cause of Anglo-German relations – and perhaps for the future of cricket in Germany – she hits her first ball straight into a Fraulein's face who is led away, weeping bitterly with a bleeding nose. Upon being 'ignominiously run out', Helen decides cricket is not for her: 'Moral – stick to business'.

The circumstances of the nineteenth century made the Victorians great readers. Books enjoyed a monopoly not yet challenged by film, radio and television. Many a novelist, with a string of titles to his or her name and who enjoyed a contemporary vogue, is quite unknown today; some do not even merit a byline in the reference books. Among them one finds novelists combining romance with a high moral tone and an appeal to duty – the path of true love did not always run smoothly. Cricket has its part to play in such books and a few examples serve to illustrate. Horace Hutchison, a writer on golf for the Badminton Library on Sport series, wrote *Creatures of Circumstance* (1891) and *Peter Steele, the Cricketer* (1895). In *Creatures of Circumstance* Sybil has to make up her mind – in 800 pages – whether to marry Robert, with whom she grew up, or Lord Morningham, a young nobleman of wealth and position. Both men are cricketers though. After schoolboy cricket at Eton Lord Morningham scarcely plays, but he is at Lord's when Robert makes a century against Australia. So, too, is Sybil and her delight at

Robert's century becomes confused in a strange, contradictory medley. She marries the peer and returns one day to the village of Little Pipkin, where she and Robert lived as children, to watch the annual encounter against White Cross. Robert is around but she has made her decision and has to live with it. The two matches described, at national and village level, have the flavour of the 1890s and the reader is allowed to follow them through to a result.

The eponymous hero of *Peter Steele* is the squire's son whose cricketing career, via Oxford and the Gentlemen, is central to the book. In between playing at country houses and at Woolwich, he finds time to court Lady Emily. But first he must play against Cambridge, and Lady Emily watches him reach 99 not out at lunch. Immediately afterwards, he swings at a half volley, gets it on the edge and the catch goes to Maurice Crobyn fielding near her carriage.

> Involuntarily, unconsciously, she called out, 'Oh, Mr Crobyn!' In the painful hush all heard her clear young girlish voice. Maurice Crobyn turned his head and failed to sight the ball. Peter, little knowing the incident, laughed a jolly laugh.

Lady Emily goes home to the reproaches of her family, 'Egad, though, a dreadful thing to spoil a fellow's catch,' says her father. But, unlike Sybil, she makes the right decision (there is really no competitor) and marries Peter and their wedding presents include three golden bats and a ruby ball.

Rather a different tone is sounded in a strange little book written by Phoebe Allen called *The Cricket Club or Warned in Time* (1884). It is sub-titled 'A story for mothers' meetings'. Jack and Jenny Down live in the village of Mapledene where Jack is a good-natured, long-suffering carpenter whose only vice is playing cricket. Jenny, once a pretty young girl who had admired his talents on the field, is a tired young mother with small children about her and a nagging tongue. One day Jack collapses on the field of play. Jenny's reaction is to hope he will have the sense to give up the game. He doesn't, and soon afterwards collapses again. This time it proves fatal. Jenny is distraught with grief and wishes she had been a better wife. As the reader comes to share her misery, so he shares her joy. Jack's second collapse had happened in her dreams! As in any good fairy story they now live happily ever after: no more grumbling or fretting or complaining; no more sulking if he went out to his cricket practice; no more reproaches if he took a shilling for his club expenses.

A world away from the village green where Jack played is the image given of Lord's on the morning of the Eton and Harrow match in *Curb and Snaffle* (1888) by Randal Roberts, a tale of secret romance in unlikely quarters. Twin brothers, a bishop and a general, have sons playing in the game, set in the 1850s.

> For two days before the match, the neighbourhood of Wellington Road and St John's Wood Road has been a pandemonium by the constant traffic. Drays, omnibuses, landaus, and every sort of vehicle have found their way inside the ground and taken up their allotted position. You must breakfast very early, spot the carriage you're going to lunch on, and, if you can find someone who knows somebody who lives in those nice little houses on the Nursery side of the ground, why *then* you're in luck. For the million this gala day has no interest; the people who are to be seen there are the crème de la crème. The daughters of Eve set themselves the gratifying task of appearing in the most ravishing toilettes.

At the very end of the century and of Victoria's reign, J. C. Snaith in *Willow the King* (1899) presents us with a very modern young lady just about the right age, background and temperament to be an active suffragette in a few years time. The lunch interval finds Miss Grace, who would have much preferred to play for Middlesex than to be the belle of a London season, dispensing ginger beer, beef sandwiches and a mixture of ecclesiastical and cricket gossip. 'Look at Toddles – Blue, Kent and the Gentlemen and just a common curate.' Toddles thinks her an awful good sort and tells her so, and is promoted from ginger beer to beer or gin. After lunch, her father insists she comes round the ground to be introduced. 'But I shan't stop long. Can't stand a set of women inquiring whether I take an interest in cricket and can I tell 'em what a maiden is. I shall cut early.' Snaith, a wide-ranging novelist, played first-class cricket for

Nottinghamshire in the last season of Queen Victoria's reign. He also played cricket for a team run by J. M. Barrie called the 'Allahakbarries' (a word bearing some relation to an African word for 'Heaven help us!'). So, too, did Conan Doyle. Barrie's team was made up of cricketing authors and writing cricketers and – with honourable exceptions such as Conan Doyle – he would argue that the better was the writer, the worse was his cricketing ability. But among those who turned out for him were A. E. W. Mason, E. V. Lucas and William Meredith, the son of George. Sir John Squires' team 'The Invalids,' founded after the First World War with players such as Alec Waugh, was the lineal descendant of Barrie's and regularly played my own club in Oxfordshire, Moreton, in later years.

We have journeyed together from Dickens' *Pickwick Papers* in 1837 to Snaith's *Willow the King* in 1899. Our task is done and, in the words of Thackeray, the great Victorian novelist who has scarcely disturbed by these pages, 'Friendly reader! May you and the author meet on some future day.'

10
England v. Australia, 1905

The Ashes contest in 2005 gripped the British public with intensity unmatched in over a century of combat between England and Australia. England, more in hope than expectation, dreamed of ending Australia's sixteen-year hold on the Ashes. But after a second-innings collapse in the First Test at Lord's thoughts of an English renaissance petered away. An agonising win by 2 runs followed in the Second Test at Edgbaston, after an Australian last-wicket stand of 49 had all but snatched success for the visitors. In the Third Test at Old Trafford, England failed to take the final wicket so that the game, as intense as the previous one, ended in a draw. The Fourth Test was yet another cliffhanger, with England's tailenders securing a win by three wickets. So to the Oval where England, leading 2-1, only needed a draw to regain the Ashes. Six runs separated the two sides after an innings apiece. Rain provided an extra dimension to the drama on the fourth day and the match seemed as if it might finish in the style of one-day cricket. Soon after lunch on the fifth day England were 126 for five, but a century from Kevin Pietersen saw them safe and their total of 335 took the Ashes England's way. Bare figures alone cannot convey the euphoria, not to say hysteria, which engulfed the British Isles. The final report took the lead in the national television news that night. It was ironic that terrestrial television, which had played such a part in bringing live coverage to an avid public, had shown its last Test match for some years. On the following day England paraded in Trafalgar

Square with Lord Nelson, the victor of 200 years earlier, looking down from his column.

By one of those coincidences of chronology which delight the composers of articles, Australia toured England exactly a century after their predecessors in 1905. Let us be honest at the start: the tour of 1905 did not have the aura of that of 1899, nor that of 1902, but there is a sufficiency of interest for us to consider it. We may also pertinently ask how much the contest for 'the Ashes' was seen as such by contemporaries.

By 1905 the Ashes may be said to have achieved their majority. First spoken of in 1882, the metaphor was principally taken up by the Australian press, with some mention also in, for example, the London *Sportsman*. There are at least four distinct accounts of their origin, the most persuasive being that associated with Rupertswood, the country house in the state of Victoria. The mythology refused to die and 'Plum' Warner, who captained the team of 1903/04 to Australia, gave it respectability in his book *How We Recovered the Ashes*, marking the triumph of the first official MCC tour to Australia. Yet an English reviewer commented that the title was 'slang and of very temporary importance'.

As far as the immediate future was concerned, he had a point. The contemporary periodical *Cricket* did not once employ the term in its lengthy coverage of the Test matches in 1905. But in the long run, the Ashes had come to stay, to remain a prize of mythical substance and elusive value, and their home a matter of controversy in our own times.

One essential difference must be declared: those who came in 1905 sought to reclaim what had been lost in 1903/04. Those who came in 2005 had (in English eyes) held them for far too long.

The England captain for the 1905 series, Sir Stanley Jackson, wrote a letter to his old friend Sir Pelham Warner in 1941 during the darkest days of war. He recalled a conversation with his opposite number in that series, Joe Darling:

After tossing the coin for the First Test, Darling said to me, 'How old are you?' and then 'When is your birthday? Then we are twins. This is a record which will never be repeated.'

One hundred years later, the 'record' stands. Strange comparisons between the two men continue. Both became legislators, Darling for the Tasmanian Assembly (of which he became Speaker) and Jackson in Parliament. Both were styled 'the Honourable' – Darling by virtue of office and Jackson by family title. Each was decorated for public service, and they died in 1946 and 1947 respectively. There the similarities end, for Jackson would win the toss in all five Test matches. When the two men met in the Scarborough Festival at the conclusion of the tour Darling, stripped to the waist, proposed a wrestling match instead of the toss of a coin. But dignity prevailed and Jackson won again.

In the series itself England were undoubtedly the stronger side, although at 119 for seven on the opening day at Trent Bridge the omens were not good. In the end they led on first innings by 25 runs, and at no time thereafter did they ever concede a lead on first innings. England won at Trent Bridge by 213 runs; the Lord's Test was spoilt by rain when England led in the second innings by 251 runs with five wickets in hand. The game at Old Trafford brought an overwhelming English victory by an innings and 80 runs. At Headingley, again after a second-innings declaration with five wickets down, Australia faced another large target. Bad light brought a close ten minutes early, with Australia 175 runs behind with three wickets remaining. The Fourth Test at the Oval saw Australia needing to get 329 runs in two and a half hours. Little attempt was made, and the match concluded with the visitors over 200 behind with six wickets left. England thus won by two matches to nil. Test matches in those days were of only three days' duration. Two of the three drawn games were affected by weather.

The averages point to the superiority of England. For the first time in an Anglo-Australia series one country took the top six places in both batting and bowling averages. Jackson led from the front with a batting average of 70.28, and was a useful enough bowler, having taken thirteen wickets at 15.46 apiece. England's top batsmen after him – C. B. Fry, J. T. Tyldesley, Wilfred Rhodes, R. H. Spooner and A. C. MacLaren – all topped the Australian R. A. Duff. Collectively, they represent the outstanding batsmanship of Cricket's 'Golden Age'. Frank Laver came top of the Australian bowling averages, but still trailed behind all the English bowlers bar George Hirst. A contemporary remarked before the tour, 'English bowlers have little to learn from the Australians.' The achievements of Laver call for comment. Before the tour, the Australians regarded him as a player 'whose services might occasionally be sought' and he had come chiefly as manager. But he would return with the 1909 side more flatteringly described now as 'a bowler whose accuracy and well-concealed variation of pace suited English wickets well'. (His selection, yet again, as player-manager for the triangular series of 1912 was blocked by the Board of Control. This conflict between players and the administrators led to six of the leading Australians refusing to tour, missing out on what proved to be a rather less-than-successful experiment.)

The strength of England's batting explains why Warner was never picked at home for any of his fifteen Tests, despite being the successful – and reigning – captain at the start of the 1905 series. His leadership qualities were never in doubt and he would captain England twice in Australia (though illness almost totally spoiled his tour in 1911/12). In other matches, against the 1905 Australians, he lay 18th in the list with an average of 28.

The British public flocked to the Tests and *Cricket* commented that 'people who pay a shilling to see an Australian match are apt to economise by saving two sixpences over other matches for in these hard times there is not much money to spare.' A striking comparison between 1905 and 2005 is in seat prices. Where a Test match ticket may today come close to £50, it cost a thousand times less a century ago. Among those who watched a day's play of the Fifth Test in 1905 were the future Edward VIII and George VI. They were accompanied by Prince George of Sparta, whom the press described as 'an enthusiast over the game' – with, presumably, few opportunities to display his enthusiasm.

Those 1905 Australians, remarked *Wisden*, 'apart from the

matches against England, had a brilliant tour'. The only county match lost was against Essex, 'with far less than their full strength . . . and stale and tired after a long journey from Dublin'. They had their moments of great triumph when, for example, Warwick Armstrong made the then highest score ever made by an Australian in England: 303 not out against Somerset. Yorkshire and Lancashire were beaten in successive matches by 174 runs and 244 runs while, at the very end of a long tour, Northamptonshire, Lancashire and Kent were beaten in successive matches each by an innings.

A century ago Anglo-Australian Test matches held our ancestors in thrall just as they do today. The Ashes Tests, and the term has come to stay, provide a constant in a changing world where sport faces up to challenges undreamt of in the Golden Age of 1905.

11
England v. Australia, Lord's 1930

King George V, by meeting the players and interrupting the course of play, had taken the 'monarch's wicket' and Bill Ponsford was walking back to the Pavilion, caught in the slips by Walter Hammond immediately after the royal presentation. Thirty thousand English supporters were not sorry to see him go – a man with two quadruple-centuries behind him in Australian first-class cricket. However, he was replaced by someone who had amassed 452 not out only six months previously.

Don Bradman came out to bat at Lord's at 3.40 p.m. on Saturday, 28 June 1930 in blazing sunshine. If there were a point when he set his sights on double- and triple-centuries in Test matches, on figures that dwarfed conformity, on the ruthless exploitation of the greatest bowlers in the game, it was in the two-and-a-half hours of play remaining that afternoon.

By close of play he had scored 155 not out in exactly 155 minutes. Old campaigners like Maurice Tate and Jack White, as well as newcomers to Test cricket like 'Gubby' Allen and Walter Robins, were flayed without mercy. Hard as Percy Chapman, the captain, strove to set his field, every gap presented to Bradman seemed an inviting chasm. A maiden over from Tate earned a mighty cheer from the crowd, appreciative of his endeavours. Not a ball was put in the air by Bradman and only the remotest of chances was given when he nearly played on. Percy Fender, watching from the press box, thought that only two balls beat the bat all day. It was an innings of ruthless efficiency. Neville Cardus, in calling it a massacre and searching for some new and expressive word, wrote: 'Never before this hour has a batsman equalled Bradman's cool deliberate murder or spifflication of all bowling.'

On Friday and Saturday each side had scored 400 runs apiece – figures tauntingly similar until one adds that the Australians had only lost two wickets. Before the match England had been rated the slightly better side: holders of the Ashes and with a victory at Nottingham behind them. The England openers were Jack Hobbs and Frank Woolley, both close (Hobbs very close) to the end of their Test careers. Woolley scored 41 in the first half-hour of the match, playing a little below his best. Then came Hammond. The hallmark of England's innings was 173 by Duleepsinhji who, on debut, made the then highest score by an England player against Australia at Lord's. As for the Australians, their innings had been structured on the rocks of Woodfull, Ponsford and Bradman.

The Sunday papers praised Bradman and deplored Britain's 'black day' at Wimbledon where only Fred Perry now remained as a representative. Sections of the press took the selectors to task for picking the Australian-born Allen and the Indian-born Duleepsinhji, something very properly defended by 'Plum' Warner. Had not he and Lord Harris, both former England captains, been born in the West Indies? Nor did the Sydney *Referee* have any truck with such nonsense, reminding its readers that Archie Jackson of the current Australian party had been born in Scotland.

Bradman returned to business on Monday morning. Somehow the England bowlers kept the scoring rate below 60 an hour before lunch. Bowlers in this match on both sides needed commiseration and not condemnation. There was nothing for them in a benign, over-prepared wicket and England lacked the injured Harold Larwood (as indeed they did the batting of Herbert Sutcliffe). There were 140 runs before lunch and another 185 before a tea-time declaration. Bradman added a further 99, and his 254 was the highest score in an Ashes Test in England. The rest of the Australians, Alan Kippax, Stan McCabe, Victor Richardson, Bert

Oldfield and Alan Fairfax, helped Australia to a declaration total of 729 for six and to the highest score in the history of Test cricket. No proper '7' could be found for one of the scoreboards.

To stave off defeat by an innings England needed just over 300 runs. Cardus, a little pessimistically for an England supporter, thought that Australia ended the day on the verge of victory. Hobbs and Woolley had both fallen to the leg-breaks of Clarrie Grimmett. At the close Hammond and Duleepsinhji were still there. Hammond, with over 900 runs in the 1928/29 series against Australia, was due a large score. The 25,000 who found a reason for not going to work on a Tuesday turned up at Lord's without any expectation of victory, hopeful of a good fight, doubting that England would lose and perhaps aware of sharing in an occasion of classic proportions.

Within an hour Grimmett had got the measure of Hammond. He had dismissed him twice at Nottingham in the First Test and he did so now for a second time at Lord's. Eighty-two runs in four innings was a long way from vintage Hammond. 'Patsy' Hendren also fell victim to Grimmett's flight, spin and varying delivery height while the slow left-arm bowler Percy Hornibrook disposed of Duleepsinhji. At 147 for five before midday England's fortunes looked low and people who lived in Deal or Weymouth started consulting timetables for an early train home. Chapman put a ball from Grimmett in the air and farce intruded on the drama. Three Australians stood and watched and left the catch to one other. Chapman – dashing, stylish, debonair – rode his luck and made a century in the cavalier and carefree manner so in the nature of the man. To a left-hander, Grimmett was bowling off-breaks and Chapman hit him for three mighty sixes, making mincemeat of his analysis. His partner was Allen, who usually worked for his living on Tuesday mornings at Debenham's, though Test match selection was not counted by them against his annual leave. He had a point to prove to those members of the press who had chided him for being an 'Aussie', not to mention being an amateur cricketer who was 'not quite good enough'. Always at his best when niggled – he once won a match for MCC against the Gunners virtually single-handed after hearing the opposition pour scorn on the side he had brought –

Allen made a half-century. The partnership of 126 between him and Chapman gave England a fighting chance of a draw, somewhat squandered by the tail-end batsmen. The total of 375 brought an England match tally of exactly 800: not the sort of aggregate with which to lose a match, but then it was not usual for the opposition to be already 729 on the way.

In the final three hours of the game the Australians embarked on their pursuit of 72. Scarcely had Ponsford gone at 16 when Bradman left to a catch by Chapman in the gully, which led Sir James Barrie to turn to Cardus with the remark, 'What evidence is there that the ball which Chapman threw up into the air is the same ball that left Bradman's bat?' Catches like that were not taken by those who played for Barrie's 'Allahakbarries', a team of writers whose greatest performer was Conan Doyle, who had died a few days earlier. Just as Conan Doyle is remembered for creating Sherlock Holmes rather than for having bowled W. G. Grace, so Barrie is remembered for creating Peter Pan rather than for being a cricket fanatic. But fanatic he was and he had just written a letter to *The Times* inviting an imaginary brigadier to dine with him, 'Though I am not a brigadier, I too led my men into the tented field.' Barrie asked himself what they would talk about: 'Mr Hornibrook, their only slow left-hand bowler, I am a slow left-hand bowler. Mr McCabe, Mr Jackson and Mr Bradman; such a talk we shall have, if you will dine with me'. So Barrie and Cardus, old acquaintances, watched together in the Long Room. Nearby sat the essayist, E. V. Lucas and Edmund Blunden, whose *Cricket Country* would be a cheerful beacon written during the darkest days of the Second World War. It was as if men of letters had conspired to be together on an occasion which would imprint itself in the literature of cricket. Lord Harris, who had captained England exactly fifty years earlier in the first Test played in England, talked to 'Plum' Warner, who had led the first MCC side to Australia in 1903/04. A few yards away a very young journalist named E. W. Swanton was reporting his first Test match and boldly declaring that in Bradman a star of the first magnitude had arisen.

Kippax went immediately after Bradman and the Australian total was 22 for three. Improbable hopes of victory were entertained and

Warner later wrote in the *Cricketer*, which he edited, that for a moment it had looked as if there might be a hard finish. But the Australians had come determined to wrench back the Ashes, relinquished to Chapman at the Oval in 1926, and Woodfull and McCabe saw them home by seven wickets.

As both teams trooped from the field, a romantic would have maintained that, in such a game, there was no loser. But to what extent did contemporaries really see it as a great occasion – symbolic of the best of cricket since the end of the war? They recognised that one generation was at a rendezvous with its successors. Warner, always perceptive to young talent, wrote that 'Bradman stands on the threshold of a career which will equal and probably surpass that of any other batsman'. *The Times* wrote that King George V had been able to see an innings destined to be famous as long as the game exists and compared the batting of Bradman to the acting of Marie Tempest, 'Both so exquisitely right in design and of execution'. It also adjudged, with perhaps more guesswork than informed knowledge, that Chapman's fielding had 'probably never been equalled in a Test match'. It was a time when the two great cricketing countries were evenly balanced. Hammond might be set against Bradman, Tate against Grimmett, man for man the two sides could be matched. That many of the greatest cricketers of the day had come together was generally agreed. Contemporary reports noted the record-breaking crowds, the glorious weather and the splendour of the occasion.

There is another sense in which this match may be seen in the context of its setting – England in the year 1930. The worst scars of the First World War were healing. Men and women flocked to see a play called *Journey's End* by R. C. Sherriff, which portrayed the inevitability of death for men in the trenches, and they could also find relaxation in the same playwright's portrayal of cricket in an English village. On *Badger's Green* people lay under the trees and heard the chock of ball against bat whilst old Hobson's mare watched over the gate. The sun shone in fiction as it had done in fact during those June days at Lord's.

The infant sons of the men who fell in Flanders were old enough now to be watching, sent off for the day with their sandwiches by middle-aged mothers who had learned to cope as single parents. During the Test match the last French troops had left the Rhineland, and German pride, as an equal nation, was restored – though there still remained the matter of the Saar coalfield. No one in June 1930 was paying much attention to the internal politics of Germany. The House of Commons, conscious of the value of those twenty-two miles separating England from France, threw out by seven votes a Bill for a Channel tunnel on the Tuesday. Ramsay MacDonald, the Prime Minister, and Stanley Baldwin had found time to get to Lord's. In India Pandit Nehru was sent to prison on Monday for his membership of an unlawful association and, after the ensuing riots, MCC felt it safer to cancel the proposed tour of India for 1930/31. In the United States the stock exchange on Wall Street had crashed but the crisis had yet to make a mark on those who went to Lord's – or Badger's Green – though a poignant advertisement in *The Times* on the Saturday was a reminder of one kind of poverty which had been around since 1919: 'Ex-Officer, aged 39, willing to work at anything'. There was a world outside.

For those more fortunate and whose world was cricket a house might have been rented in St John's Wood with four bedrooms, three reception rooms and a good garden for £100 a year: convenient for Lord's and for that 1930 Test which conveyed so much of all that was best in the cricket of the period. The Test, wrote Bradman in his memoirs, was 'one of the golden chapters in cricket which connoisseurs revel in discussing by the fireside'. 'This was also a golden age,' conceded Cardus, 'the match of every cricketer's desire.'

12
A Second Golden Age

'Cricket reform has always attracted the attention of the eccentric,' wrote Robertson-Glasgow towards the end of the Second World War at a time of debate about the game's post-war future. He had, he admitted, little cause for worry: 'An interesting little battle ended in the rout of the hustlers and the triumph of conservatism.' He was right in identifying the heart of the controversy: the 'hustlers' in their plea for faster cricket and one-day cricket were using coded language for money. He would be proved wrong in his judgement that one-day cricket 'would empty the ground as surely as the rain'. Meanwhile cricket resumed in 1946 even less changed than after the First World War, when the two-day experiment was introduced. Those whom Robertson-Glasgow called 'honest, if deluded, zealots' were no match for the establishment.

Yet it would be unfair to assume an utterly laissez-faire attitude upon the part of the cricket authorities in England. MCC had set up a Commission in 1937 under William Findlay, a former Secretary, which examined the financial problems of first-class cricket and called for more attacking cricket and for matches to be brought to a conclusion. During the war, a committee met under Sir Stanley Jackson which proposed changes of a minimal nature, none of which affected either the number of counties playing or the length of matches. Groundsmen were instructed to prepare fast wickets and there was worry at the extent to which they had been 'doped' before the war.

G. O. Allen expressed his concern about doctored wickets in an article in 1938. In his view, easy-paced wickets caused even the most menacing bowler to lose his sting and, in self-defence, adopt negative tactics. Groundsmen had advanced their skills. Gang-mowers and lawn sand came into popular use in the 1920s and relieved the tedium of cutting and weed killing. There had followed greater study of the value of aeration and fertilisation in soil conditioning. But increased knowledge could bring increased contrivance, and the wickets, saturated with liquid manure and other forms of dope, brought the lifeless conditions condemned by both Allen and the Jackson Report.

Sir Stanley's report made a positive recommendation that there should be a knockout competition (of three-day matches), though it added that there were 'many practical difficulties'. Despite all the success of one-day cricket in war-time – and he himself had been responsible for organising much of it – Sir Pelham Warner's remarks at the Middlesex Annual General Meeting in 1942 conveyed the viewpoint of the majority and ensured that what had been good enough for 1920 (when he retired) would be carried into the immediate future: 'Do not be led away by the call for brighter cricket. It is a leisurely, intricate game of skill. We live in an age of speed and people are apt to think that cricket must be speeded up.' Robertson-Glasgow was on the side of the angels – though he admitted that his preference for three-day cricket was related to his preference for the three evenings which followed play: 'I should never have listened to nightly conversation on cricket, compared with which all books that have ever been written on sport are like cocoa and hot water'.

The Findlay and Jackson enquiries had been concerned with cricket in its English context – one aspect only of MCC's obligations. MCC was both a private club and the executive body of the game. In its essential role nothing changed – it remained (as it still does) the custodian of the Laws of the game; it was responsible for overseas tours and Lord's was seen as the headquarters of cricket. Test matches were administered by Boards of Control; each country sent delegates to the Imperial Cricket Conference, which had met since 1909 and with more frequency after 1930 as its membership increased, though the ICC in those days did little more than determine the dates of Test matches and rubber-stamp MCC resolutions.

The one great controversy MCC faced was the bodyline affair of 1932/33; almost a trial of Empire as well. Officialdom at Lord's had to think on its feet and politicians in both Westminster and Canberra had anxious moments. No other crisis emerged for either MCC or the ICC, though lurking in the shadows, never in the limelight, was the issue of colour. South Africa simply did not play against the new members of the ICC from 1928 onwards in whose ranks were coloured players. In the first Test against South Africa in 1929 England selected Duleepsinhji. He only made a dozen or so runs in the match, and that was perhaps the excuse for dropping him for the rest of the series (despite the fact that he enjoyed a season in which he finished seventh in the national averages). E. W. Swanton has written that 'there was evidence of political pressure from the South African end' and of the distress it had also caused to Duleepsinhji's uncle, Ranjitsinhji, who had experienced something of the same thing himself when an undergraduate at Cambridge.

Not until the 1960s would the 'D'Oliveira Affair' bring the racial issue out into the open, by which time the Imperial Cricket Conference sounded like an anachronism (in 1965 it became 'International'). As for MCC, the committeemen at Lord's would eventually have to share power with new bodies such as the Cricket Council and the Test and County Cricket Board. From 1947 onwards Empire gave way to Commonwealth. Neither Lord's nor Westminster could be seen any longer as the fulcrum of imperial authority and the duo of cricket and Empire had played its last tune.

Cricket in the Second Golden Age avoided radical change because, as much as anything, the game sustained its popularity. At international level it still had a rarity value, and was unchallenged by the fiesta of international competition which sponsorship, air travel and supporters' package tours brought to a later generation. Despite the misgivings of *Wisden* at the arrival of new countries on the Test scene, they brought a certain magic to the game. By comparison with today, when virtually every Test cricketer is well known to every other through constant meetings in Tests, in one-day internationals and on the English county circuit, cricketers of the Second Golden Age were often strangers both to one another and certainly to the watching public. Every cricketing country enjoyed the excitement of players arriving from another land, perhaps with distinct cultural differences and bringing to the descendants of emigrants a whiff of the land of their forebears. A Test match or the tourists playing against county, colony, province or State was an event to be cherished for its infrequency, its appeal undiminished by familiarity. Only the English tourists of 1932/33 to Australia were sent on their way at the end of the tour in no doubt of the low esteem in which their hosts held them. Yet even then, when Anglo-Australian relations were at their lowest ebb, the *Sydney Morning Herald* compared the imperial bond through cricket to 'hooks of steel'.

Domestic cricket too maintained a strong following. Crowds, still without the intrusion of television into their homes to set standards of excellence, were content to watch the fortunes of some lowly county, the aristocratic combat of Oxford v. Cambridge or Auckland v. Otago.

The social expectations of spectators everywhere were not high. The great majority sat on uncomfortable benches or stood, often exposed to the elements whether hot or cold. The game remained reasonably priced – even cheap – and the whole structure of cricket was shored up by the evidence of countless lovers of the game for whom the long day of travel and watching was one of pleasure, appreciation and fellowship.

The players were not unaware of these perceptions. Many felt a sense of obligation to the crowd and, according to individual temperament, would show it by some piece of buffoonery, the signing of autographs or the exchange of quips over the boundary fence. Batsmen who were 'stars' were aware that they should make runs because people had come to see them. Yet with obligations went a sense of fun. Len Hutton, in a phrase he half-regretted later, once declared that the game was not played for fun in the sense that A. P. Herbert told the House of Commons, 'People are not here for fun.' But Hutton enjoyed his cricket and retained a zest for it right to the end, and few men had more fun out of politics than APH. At one end of the scale was the guileless fun experienced by the South African, Ronnie Grieveson, who simply wanted the 'timeless' Test in 1939 to go on and on; at the other, there was the utter dedication of the Yorkshire professionals Wilfred Rhodes and Emmott Robinson, whose universe was cricket and who grudged a Sunday on which they could not bowl.

To the first-class cricketers of the Second Golden Age fun prevailed. Like the spectators who watched them, the players did not have high expectations. The player did not expect to take home a silken purse, nor did the watcher arrive at the ground expecting to be cosseted in comfort. There was never much money for the run-of-the-mill English professional. Cricket, one of them wrote, lifted his fellows 'for a period from the rut of the commonplace and gave them in their palmy days an entrance into realms far above their station'. It was a remark heavy with Victorian undertones in its acceptance of social distinctions. Sutcliffe would have given it little credence, although even he thought it better to decline the Yorkshire captaincy rather than cause embarrassment to some of the Committee. Hammond, by choosing his friends among the amateurs, distanced himself from his fellow-professionals and found it a financial struggle to keep up standards of dress and entertaining in the social ranks to which he aspired. To a young professional like Hutton, success meant being able to get married when he was twenty-three, and to buy a house without a mortgage, though the purchase owed more to a benevolent patron than to his Yorkshire wages. Wages paid in cash were, indeed, the normal way to reimburse professionals. When Parsons returned to professional cricket after his career as an Indian Army officer, his county made a special exception to allow a cheque to go to his officer's account with Cox and King's. Touring sides would wonder at all these very English distinctions and be mystified when they entertained MCC in their own countries containing players who were neither MCC members nor permitted to walk within the portals of Lord's. Touring captains such as Gilligan, Tennyson and Allen did much to reduce discrimination among players travelling together for months.

In essence, the capped English professional cricketer was seen, in his own country, placed at the head of working-class society while those who displayed an independence of attitude, social ease, business acumen and cricketing talent would move into a middle-class milieu. Sportsmen will always be distanced to some extent from conventional social judgements and, as J. M. Kilburn observed, the professional cricketer of the 1930 'held a high ranking in sport' even in the sombre economic climate of the times.

One can exaggerate, and much of this must be seen in the perspective of public attitudes. Players were appreciated for their talent and liked for their personality, irrespective of whether their initials appeared before or after their names. The triumphant Yorkshire side were feted throughout the county with complimentary rounds of golf and theatre tickets there for the asking.

These were still the years of the amateur. From the Indian princes downwards, there were those rich enough or independent enough to play first-class cricket: the sons of business houses with, for a few years, indulgent fathers; those who found ways and means to play at some personal sacrifice or those who simply put cricket above climbing the rungs of their chosen occupation. It became less possible in the 1930s as the effects of the worldwide Depression began to bite.

The status of the amateur cricketer was not seriously under threat, and he enjoyed a variety of conventions, perks and quirks which distinguished him from his fellow professionals. He would use different hotels, dressing-rooms and railway compartments. He might, if he played for Warwickshire in the 1920s for example, drink what he liked at lunchtime while his professional colleague was permitted to spend no more than nine pence on drink. J. H. Parsons of Warwickshire had once been the professional Parsons, J. H. and would revert to his original status. The Second World War made a nonsense of much of this – there was a wartime game in which the participants included Aircraftman P. A. Gibb and Private N. W. D. Yardley and Major Sutcliffe, H., and Second-Lieutenant Verity, H. – but the fact remains that it would not be until the 1960s that the distinction between amateur and professional disappeared.

Whatever the labels and the order of initials, cricketers were recognisable figures featured in lurid colours on cigarette cards, in the tabloids or fleetingly glimpsed by the cinema newsreels. They flourished in an age of increasing press publicity and the evolution of broadcasting.

Those who reported upon first-class cricket knew that they had a duty both to their editor (since continued employment depended upon his good favour) and to the public. Neville Cardus has told of his summons to C. P. Scott, the editor of the *Manchester Guardian*, for supposedly describing the 'wrong' arm when Woolley was batting. On being informed by Cardus that Woolley was a left-hander, Scott declared he would never again criticise a specialist member of his staff. Nevertheless, such editorial regard kept young journalists on their mettle and Cardus left feeling the offender for having led the great man into error. Editors, after all, decided who reported tours and the preference for Bruce Harris, who knew more about tennis than cricket, over E. W. Swanton to go to Australia in 1932/33 probably deprived the English public of a quicker insight into what was happening.

As for the public, reporters were aware that they were expected to give a portrait of a day's play for those who might not know the scores when the paper arrived on the breakfast table the following morning. Much of the reporting was generous in both quantity and in attitude. Compared with a later age the press was more ready to create heroes rather than to destroy reputations. Even when he was going through a very bad patch in 1934 the journalists, as a whole, stuck by Hammond. Because his batting failed, they were at pains to praise his bowling and fielding, for which 'he was worth a place alone,' said the *Daily Mail*. Hutton was 'spotted' early, particularly by J. M. Kilburn in the *Yorkshire Post*, and he was praised to the point of embarrassment in the national press, only *The Times* offering more sober, and even caustic, judgements.

Those who had played the game at first-class level might be employed either on a regular basis or under contract to report a tour. C. B. Fry was the doyen of a distinguished group of English players which included Warner, Jardine, Fender, Gilligan, Hobbs and

Robertson-Glasgow. Warner, for years, depended on journalism for a personal income. He had learnt the trade before 1914, sometimes reporting on matches in which he had himself performed well. It was not unreasonable for him to write, anonymously of course, in *The Times* that 'Mr. Warner played a faultless innings of 150' when it was probably true! After he retired in 1920, this particular conflict of interest disappeared (he would have others) and he was a faithful correspondent for the *Morning Post* from 1921 to 1932. His writing was at once factual (if sometimes mildly inaccurate) and historical though there were times when the reader got an essay on great players rather than the 'evidence' with which he might confront his colleagues on the 7.40 to the office.

Much more than Warner, it was Cardus who pioneered the cricket essay as an art-form, closely followed by Robertson-Glasgow. Cardus drew heavily upon the imagery of music (Beethoven for preference) while Robertson-Glasgow turned to the classics, especially Virgil. Musical analogies and classical allusions could enhance the word-picture of a dreary day between the showers at Southend, Lancashire doing battle with Yorkshire at Old Trafford or Gimblett smiting the attack at Taunton. Cardus gained followers in abundance and his published collections were among the successes of the comparatively small market for cricket books of the day. Players to whom cadences and hexameters were as remote as playing cricket in Alaska might grumble or chuckle, as the mood took them, when they saw their names in some Cardusian or 'Crusoeian' flight of fancy but, on the whole, they welcomed the publicity he gave them. Sir Leonard Hutton has remarked that these were the two cricket writers who appealed to him most, and on whom he tried, in a modest way, to model his writing for the *Observer*.

Cardus was the *Manchester Guardian* so far as its cricket readers were concerned, but for a few years in the 1930s he had a colleague making his own claims. C. L. R. James was a Trinidad journalist writing on cricket and laying the mental foundations which would produce his post-war classic, *Beyond a Boundary*, in which he crystallised his ideas on the evolution through cricket of a national West Indian identity.

Cricket writing in *The Times* was in the hands of Dudley Carew and Major R. B. Vincent. Both were typical of a generation of writers who turned their hands to many sports. Vincent, for example, was primarily a golfing and rugby man. Neither attempted flights of fancy but rather offered their readers a detailed account of a day's play which stands the test of time. If the reader, fifty years later, wants to know exactly how Bradman was bowled by Bowes, the chances are he will be told. Whether or not a particular match is reported (apart from the obviously great occasions) depended on whether an editor could spare a reporter.

The 'nationals' might fail to give more than the cricket scoresheets supplied by the Cricket Reporting Agency but the 'provincials' would often remedy the deficiency: cricket was well served by provincial journalists. A. W. Pullin ('Old Ebor') of the *Yorkshire Post* was typical of the dedicated writers who would travel around with county sides writing lengthy reports upon their doings. He worked to the last, dying on the bus to a Test match at Lord's in 1934. In his early days his 'copy' was dispatched by pigeon from various Yorkshire grounds. Men such as he and his successor, J. M. Kilburn, and many another provincial journalist, wrote with shrewdness and authority and they were vital in sustaining the links between the players and the public. Even cricket at county second XI level received plenty of coverage. When I first met Canon Jack Parsons, on becoming his biographer, he was approaching his ninetieth birthday. I dared to doubt a very old man's recollections of a double-century on his debut for Warwickshire second XI. The files of the *Birmingham Post*, in considerable detail, soon confirmed his achievement.

The amount of first-class cricket played in England meant that a great number of journalists found employment. In the other cricketing countries particular writers built up a reputation, among them Louis Duffus in South Africa, Ray Robinson in Australia and Dick Brittenden in New Zealand, and – among the players – Arthur Mailey. Jack Fingleton was the professional journalist who happened to be a very good cricketer.

The distinction between good press reporting and what makes

literature can be blurred. Cardus wrote with an eye to publication in a more permanent form and his was the cricket prose which commanded the largest support in his time and which (despite the revisionists) stands examination in our own. Warner – no mean trafficker in cricket writing himself – was flattered to receive the great man's accolade in a private letter: 'through your pages come the glow of nature, civilisation and courtesy' – a commentary, perhaps, on both men. A. G. Macdonell, in one book, and Hugh de Selincourt, in several, wrote fictional cricket classics set outside the first-class game which were the stuff of romantic escapist literature, while the two great chroniclers and historians F. S. Ashley-Cooper and H. S. Altham published seminal works which consolidated decades, almost centuries, of cricket history. The famous series of books in which different authors dealt with 'The Fight for the Ashes' belonged to a period before instant reporting supplied every known fact about a Test series between England and Australia. Cricket writing remained selective: not until the 1970s was there a plethora of authors whom a later generation of enthusiasts kept in business.

Of the writers from cricket's Second Golden Age, E. W. Swanton would still be active in the 1990s. Sixty years earlier he had embarked on a career which took him to the top of his profession – his hallmark is his sheer professionalism. To have sat beside him at some match is to have observed a man who watched the game carefully, made notes and prepared his piece. The resulting article would declare his mastery of the game's technique, be fair but penetrating in its judgements, acerbic if needs must, and – with the ease of a novel – pass backwards and forwards in time. Swanton would put a match or an incident in its historical context and offer some conjectures on the future for a team or a player. If something needed to be said without beating about the bush, he could be relied upon to do so with judicious impartiality and measured tones. Swanton was on the edge of the first-class game as a player, wryly observing that he would have liked a few years with Middlesex to see how he might have done.

At the very end of this period, the young John Arlott left his policeman's beat for the press box to make his own magisterial contribution to cricket journalism. Both Swanton and Arlott won distinction in the related medium of broadcasting. Swanton, in measured deep tones, became something of a specialist in summarising a day's play. Arlott, in a voice that seemed to evoke the cricket of Hambledon and Hampshire, made poetry of his prose and gave a word-portrait of those who, as with Cardus, were always very close to being his own perpetual heroes.

No one in 1919 had ever heard a cricket commentary, but the technology which made broadcasting possible was known and the basic patents necessary for its operation were being secured, primarily in America, by business interests. The British Broadcasting Company (later a Corporation) was formed in 1922 and one of the earliest broadcasts on cricket was a talk in 1925 by 'Plum' Warner on 'Prospects for the Season' for a fee of eight guineas. Twelve months later, as Chairman of Selectors, he gave a talk on the eve of a Test discussing the team he and his colleagues had selected against the Australians and he was involved in the discussions which led to the introduction of 'eye-witness' reporting on county matches in 1927; he and Canon F. H. Gillingham being the BBC's first performers. The art of commentating came to be associated with the names of H. B. T. Wakelam, Michael Standing and Howard Marshall – in the 1930s their voices were synonymous with the presentation of first-class cricket in England. In 1939 the series between England and the West Indies brought the first sustained ball-by-ball commentary. Elsewhere, the impact of wireless on huge countries such as Australia and South Africa brought cricket to those who might never expect to see a first-class match in their lifetime. Broadcasting between one country and another developed more slowly because of commercial and technical difficulties. In 1928 Warner gave the first cricket broadcast (though not a commentary) from England to Australia and the 1932/33 series was relayed through Paris from Australia. Swanton broadcast the MCC tour of South Africa in 1938/39 back to England.

During the war some one-day games in England had time allocated by the BBC and a feature of Learie Constantine's important weekly broadcasts to his native West Indies – ostensibly on the British war effort – were his remarks on how West Indian XIs were performing against wartime sides such as London Counties, the British Empire XI, the Dominions, or an England XI.

After the war Constantine continued as a commentator – 'the equal of anyone else and superior to most,' remarked a colleague. By then the voice of Alan McGilvray was becoming familiar: a symbolic link between Australia and England first heard during the bitter British winter of 1946–47. Gradually the structure of large commentary teams became established in the immediate post-war period, with the voices of Swanton, Arlott and Rex Alston. They were joined by what H. F. Ellis has called a 'mighty cloud of witnesses' as experts and statisticians trooped in to air their opinions and figures and ensure that silence would never be golden.

On the other hand, silence on television was sometimes a virtue and commentators had to learn when to let the picture tell its own tale. Television in Britain had begun in 1936 and two years later the cameras were at Lord's for the first time to record the Test match against the Australians. Wakelam did the first commentary and was lucky enough to have Hammond's great innings of 240 to talk about. Two months later he was at the Oval to comment on Hutton's 364. After a total closedown during the war, television took some time to re-establish itself. By 1948, when the Australians came again, there was a British viewing public of millions able to watch on their black-and-white screens snatches of play, though it would be 1950 before a Test match outside London was televised. What might be accomplished and the relationship between television and sponsorship – not to mention World Series cricket – lay far in the future.

All the attention which cricket received from what we have learnt to call 'the media' was bestowed on a game which Lord Harris called (significantly in 1931 rather than a year later) 'more free from anything sordid, anything dishonourable than any game in the world'. In an ideal world it was a contest between bat and ball in which it was as essential to see a man dismissed as to see him get runs. Conditions would allow the ball to come on to the bat with an even bounce off a firm pitch so that strokes could be played with assurance and confidence. For the bowler, there would be the expectation of sufficient pace in the wicket to give him a chance, while the effect of rain or the passage of the match into its later stages might allow the spin bowlers to come into their inheritance. In many ways this simple philosophy prevailed whether applied to the black marble tables in Australia, the natural soils of England with a deep-rooted growth of grass or the matting wickets elsewhere. When concern arose that batsmen were making rather too many runs, the laws were changed to make the stumps slightly larger and to give the bowler a greater opportunity to secure a leg-before decision.

Both batsmen and bowlers in the first-class game profited from the absence of any demands made upon them to play one-day cricket. In the stock phrase, nos 5 and 6 in the order had time 'to build an innings' while a bowler was constrained neither by limitations on the number of overs nor upon field placing. Modern devices designed to give high drama and constant action in a game in which money is the prevailing force would have found no abode. Perhaps in this lies the essential difference between then and now. No game stands still and an observer from (say) 1949 would say of cricket fifty years later that batsmen had things less their own way, that bowlers lacked variety, that fielders were more athletic and that more time was wasted.

So there ended a golden age – golden in its personalities and appeal. Cricket in the Hammond/Bradman years drew the crowds for the ferial as well as the festal days. Albeit the counter-attractions were fewer and the pace of life slower, yet people went to the cricket when they might have stayed at home. The game had a pleasurable purpose about it: not yet shackled by the bonds of commerce. Even the ongoing English County Championship did not detract from the rarity value first-class cricket enjoyed. Test matches were infrequent and thereby glamorous; visitors were exciting guests from faraway lands; Sunday was a day of rest.

It is all relative. The past has perfection and the present seems imperfect. The past cannot hurt us and the present can bruise. Only politicians tell us we have never had it so good; cricket-lovers are more ready to proffer such judgements on generations other than their own. Old men watching praise the virtues of those they saw when they were boys. Gold Medals are for winners of Man of the Match awards – instant glory. Golden accolades are for Ages – times remembered.

13
Faded Memories – Essex, 1939

As Ottomans go, it went: a tatty, decaying piece of furniture whose coverings had long since abandoned any attempt to preserve their shape and texture and whose legs appealed for splints to support their declining years. Someone had once loved it, but it had known better days. For the price of a few pence, it could finish up in my back shed – something to tinker with on winter evenings. As a child who has bought a goldfish at a fair and who goes home uncertain of its reception, I crept warily into the house with my purchase. My wife looked surprised. 'What on earth are you going to do with that old thing?' she asked.

That evening we were due to play the last evening game of the season but the rain came down at 5.30. The landlord of the Bear lost some potential trade and I stripped the hessian off the undercarriage of my trophy. Then came the great discovery, and I had my evening's cricket after all, for out cascaded faded newspaper cuttings of Essex cricket in the July of 1939.

How generous was the press coverage! A whole page bore the details of the weekend performances of Walthamstow, Chingford and Adelaide; of the Finchley Ramblers, Leytonstone Nomads and Plaistow Wanderers; of Buckhurst, Ranlegh and Epping. Full scores were reported, each with a pithy introductory sentence such as: 'Ranlegh were in a bad way when seven men had gone for 54 but T Crosthwaite senior and T Crosthwaite junior put a better complexion on the game.' There was a contest between Essex County Council officials and the League of Three. What an intriguing name! Who was in league with whom? Did three men conspire (like the Graces, WG, EM and GF) to take on all comers? For this occasion, at least, the League signed on a further eight – all to no avail against such consular efficiency. The ECC XI dared to declare at a mere 92 and deposed of the League for 66.

But, of course, part of the charm of old cuttings lies in what is 'on the other side'. We keep some item of interest to ourselves, tuck it away in a drawer and years later find it again – what is on the back is of just as much interest. My paper told me that Wanstead Fire Station hoped to take a Cup at the Billericay Auxiliary Fire Service Bank Holiday Festival; that there were houses for sale in Wanstead for £695 provided you paid a deposit of £3– (the page was torn); that Hornchurch had some seven hundred satisfied purchasers of bungalows so far – and well they might – at weekly repayments of 13s 5d (67p); that there was space for 4,000 cars at West Ham Speedway where Invincibles, 'the greatest side ever opposed to a League team', would meet West Ham – yours to watch for 1s 3d (7p).

What had brought the Ottoman from Essex to my Oxfordshire village? And why all the cuttings about cricket? Had the owner so loathed the game that everything about it one July evening had been stuffed into the lining? I burrowed again among the fraying pages and found a banner heading: 'Cricket and the Weather – Walthamstow unlucky in recent weeks'.

It was the era of prosperous 2nd and 3rd XIs: Old Heronians II lost to Theydon Bois II; Epping II slaughtered Chingford III. They must have hoped for a fixture against Chingford II in 1939 had not Hitler intervened. J. H. Leiper, a schoolboy at Chigwell school, was tactless enough to score 136 not out and take six for 36 against the staff on Saturday and would have to face his masters in class on Monday.

There were cricketers who bore famous names. Constantine appeared for Goodacre while his namesake toured that summer with the West Indies. P. F. Warner scored 32 not out for Woodford Wells

II while the famous PFW managed an MCC tour to Denmark. Why had Clapton and District Cricket Association announced a mid-season meeting to discuss matters affecting their Sunday Cup? And the heading in the Court News caught my eye: 'Watching a Cricket Match'. 'PC Bell said he saw the defendant sitting on a seat and using bad language'. 'I only had one drink,' said a domestic servant, aged 56, of no fixed abode. Nevertheless, the magistrate fined her 10s (50p) or seven days.

For me, the most intriguing item was the report of Wanstead's Sussex tour. They played Storrington, the little village immortalised as Tillingfold by Hugh de Selincourt, lying in a fold under the Sussex Downs where dear little cottages looked out over the mill-pond and there was the pleasure of simple things. The real Storrington used stumps painted white, made tea on a primus and got water from across the road. The make-believe Tillingfold beat the Australians. The players of Storrington became the characters of Tillingfold, and on that July day in 1939 de Selincourt himself took five Wanstead wickets. Did Messrs Logue, Wynnes, Hudon, Alcock and Ewer realise they had fallen to one of the great classic writers on the game? De Selincourt once said he lived for white shirts, not black or brown ones. Alas! The black and brown ones were to triumph for a spell. War was in the air and our faded scraps of paper said so: 'It is hard that at a time when we look forward to our holidays, our future should be overclouded and uncertain because of one man,' declared Mrs Winston Churchill, opening a fete at Chigwell. In the 'Leytonian's Log', plans were outlined for an ARP display. Soon the cricketers of Essex would be defending their coastline.

14
Cricketers well met

In the course of writing numerous books and articles on cricket I have been privileged to meet many of the game's greatest players and journalists. All were willing to see me and the great majority gave invaluable help. In this chapter I present some reminiscences of a dozen of these famous figures. In determining an order of 'batting', in the end a team selected alphabetically seemed the least controversial method.

Sir George ('Gubby') Allen of Middlesex and England played in twenty-five Test matches and led his country in the tour of Australia in 1936/37, designed to heal the wounds of bodyline. Subsequently, he was President of MCC, its Treasurer for a dozen years, a very good Chairman of Selectors and a powerful voice at Lord's for two generations.

In talking to Allen, I found him a shrewd and fluent commentator on people and events. There was, perhaps, not a great deal of warmth in his personality, but he was gracious in his home in Grove End Road beside Lord's and I recall him, as an old man, turning out on a bitterly cold night to come to the launch of my biography of 'Plum' Warner. Indeed, that book had caused him some agitation.

He believed that I had in mind to re-tell the tale that he was the natural son of Warner. Coolly, he indicated that he would take me to court if I did. I assured him that the facts did not give credence to the rumour, whereupon he said, 'Well, let's have some coffee.' His portrait in the Committee Room at Lord's is a reminder of the influence and authority he wielded (without arrogance) at the game's headquarters.

Leslie Ames, the great Kent and England wicketkeeper-batsman, who played in nearly 50 Tests, was the first professional cricketer to be appointed a Test selector. He became successively secretary and president of Kent and was manager of three MCC tours. My association with him was brief. I drove across from Oxfordshire to Kent one winter's morning to be greeted with, 'You must have a good breakfast before we talk,' and a splendid meal was produced. There followed a fascinating discussion, mainly focusing on the events of the Australian tour of 1932/33. Ames took a more kindly view than most of Warner's management of the bodyline tour. He was a man of immense courtesy, a natural leader – as his war-record showed – and I had happy memories to reflect on during the long drive back to Oxfordshire.

John Arlott was one of the most distinguished commentators on the game, in a lineal inheritance from Neville Cardus. Both men were in the romantic rather than the classical tradition of writing and both men were endowed with both a deep love of cricket and a command of language. My first meeting with Arlott proved traumatic in my career. He had guardedly suggested that I might try a book on Constantine and would like to meet me. The 'interview' did not go well. I had tactlessly taken my son Michael with me and Arlott was a man who deeply mourned the tragic death of his own son. Just as I felt there was no more to be said and the encouragement was not forthcoming, the front door bell rang. The unexpected guest was Gerald Seymour, by now a well-established thriller writer, who knew us both. I had once taught him as a very lively VIth former, and we had kept in contact. The mood changed, and when I eventually left Arlott assured me of his good will and assistance in finding a publisher. Winning the Cricket Society's award for the best cricket book of 1975 was a welcome bonus and it launched me on a new career in writing cricket books.

Arlott and I kept in touch over the years, and there was always generosity and a welcome from him. David Rayvern Allen's fine biography does him full justice.

Xenophon Balaskas bowled South Africa to their first Test victory in England at Lord's in 1935. He subsequently played in eight other Tests, picked primarily as a slow leg-spin bowler, though he was a good enough bat to score double-centuries in first-class cricket. He appeared for several provincial sides in his country. I met Balaskas at his Johannesburg house, where he had set up a net with a concrete pitch. We had time for a chat before two groups arrived: youngsters whom he would coach almost daily and the survivors of the famous 'timeless' Test of 1939 whom he had invited to meet me, though he himself had missed out on that particular Test. I recall the delight of Ronald Grieveson. 'I just kept wicket day after day and I had a Test average of 57 in my one Test!' They talked to me about Wally Hammond and reflected on his captaincy in that series. It had been a tour of great harmony and they credited Hammond's leadership. It was an imaginative gesture of Balaskas to invite them.

Sir Alec Bedser, one of the great bowlers of all time, played for Surrey and England and was the mainstay, in his fifty-one Tests, of England's immediate post-war attack. He is regularly to be found at Lord's at Test matches and, in the Committee Room, sits avidly watching. He is a good talker with strong memories of the past, and is generous in sharing them. I have not so much 'interviewed' him as been the beneficiary of his recollections. If cricketers today – and especially bowlers – lack the ability of the players of his day, it is his privilege to say so.

W. J. Edrich, the Middlesex hero, with Denis Compton, of the summer of 1947, made thirty-nine appearances for England. He shared, with Compton, the winning partnership against Australia at the Oval in 1953. We met at his house in North London. I think it the only time I have been pressed to have a gin and tonic at 10 a.m! We talked about Hutton and his great innings of 364 in 1938; of Edrich's failure in that match and the bad run of form which followed; of Hammond's faith in him in South Africa in 1938/39, when he made 219 in the last Test, having made 20 runs in the previous four Tests. Naturally a cheerful soul, he spoke of his gathering concern for his career as he failed in innings after innings.

Tom Graveney of Gloucestershire, Worcestershire and England is the first former professional to be President of MCC. He was a stylish right-handed batsman who made seventy-nine appearances for his country. He was a prolific runmaker, scoring nearly 48,000 runs including 122 centuries. He was elevated to the presidency at Lord's in 2004 ('I can't believe my good fortune'). I met him several times but two instances suffice: I was going to the funeral of the cricket celebrity Hugh Pickles. Tom Graveney heard of his death on his car radio, changed direction and joined the distinguished group of cricketers (and clergy) at Blewbury Parish Church. I gave the address – or rather was one of two who did. The other occasion was when my son Michael was with Gloucestershire and we went to watch him – with our cat whom he had called 'Graveney'. The cricketer was desolate that we did not introduce him to the cat. 'I've never had a cat called after me before,' and nor has he since.

Jack Ikin of Lancashire and England made eighteen Test appearances as a left-handed batsman. For his county he was a right-arm leg-break and googly bowler, taking over three hundred wickets. He shared a partnership with Hammond in the only Test against New Zealand in 1947 and never met Hammond again. Ikin met me as I turned off the M6 on to the A500 road and there we talked about that tour to Australia and New Zealand in 1946/47. He had appealed for a catch when Bradman was 28 in the First Test, which was disallowed. 'What a way to start a series,' Hammond allegedly hissed at Bradman. The 'catch' was of historic importance. Had Bradman gone, he might well have retired from Test cricket instead of going on to average 97 in the series and coming to England in 1948. But Ikin admired Hammond, who had protected him against the left-arm spin of Tom Burtt and 'ensured that he himself faced him while I gained confidence. The sense of hero worship never left me.' It was a strange place to conduct an interview – in a car close to a motorway. I sensed that Ikin was a sad man, not in good health. When he discovered my wife was a psychiatrist, cricket faded from the conversation and more personal matters took over.

Harold Larwood, the Nottinghamshire and England fast bowler, retired to Australia – despite the furore of the bodyline bowling series twenty years earlier. I chatted to him in Sydney in the 1980s. He was a small, even frail, old man. It was difficult to see him as the terror of Australian batsmen all those years ago. There was no rancour but a fierce defence of what he had done and the stern assertion that he was a professional, under orders from his captain, Douglas Jardine. The legacy of the great social gulf in his era between Gentlemen and Players was clear in his conversation, though any personal bitterness that remained focused on his virtual rejection after the tour was over.

Reg Sinfield, Gloucestershire all-rounder, had one game for England against the 1938 Australians. His first-class career exactly spanned the inter-war years. He later became a coach at Colston's School, Bristol and when he was deemed too old for that post Clifton College took him on. One of his protégés was the England batsman Chris Broad. We had a wide-ranging conversation. He showed me proudly the silk copy of the score-sheet of Gloucestershire's famous tie with the Australians in 1930. He had, he said, 'never seen Wally Hammond so excited'. He remembered Hammond declaring against the New Zealanders a little later when he was 92 not out – 'never thought himself greater than the game'. Sinfield also recalled his hard upbringing on the training ship *Mercury*, which C. B. Fry ran at Hamble. It was an institution so formal in its structure, so efficient in its organisation and so severe in its discipline that Hitler sought Fry's advice when setting up his own Youth Movement in Germany. But Sinfield was ready to praise the institution rather than condemn it. He was a man of serene temperament who accepted his lot in life and was the epitome of the professional cricketer of his day.

So, indeed, was 'Tiger' (E. J.) Smith, a wicketkeeper-batsman for Warwickshire and England before the First World War. Later he became a Test match umpire and the county coach. When I visited him in 1978 he was over ninety but, as so often with the old, had crystal-clear memories of cricket sixty or seventy years' earlier. He told me how he successfully negotiated a fee of £300 for the season of 1920. He described the economic straits into which the professional of those days found himself. 'You stayed in as cheap a hotel as possible. I got supper, bed and breakfast for seven shillings and sixpence.' But in a revealing sentence, full of social undertones of the day, he added: 'the game lifted you from the rut and gave you a place above your station.' Smith was full of praise for Jack Parsons, the professional turned amateur, who switched again between professional and amateur status, and who led Warwickshire towards the end of his unique career. 'He was one of the greatest players we've had in front of the wicket [and] he led a disciplined side and knew what he wanted.' Parsons, like Hammond, was one of the players of the inter-war years who bridged the 'social divide'. I have one last thought on 'Tiger' Smith'. Wicketkeeper as he was, he looked at my hands: 'schoolgirls' hands,' he said disparagingly, with a look at his own gnarled and aged pair. It was not for me to disagree but to thank the glove manufacturers of later generations and modestly admit that he had 'taken' tougher bowling.

John Woodcock at one point had reported more Test matches than any other journalist, and his dictates on the game have the same magisterial authority as those of his mentor, Swanton. Yet they differ so much: the one an imposing, dominant figure; the other a diffident man, modest and slight in build. Woodcock I first met when I was an elderly yet utterly inexperienced journalist – very much an 'Officer under Instruction'. He was helpful and kind and led me up the proper paths. Subsequently, we have been associated for almost twenty years in the deliberations of MCC – and for some of those I had the great honour to be his chairman. His contributions were always worth listening to – measured, balanced and endorsed by great experience and deep wisdom. If Swanton had been the commanding officer, Woodcock was a first-rate adjutant; but then, of course, he took over his own 'command' in writing so purposefully for *The Times*.

Bob Wyatt of Warwickshire, Worcestershire and England played in forty Test matches for his country and captained on occasions. Subsequently he served as a Test selector and chairman in 1950. I met him at his home in Cornwall when he was in his late eighties and living in a house with a staircase dangerous for a man of his age. But he would survive many years more, dying in 1995 at the age of 93. We talked about the bodyline tour and he was generous in his views on Warner, as manager – 'the ideal man when selected,' he remarked, 'and did his best to ensure better relations after the drama of the Brisbane Test. Warner kept in close touch with the players and he did not lose credibility.' Wyatt was more sympathetic to Warner than many another; the more surprising as he believed Warner was principally responsible for him being sacked from the England captaincy in 1930.

They were a splendid bunch of men and I look back with some pride to have met them. All of them had tales to tell, delighted in so doing and gave a warm response to my questions. Collectively, it was a rich experience.

15
Three England Captains

In the 1980s I wrote biographies of three England captains – 'Plum' Warner, Walter Hammond and Len Hutton. They posed different problems for a writer and I discuss some of these below.

On my first visit to Lord's, in the closing weeks of the Second World War, I was taken in to the Pavilion and met Sir Pelham Warner. He delighted in meeting a newcomer to his 'kingdom and his cathedral' and he gave me a conducted tour. I had experienced his 'charm' – as so many had done and would do for so long. It was a word he used so often of others when he wrote their obituaries.

To Warner's 'charm' must be added his commitment to cricket. He invested time, knowledge, judgement, affection and dedication, which the circumstances of his life and generation permitted. Such an opportunity to dedicate one's life to cricket is unlikely to be repeated in this or forthcoming generations.

Some forty years after my meeting Warner at Lord's I was invited by Urwin Hyman to be his biographer. The challenge was a formidable one: after his cricket career was over, there were as many years in which cricket was the beneficiary of his lucidity as a writer, his perseverance as a broadcaster, his urbanity as a chairman and his ubiquity as an observer. A biographer needs friends and allies, and I found one at once in his granddaughter. Marina Warner is a distinguished writer, critic and broadcaster who gave me all the help she could and who understood the need for primary source material. There was certainly plenty of it. Some four thousand letters, postcards and scraps of information were my starting point.

Broadly, a biographer follows a traditional pattern, taking the reader through the decades of his subject's life and providing a pen-portrait of the passing of the years. Warner required some variation in balance. For almost the first sixty years one covered his life in six chapters. The final four dealt with Warner's final thirty years. But there lay a period of six months which commanded two chapters in the middle. 'The Burden of Management' and 'The Legacy of Discord' describe the events of 1932/33, during which Warner visibly aged, despaired of his love of cricket and sought some consolation in the friendship of a lady who remained a financial charge for the rest of his life. Warner's management of the bodyline tour of 1932/33 would be a millstone and present him with conflicting obligations of loyalty. His relationship with the England captain, Douglas Jardine, was fraught and he poured out his troubles in his letters home to his wife. Part of his problem lay in the fact that he had worn too many hats. He had, as a journalist, criticised the leg-theory bowling of W. E. Bowes in the summer of 1932: 'If all fast bowlers were to adopt his methods there would be trouble.' He had, as a selector, picked both Bowes and Jardine for the tour. As a manager he had nothing to declare when Larwood and Voce, with Jardine's approval, employed tactics similar to Bowes'. I devoted some 20,000 words to what remains an ongoing saga in cricket's folklore. As late as 2005, a book was nominated for the Cricket Society book award of 2005 entitled *Gubby Allen – Bad Boy of Bodyline?*

Warner could be two-faced; that proved the heart of the problem in writing his biography. All the accolades are there – and rightly. But I could not ignore the evasion of responsibility when things went wrong; when a player was selected (by him) and failed, and could not gloss over the variance between his public and private image.

At the same time, it made him a more interesting person to write about. In a long life, often plagued by the pain of a wretched digestive system and with a mind which shrank from contending with the ugliness of dispute, there had been moments of triumphal ascendancy – when he brought back the Ashes in 1904 and got married in what the press called the 'wedding of the year'. There followed a period of halcyon calm up to the First World War when he was in the front rank of batsmen, outstanding for his county, and lived a life of comfortable, upper middle-class affluence. The graph dropped perceptively after 1914 and in the 1920s. Then came bodyline. The final years – and there are thirty more of them – find him busy as an author (three books written in his seventies), worried about money (the books, he sees, as a financial necessity), dreading 'rejection' at MCC's AGM, where not till he was eighty was he appointed President, and disturbed by the lady-friend of Australian days living a stone's throw away (and relying on him for money).

Yet he could still, even to the end, muster the confidence and passion to go to Lord's, write generous letters to his friends and remain 'the survivor'. This he had always been, from the days at Rugby when the frail but tanned West Indian went for nature walks rather than play football – but no one dared bully him. His was a life worth writing.

Warner was one of the first to recognise the outstanding talents of the young Hammond. Writing in the *Morning Post*, when the younger man was only twenty, Warner 'watched him with special interest [and] liked his cricket immensely'. It was the beginning of a friendship confirmed when Warner visited the desperately ill Hammond in hospital only three years later – in 1926. Hammond would write that he 'gave me the strength to turn the dark corner from hopelessness back to life'. It was a friendship which lasted the years, and it owed much to Warner's influence that Hammond became the first professional to turn amateur and captain England.

Friendship is not a word which immediately comes to mind in thinking of Hammond. When I was approached by Allen and Unwin (three years before the same publishers asked me to write on Warner) to be his biographer they set out their approach from the start. There was an existing biography on Hammond, written some twenty years earlier by Ronald Mason. It was typical of many biographies of the 1960s: the hero was admired from afar, seen only as a performer, praise flowed from the pen of the writer and no hint was given of a world apart from cricket.

Allen and Unwin wanted something more. They wanted to reveal what made Hammond tick, and to ask why he found relationships so difficult, whether he was conceited or arrogant, what happened in South Africa and if he died in poverty. Clearly, I was being invited to give a much fuller picture of the man than that found in Mason's book and answers had to be found. I struck a deal with the publishers. Normally, an author meets his own expenses and sets them against his profits in filling his income tax return. I insisted that I must go to South Africa to meet his widow. Allen and Unwin agreed to pay the airfare and I would pay for internal travel in South Africa.

But where should I travel to in South Africa? I looked up the telephone directory – conveniently available in Oxford – for the major cities in South Africa and selected some dozen people called Hammond. After four or five false starts, I tracked down Mrs Sybil Hammond. My journey to meet her in Durban ended with the not inappropriate greeting, 'Mrs Hammond, I presume.'

Although 'South Africa' would be the final chapter or two in the book, I felt it had to be examined first. And so it proved. There was not only Mrs Hammond but also the vice-chancellor of Natal University, Owen Horwood. He had given Hammond a job at the University as its first Sports Administrator. Far from being 'the man who cut the grass' (as much conventional view believed him to be) Hammond was a major influence in the development of South African University cricket in the 1960s and on Provincial and Springbok cricket itself.

Hammond found in South Africa a peace of mind which had eluded him in England. His happiness came from his marriage to a South African, Sybil Ness-Harvey, in the birth of three children and – paradoxically – by his not being seen in the context of a great cricketing figure. Anonymity was part of the clue to his pursuit of happiness. If South Africa did not make him rich, it gave him a modest income. His death, at the age of sixty-two, left his young family grateful for the help of an Appeal launched by the Dukes of

Norfolk and Beaufort. A Trust Fund, on which I serve, was set up and still benefits deserving ex-first-class cricketers and their dependants every Christmas.

Hammond struggled to cope with fame, found it difficult to give praise where it was due and could not relate to those who saw him in the context of cricket. There was a strange tea party when he was a youngster. Marie Lloyd, the great Victorian actress of the 1880s, met the shy eighteen-year-old (already a professional with Gloucestershire) and remarked: 'All that boy wants to do is to hit a cricket ball as hard as he can.' She had, in a nutshell, identified his dilemma. He sought achievement but shrank from its concomitant fame. Hammond's shyness, for that was what it was, explains many of his traits that attracted most criticism: remoteness as captain, aloofness as a player and awkwardness as an individual. There were people who could break through the shyness, but they were in the minority.

Hammond had been a colossus from the start. At Cirencester Grammar School he had averaged 613 in house matches (the next boy had 17). As a bowler, he took almost a wicket an over. In my biography that 'greatness', sustained throughout, had to be conveyed to the reader. Hammond was to be shown at the apex of his career, after a memorable 240 at Lord's against Australia. And his flawed character had to be shown as well: the man who found it impossible to congratulate a colleague when all around him were doing so.

In a sense, Hammond was the victim of the age he lived in. He was sensitive to his social class. He neither fitted into the artisan circles of the professional cricketer nor into the amateur ranks of public school and Oxbridge men. And yet he was an officer's son and a grammar-school boy. Hammond chose to identify with the amateurs. In manner and dress he aped their style, but lacked the financial resources to fit comfortably into their world. The professionals, not just on account of his talents, felt more comfortable calling him 'Mr Hammond'. He was not quite one of them. Turning amateur in 1938 provided something of a solution. He was, in the end, the man whose mastery of technique delighted the cricket purists but whose philosophy of life faltered; who amassed runs yet failed to amass the personal assurance that men crave; whose cover-drive was a gift from the gods but whose craftsmanship in the building of relationships was frail. He was a great public figure, but a very private man.

Sir Leonard Hutton kindly agreed to write the foreword to my book on Hammond. He had admired the man as the cricketer 'who, on all types of wickets, had no superior' but also as a man of modesty: 'I never heard him say an unkind word about anyone.' It was Sir Leonard who asked me to write his own biography – which appeared in 1988 under the imprint of Heinemann. There was a difference: the other two England captains had both died some twenty years before I started work on their biographies; Hutton would see what I had to say. A pattern of work evolved. I would visit him at his home in Surrey, after navigating the M4 and M25 (well past rush-hour), arriving for coffee-time. The first twenty minutes would be spent discussing the great man's health until Lady Hutton reminded him why I had come. He would respond to my questions in the enigmatic vein commentators and journalists the world over had encountered so often. There were also requests for me to mention things which I felt unable to include, usually dealing with money. Hutton, in a working career as long as his cricket one, felt he was undervalued and wanted me to say so. His wife demurred but gave me some wise advice very early on: 'You are not writing a book to please us.'

There were some parallels with Hammond. Both men, from lower middle-class backgrounds, became captains of England at a time when that honour usually went to their social 'superiors'. The great offices of English cricket are a closed shop – it would be the twenty-first century before a former professional cricketer became President of MCC. Both Hutton and Hammond were conscious of the burden of fame, but Hutton handled it rather differently.

The 364 at the Oval in 1938, under Hammond's captaincy, became as much a millstone as a milestone in Hutton's life.

Holding the world record he was conscious, ever after, that when he went out to bat some youngster had come especially to see him and he must not fail.

Of Hutton himself Neville Cardus had written: 'this was a cricketer, an artist, with more than Hammond's strokes – much more.' One of the problems facing the cricket biographer is the relative evaluation of talent. He can, of course, follow Cardus's line, giving praise but always inclined to see the generation before as greater. But wherever we place Hammond and Hutton in the hall of fame, we give the accolade of greatness to them both.

'Greatness' was something that Hutton coped with better than Hammond despite the burden he felt it imposed upon him. Like Hammond, though less self-evidently, he could shrink from the crowd and distance himself from the players but always as a transitory act rather than a permanent projection. And his sense of humour, if once one could penetrate it, had a whimsical streak. It was easier to discern the rigid foundations of discipline, self-denial and achievement which were the groundstones of his Moravian background – that strict, demanding Protestant sect. One had to grasp this background in order to understand what motivated Len Hutton and made him the model pupil. 'I've taught him all I know,' was the judgement of the great Yorkshire coach, George Hirst. None learned better.

Yet there remained a certain underlying insecurity. He would be the first professional captain of England and there were always conservative swords out to attack him. Despite Cardus's eulogy about his strokeplay, he was accused, through much of his career, of being too cautious and defensive. Many, many years later I sat next to him in the Long Room at Lord's at an autumn dinner. 'The best cricketer in the room,' he murmured, 'but they don't put me on top table.'

Hutton was not vain or conceited, but he had a Yorkshireman's appraisal of his worth. In the many visits I paid him I detected a certain sense that cricket and the world in general had not given him his due. Yet the affluent circumstances of his life in the south of England seemed to belie it. We went to Yorkshire together, in tandem, as the joint speakers at a Pudsey celebration. For all his reputation and achievement, I sensed he wanted me there as well, as if he were not entirely welcome in the pastures he had left behind. Nor was I, indeed, welcome when I was bidden to speak on the edge of midnight after a lawyer who preceded me had gone on for so long. 'I have had to wait a long time to bat,' I began and, as the clocks neared 12.15 a.m., I closed my innings.

Some of these judgements I hesitated to use because I was writing a biography of a man who was still alive, but the 'good' things I could – and did – say. No one had ever remotely challenged Hutton's quality of modesty. Indeed, as a person, he tended to undervalue himself. The imp of vanity could dance elsewhere. He became cricket's 'verray parfit gentil knight' and deservedly so, displaying the knightly virtues of chivalry, honour and valour as a player and a man. His folio of figures was the ledger of his life.

16
Three Cricket Characters

Cricket, like other sports (but perhaps rather more than most) has always produced 'characters'. They are those who by their personality, conversation and larger-than-life characteristics win the affection of the populace, make a mark and (in due course) bequeath a memory.

One such is the broadcaster Henry Blofeld. No mean performer himself until injury put him out of the running for the great things in the game, he became a commentator in that long list of distinguished performers whose utterances are unique, and whose observations ornate. With Blofeld his obsession with the natural world dominates, and while he is in the press box no robin redbreast can fly past unheralded. Yet no bird may intrude on, or indeed passing bus invade, his critical judgements on the game itself.

'Blowers' brings a breath of fresh air. His catch phrase, 'my dear old thing', immediately addresses his public and arrests them to his acute, critical and temperate judgements. But there is excitement too: no one can convey the sense of infectious enthusiasm as he does when a game is at a dramatic point. You, the listener, are at one with the commentator in sharing the experience, being aware of the occasion and getting in tune with the mood. You have not paid your money to go to the ground and you almost feel glad that you did not. There, pitchforked into your living room, is the atmosphere of the unfolding drama. You can hardly keep your seat and the everyday noises around you pale into insignificance. You are captivated and, if not already a devotee, you become a convert.

Part of the broadcaster's task is to win converts to the game. Test Match Special has always been a good recruiting ground and Blofeld is high in the batting order. He may talk to millions, but he has the broadcaster's gift of addressing just one. Your devotion is won, your conviction secured and you have joined the ranks of cricket's following.

When that admirable reporter on the staff of the *Daily Telegraph*, Sue Mott, commented that she could 'hardly think of a greater loss to English cricket' than Stephen Green, there was a good-humoured chuckle among those who knew him. Green had just retired from the post of curator at Lord's, which he had held for thirty-five years. He was never the best-dressed curator – indeed, his only predecessor was a woman and his successor the immaculately dressed Adam Chadwick – but the crumbled suit with bulging pockets was a trademark. So, too, was the care and detail with which he dealt with endless queries and minutiae. The wetter a Test match day, the more people flooded into his rooms at Lord's. He would be affability itself to them all, with his own particular catch phrases such as 'My lord' – however lowly the recipient of his accolade – or 'I haven't shares in it, of course,' when making a case for a particular project or enterprise.

But perhaps he was as popular out in the field as at Lord's. It was never, of course, the cricket field. He once said that being bowled by a lady on the Cross Arrows ground put an end to activities in that direction. It was the wider field of cricket societies where he was such an outstanding success and where institutions would ask him back for a second or third visit. He thought nothing of giving a talk somewhere in England, getting to Portsmouth and catching the last ferry (at midnight) back to his flat on the Isle of Wight. One sensed that Green cultivated the role of an eccentric. He can be erudite in his conversation and the tortuous paths of church history are never far from his thoughts. The acquisition for Lord's of a portrait of Frederick Beauclerk, cleric and cricket enthusiast, was a particular delight for which he took some credit. Green, one feels, could equally be at home in the eighteenth century and, as a non-driver, would not miss possessing a car. Mechanical things, still less the complexities of computers, remained a mystery for him to the end, compensated by his retentive memory. Since leaving Lord's he retains a vast coterie of friends. Many came to his party on the Isle of Wight to mark the bicentenary of the Battle of Trafalgar. People of all ages came to be greeted, as ever, by a happy mixture of bonhomie and skill in blending all sorts together. In a sense his retirement has been a great loss to English cricket after all.

I was keeping wicket industriously for Hugh Pickles' XI against his former club, Wantage, in the annual fixture. One never knew whom Pickles would invite to play there, though it was a reasonable guess there would always be two or three of the current England women's team. Bill Frindall might be present and once a Pakistan player, Nawaz Sarfraz, fielded at first slip in carpet slippers because he had injured a toe. It was an interesting combination, but not half as interesting as what followed. A lady walked – no, stormed – across the pitch bearing a threatening umbrella (on a sunny day) and demanded to see Pickles. Without a word, he disappeared with her and Frindall took over the captaincy. When he returned, three hours later, looking somewhat ashen, it was with the remark: 'Never take weddings on the second Saturday in September: Wantage match.' Gradually, in the bar, we pieced together the story of the bride who had waited in vain for the parson.

When it rained at Lord's, Test Match Special (and especially Brian Johnston) would fill in with stories about Pickles – a legend in his lifetime. He must have been unique in receiving permission from his bishop to take Holy Week off and go as chaplain with the MCC team to the West Indies. His absence from his parish was often explained away by the slurred words, 'got to go to Lourdres'. Yet it would be unjust not to mention that he was a faithful parish priest at Blewbury on the Berkshire Downs. Though the Church of England did not recognise him with a canonry, the Church in Japan did and he was a canon of Kobe.

In what proved to be the last year of his life, I played for his XI against his old theological college at Oxford. Tea was in the common room. What was once a quasi-monastic institution with no females save the housekeeper now hummed and squawked with life. There were students of both sexes, including an Anglican deacon (feminine) in a fetching black costume. After tea Hugh Pickles performed a hat-trick in what was almost his last match.

At the end Canon Pickles joined the students in the college chapel – his doubts about the ordination of women mollified by the 'beautiful reading of one young lady,' as he told the rest of us in the Bat and Ball later. His funeral, only a year later, drew a distinguished congregations of clergy and cricketers. I was one of two who gave the address. 'Who else,' I told the vast assembly, 'would have two preachers – one for each end of the wicket?' And no less a cricketer than Tom Graveney, when he learned of the funeral on his car radio, turned round and arrived in time. Such was the respect which Hugh Pickles attained in the cricket world.

17
Sir Neville Cardus

Sir John Frederick Neville Cardus (1888–1975), writer on cricket and music critic, was born on 3 April 1888 at 4 Summer Place, Rusholme, Manchester, the illegitimate child of Ada Cardus (1870–1954). His forenames were registered as John Frederick. His father may have been John Frederick Newsham (b.1867), whom the seventeen-year-old Ada married three months later on 14 July 1888. The marriage, however, did not last long, and the description of Newsham as a 'smith' hardly fitted Cardus's own comment that his father may have been 'one of the first violins in an orchestra'. The boy lived with his maternal grandparents. Robert Cardus, his grandfather, had a policeman's pension, Ann Cardus took in washing, and the household finances were augmented through the activities of Ada (who briefly returned home) and her sister Beatrice as prostitutes.

Yet the home was not quite the slum Cardus suggested and, even for the poor, the community of Rusholme, in late nineteenth-century Manchester, offered cultural expression in its cosmopolitan nature, free libraries, and music halls. The young Cardus took what he could from his working-class background, learning to read and write at the board school in Rusholme, using the libraries and reading his grandfather's *Manchester Guardian*, and getting his taste for music as a chocolate seller in the Comedy Theatre. Variously, he had delivered his grandmother's washing, boiled type in a printer's business and driven a carpenter's handcart before, in 1904, he became a clerk in an insurance agency with the Fleming brothers, benevolent employers who encouraged him in his self-education and would let him off to watch cricket at Old Trafford. This was the time when he acquired his deep affection for Lancashire cricket and for the game's 'golden age'. He remained indebted to the Flemings, who for eight years (1904–12) 'stood between me and destitution'.

Great literature, especially Dickens, and philosophy had their place in Cardus's grandiose pursuit of culture, but it was music that mattered most. He attended concerts at the Free Trade Hall and heard the first performance of Elgar's first symphony on 3 December 1908. He saw Sir Thomas Beecham conduct *Madama Butterfly*, and his own first musical criticism, 'Bantock and style', appeared in the monthly *Musical Opinion* in 1912.

Yet in music, unlike cricket, Cardus was no performer (though he briefly took singing lessons) and it was his cricket in that same year (1912) which gave him his first opportunity. On the strength of his figures as an off-break bowler in Manchester league cricket he successfully applied for the post of assistant cricket coach at Shrewsbury School. When war broke out in 1914, he volunteered for service but his poor eyesight brought rejection. The headmaster, C. A. Alington, was aware of his unusual interests – he had spotted him reading Euripides in translation – and appointed him as his secretary. The idyll of Cardus's four years at Shrewsbury – 'because of Alington, I call myself an Old Salopian' – ended when Alington went to Eton. He was willing to take his secretary, but only if he could be assured that Cardus would not be conscripted.

C. P. Scott, editor of the *Manchester Guardian*, took the persistent 28-year-old into his office, just as Alington had done, as a secretary. By 1917 Cardus was learning the all-round trade of reporting and writing briefly on drama and music. Two years later he reported his first cricket match. Throughout the inter-war period, readers of the 'M. G.' would be avid followers of 'N. C.' on music and 'Cricketer' on cricket.

A measure of financial security (although all his life he was fearful of being poor again) allowed Cardus to marry, on 17 June 1921, Edith Honorine Watton King, a schoolmistress. He gave his father's name (perhaps for respectability) as Frederick Cardus. There were no children. At about this time Cardus, who had always been known as Fred, adopted the name Neville, which alone appeared on his marriage certificate.

Cricket, even more than music, provided the medium through which Cardus could display his treasure house of literary knowledge and satisfy his aesthetic appreciation of grace and movement. Neither his account of his marriage nor of his one great scoop – A. C. MacLaren's eleven beating the 1921 all-conquering Australians, with Cardus the only major journalist present – stands microscopic examination. But both show his abilities in embellishing the non-essentials to make a well-told tale.

Cardus was essentially a writer with a talent for handling words, presenting balanced and harmonious prose and drawing on his deep reservoir of reading. Above all, he wrote for others' enjoyment because he enjoyed writing. Cricket and music were the chosen media through which he expressed himself. The one gave him the greater fame, the other the greater satisfaction. In his approach to both he sought to understand emotions which lay behind technical performances. He was a romantic in the sense that he paid more attention to the spirit and beauty of what he saw and heard than to the mechanics of endeavour and achievement.

Cardus was an innovator in his cricket writing. On what had been, in earlier hands, a descriptive and narrative enterprise, he imposed criticism. To the sights and sounds of the game he brought his own use of imagery, metaphor and allusion, with which he created a mythology of characters and scenes. But elegance and wit redeemed him from pomposity.

Cricketers took on the guise of characters: Macartney, Figaro; MacLaren, Don Quixote; Spooner's batting matched the poetry of Herrick. Yet the imagery never swamped Cardus's ability to analyse. Of Wilfred Rhodes he wrote: 'Flight was his secret, flight and the curving line, now higher, now lower, tempting, inimical . . . every ball a decoy and one of them – ah, which? – the master ball.'

In commercial terms, Cardus was an immediate success. He doubled the summer sales of the *Manchester Guardian* and, as early as 1922, a publisher gave permanency to his reports in *A Cricketer's*

Book. There followed *Days in the Sun* (1924), *The Summer Game* (1929), *Good Days* (1934), and *Australian Summer* (1937). All were distillations of his 9,000 words a week. In the twenty years between the wars he wrote some two million of them, even submitting 1,200 words on an August bank holiday totally spoiled by rain.

In 1927 Cardus succeeded Samuel Longford as the chief music critic of the 'M. G.' and now held two of the paper's major portfolios. As with cricket, he got to know the performers, notably Beecham and (later) Sir John Barbirolli. Cricket was for watching: Cardus cultivated the art of listening and the ability to interpret for his readers what he heard. The fame he had quickly acquired as a cricket writer came more slowly as a music critic. Even when he had made his name, year by year, with some 4,000 words a week from two or three concerts, he remained aware that a musical error of fact might bring two dozen letters of protest; a cricket one, possibly a thousand. Others, such as his friend and rival Ernest Newman, were already established. What made him different was his total independence of judgement. He could be out of step with his contemporaries and sometimes ahead of them. He wrote intuitively, conveying his own aesthetic delight and putting an essential truth into a telling phrase; Sibelius, for example, composed 'mainly in nouns and verbs with eloquent dashes of silence'. As in much else in his life, he was 'his own man', to quote J. B. Priestley.

Cardus was ready to champion little-known composers such as Gustav Mahler and Anton Bruckner – both of them in the central European tradition in which he delighted. Pursuit of that tradition took him to Salzburg, whose festivals provided some of his finest moments. Arturo Toscanini conducting the opera *Die Meistersinger* there in 1936 would 'remain in the mind for a lifetime because of its beauty and dignity. The banner of song opened with a width and nobility that caused happiness and sadness, Toscanini held us like children.' Perhaps in the end the danger, in both cricket and music, was that readers came to appreciate the words more than the deeds they portrayed. Yet there were no concessions to the faint-hearted and 'M. G.' readers had to keep up with him. This approach would later cause problems for him in Australia.

In the early years of Cardus's work, Manchester and the Hallé Orchestra were central to his writing, though some adverse notices in the 1930s during the Depression, when audiences fell, caused economic concern to performers. London came to make greater claims on him, while the outbreak of the Second World War in 1939 brought an end to his work as both cricket and music critic for the *Manchester Guardian*. In 1940 he took himself off to Australia (and there were critics of this decision) to work for the *Sydney Morning Herald*.

At first Cardus enraged his readership by the savagery of his attacks. What he viewed as a genuine attempt to raise standards was seen as arrogant and insensitive. Once he had mentally accepted that Sydney was not Salzburg, he struck a balance. By 1942 his writing was acceptable and understood, while he made a major cultural impact on Australia with his Sunday evening broadcasts called *Enjoyment of Music* and a similar midweek programme for children. With fewer demands on his time and living, at first, a somewhat solitary life in Sydney, he found time to write his *Ten Composers* and *Autobiography*.

Then, in a period of uncertainty, Cardus travelled between Australia and England five times in two years, before finally settling in England in 1949 for the rest of his life. Yet a post-war England was alien to him and he was conscious he had not shared its hardships: 'My exile in Australia had disqualified me.' After some false starts, notably with Beaverbrook's *Evening Standard* in 1948, he returned to the *Manchester Guardian* as its London music critic, where he wrote 'Music surveys', introducing readers to the music they might be going to hear or at least might read about later. He tended to remain faithful to his pre-war interest in the classical tradition, and made little concession to modernism. There was more on Mahler than could be justified, Cardus's articles a prelude to the analytical study *Gustav Mahler: his Mind and his Music*, published in 1965.

Two further volumes of autobiography, *Second Innings* (1950) and *Full Score* (1970), followed, the final volume written when Cardus was over eighty. Several of his earlier cricket books were reprinted. He also wrote a biography of Beecham (1961) and edited a memoir on Kathleen Ferrier (1971). His devotion to the singer was so profound that some critics suggested that it obscured his objective judgement of her talent. His relationship with Beecham had its ups and downs, but the book allowed him to dwell on a past from which he gained more and more comfort.

Cardus made few forays into the post-war cricket world, although he reported two MCC tours to Australia in the 1950s and the Ashes series in England in 1953. *Wisden Cricketers' Almanack* claimed him for an article virtually every year. He took great pleasure in being elected president of Lancashire County Cricket Club in 1970-71. Other honours had already come his way. He had been appointed CBE in 1964 and in 1967 became the first music critic to be knighted. In 1972 he was elected an honorary member of the Royal Academy of Music.

The death of Cardus's wife in 1968 ended a marriage which had lasted nearly fifty years. The couple had seldom lived in the same house and both valued the independence which their separate lives gave them. Yet the friendship – it was scarcely intimacy – was sustained by meals together, letters, and phone calls. After her death he stopped living in his club (the National Liberal) and moved into her flat. Cardus enjoyed the company of ladies and retained to the end of his life an old-world gallantry. He was a gregarious man, with a close circle of friends of both sexes. Good food and wine, talking, and membership of several London clubs were aspects of his lifestyle.

In his final years Cardus still wrote, though the way the *Guardian* handled his copy from the Edinburgh festival in 1969 upset him. The days of expansionist writing, untouched by sub-editors, were long since past and his association with the paper of his heyday diminished in happiness at the end. It was an opinion expressed in Robin Daniels' *Conversations with Cardus* (1976).

Sir Neville Cardus died at the Nuffield Clinic, London on 28 February 1975. Despite living to almost eighty-seven, he had changed relatively little from the lean, ascetic figure of moderate height, with sharp features, sleek hair, and strong glasses. The tributes to him as a writer were generous. Intellectually, music had been his first string, but cricket had been his passport to fulfilment. And in cricket, if not in music, he had changed the course of reporting. He would have his imitators and parodists, and no serious cricket writer would remain unaffected by him. His last entry in *Who's Who* (1975) showed something of his enigmatic approach to life: 'Recreations: anything not in the form of a game'.

18
E. W. Swanton Remembered

I was one of the judges of the Cricket Society Award for 2005. We gave it to David Rayvern Allen for his biography of E. W. Swanton, which I subsequently reviewed.

This is a magisterial biography of a magisterial figure. The author, who knew Swanton extremely well, tells – in a text closely packed with detail – of a life filled with activity, controversy and pronouncement. Something has been said (to use one of Swanton's dicta) on the subject himself in two very full autobiographies, but a great deal more has been quarried out.

Who, for instance, knew that Swanton's grandfather was German and that his mother was understandably nervous when war broke out in 1914? Who was aware that his social background was rather humbler than Swanton himself would have had us believe? There is, on this matter, an interesting, even philosophical, discussion before the conventional first chapter in which the author poses the questions: 'What shaped Swanton?' and 'Where was the small child inside the big man?'

'Big' is relevant to an understanding of the man. He dominated everyone who crossed his path and his presence cast the shadow of authority in all he said or did. While it is fair to say that much would have been omitted from this book were Swanton still alive, yet Swanton himself said to the author shortly before he died: 'They may publish what they like about me.'

Swanton's familiar foibles of snobbishness, arrogance and a tendency to fire off salvoes (usually with the pen) are duly recorded. These three characteristics define how Swanton was perceived generally. David Rayvern Allen has added some more generous observations of a Swanton we knew less about. There was his bitter opposition to apartheid (in this he was at one with John Arlott, a contemporary of whom he was always wary) and his support for the campaign for the admission of women members to MCC in the 1990s.

Then we turn to Swanton's ambition, his cultivation of the 'right' people and his taste for the good things in life. None of these necessarily endeared him to his fellow men, but then it was not his prime objective to be liked.

Rayvern Allen excels in his treatment of so many aspects of Swanton's life. He handles with sensitivity the years in which his subject was a Japanese POW – showing that even in that environment Swanton was a survivor and a leader. He understands the nuances that lay behind his service as an army officer and he explores the cushioned protection which Anglo-Catholicism and a haven at Pusey House, Oxford bestowed on him in the immediate post-war years. All these areas provide minefields for technical errors and doubtful judgements. Allen comes through unscathed and with flying colours.

John Major, when prime minister, said that talking to Swanton on cricket was like 'entering an Aladdin's Cave of History', and this book is essentially about Swanton's role in cricket over some seven decades.

Rayvern Allen has drawn on his own experience as a BBC producer to give an account, through a fascinating array of primary material, of Swanton often daggers-drawn with authority in the BBC. He clearly shows why – despite all the rancour – the Corporation accepted this troublesome jewel in its crown. Perhaps Allen quotes too much and at too great length, but it is difficult to fault him for what he selects. And, at the same time, one commends him for the sheer details of his research.

This is a book which one reads with delight for its lively style, vigorous writing, mastery of a fine vocabulary (I 'learned' at least two new words!) and penetrating scholarship. It rightly won the Cricket Society's Book of the Year Award for 2005 and did so in a year when the judges had a formidable field to discuss. No one else could have done this book on Swanton so well.

'Jim' Swanton died in 2000. David Rayvern Allen produced A Celebration of the Life and Work *the same year, to which I contributed the following piece:*

To have known Jim Swanton for the last third of his lifetime was a great privilege. At our first meeting I 'interviewed' him for his recollections of Learie Constantine for my forthcoming biography. He answered my questions with measured judgement, simultaneously making careful notes on the match he was reporting. That professionalism, matched by an acute memory, must be one of the hallmarks of his success. In later years, and to the very end, one marvelled at the way he could contribute to the debate in Committee, publishing ideas which he was unlikely to see brought to fruition. He was more liberal than many suspected in his enthusiasm for the young and his readiness to adapt to the changing times of the last decade or two.

One memory stands out. A group of us were charged with repositioning the pictures in the Pavilion at Lord's. We took the best part of two days because Jim would linger over subjects – Lord Harris, for example – and give us pen-portraits of men he had known from sixty, even seventy, years ago.

No man is perfect. One would be conscious of playing for one's place in EWS' metaphorical 'team'. Perhaps when one was invited to call him Jim one had moved up the order.

His writing output was enormous – *si requiris monumentum, respice libros.*

19
MCC in Australia, 1903/04

It was with hope rather than expectation that the England cricketers, under the captaincy of 'Plum' Warner, set off for Australia in September 1903. Since Australia had won six of the previous ten Test matches (all played within the previous twenty months) against England under the leadership of A. C. MacLaren, the English press had not been optimistic. Nevertheless, C. B. Fry, in the *Daily Express*, had written warm words of encouragement to the captain: 'Yours is a powerful team, and should do well if it plays as a team of brothers, and if you can persuade your men to scorn delights and to live laborious days . . . the prime condition of success in the game is unadulterated physical fitness.'

Fry was unable to go on the tour himself. Indeed, he never visited Australia. His absence, and that of MacLaren, Gilbert Jessop and R. H. Spooner, denied Warner the cream of England's amateur batsmen. Fry's reference to a 'powerful' team was based on the professionals and especially the professional bowlers. There were the Yorkshire all-rounders George Hirst and Wilfred Rhodes, together with the Worcestershire all-rounder E. G. Arnold and a young, untried fast bowler from Kent in Arthur Fielder. The established players J. T. Tyldesley and Tom Hayward were the mainstay of the batting. The wicketkeepers were A. A. Lilley and Herbert Strudwick. Warner, R. E. Foster and B. J. T. Bosanquet were the amateurs. Foster had made infrequent appearances in first-class cricket but he had been, in 1900, the first man ever to make a century in both innings in the Gentlemen v. Players match at Lord's. Bosanquet had had a markedly successful season in 1903, scoring over a thousand runs and taking 63 wickets as an effective slow googly bowler.

As a performer, Warner ranked low in the hierarchy of amateur batsmen at the beginning of that 'Golden Age'. Yet he had already made twenty first-class centuries with one double-century. *Wisden*, selecting him in 1904 as one of its 'Five Cricketers of the Year', described him as a 'fast-wicket batsman combining a most attractive style with a great variety of strokes and command[ing] a very pretty and effective cut'. He had made several appearances for the Gentlemen, though none for England (his century against South Africa at Johannesburg in 1899 would acquire retrospective Test status). Yet Warner's inexperience as a batsman at the highest level brought severe press criticism compounded by his selection as captain for what was to be the first official overseas tour by the Marylebone Cricket Club. It must be admitted that the press were less concerned with the status of MCC in all this than in the fortunes of a team, under Mr Warner's leadership, striving to win back the Ashes.

We should turn now to the circumstances leading to MCC's assumption of responsibility for the tour. For the previous forty years, teams from England had gone overseas, principally to Australia but also to New Zealand, the United States, South Africa and the West Indies. The tours were private ventures, some of them led by professional cricketers whose entrepreneurial instincts meant that they would drive hard bargains before agreeing to tour. Others were led by amateurs, either men of private wealth or those who organised the venture in the hope that it would pay its way. Such a touring party went to New Zealand and Australia in 1876/77, led by James Lillywhite. When his XI took on a combined Australian team at Melbourne in March 1877 no one at the time thought to describe the encounter as either a Test match or as 'England v. Australia'. Only retrospectively did history confer these titles. Six years later at Sydney (though the story is rather more complex – see, for example, *Beyond Reasonable Doubt*, Joy Munns, 1994) Ivo Bligh claimed the Ashes. Between 1877 and 1903, when the first MCC tourists arrived in Australia, there had been sixty-six Test Matches, of which Australia had won twenty-six and England twenty-eight. Major Ben Wardill first mooted the idea that MCC should assume responsibility for teams from England in 1899. Wardill (whose majority stemmed from his rank as an officer of the Melbourne Harbour Trust Garrison Battery) claimed the right to speak as the voice of Australian cricket by virtue of his position as the secretary of Melbourne CC, a position he had held for many years. But that 'right' was very much de facto, tempered by the fact that the Australasian Council was virtually moribund (it would be disbanded in 1900) and by inter-colonial rivalry between Victoria and New South Wales (whose capital was Sydney).

There exists in the archives at Lord's a manuscript volume entitled *Synopsis of correspondence between M.C.C. and Major Wardill of Melbourne C. C.* It records the letters and cables exchanged by (Sir) Francis Lacey, the Secretary of MCC, and Wardill between 1899 and 1903. Their dialogue hung fire during the Anglo-Boer War, though that event did not preclude Test matches taking place nor, indeed, a team led by Lord Hawke playing in South Africa just before war broke out. On 29 April 1903, Wardill cabled that he and Lacey should 'revive scheme' and got the disarming reply, 'Unlikely'. No doubt Lacey was stalling because he wrote on 5 June to Wardill a letter saying that MCC were not only prepared to meet his wishes but had also chosen a captain (Warner). Three weeks later Lacey sent a long (and expensive) cable which would, of course, have reached Wardill before the letter of 5 June. It served as a confirmation of the tour and an agreement upon such matters as playing conditions, gate money and fixtures. It also stated that matches should be played under MCC Laws.

There was only one 'condition' on which MCC gave way gracefully and that was in the selection of umpires. Lacey had proposed sending out James Phillips, but his name produced such a storm of protest in the Australian press (some of it cabled back to the *Daily Mail*) that MCC thought it wise not only to withdraw Phillips' name but also decide not to send an umpire at all. Phillips was one of those cricketers of the Victorian era (Midwinter and

Trott were others) who commuted between Australia and England playing in both countries, making a reasonable livelihood and never seeing a winter. Phillips also did some umpiring – again, a characteristic of the time – and his 'sin' was to have cast doubt on the action of the Australian left-arm spinner Jack Saunders, writing to the Victorian Cricket Association saying so. Phillips's stance on 'throwing' as a whole had a positive outcome, leading to an important meeting of county captains in England in 1900.

A curious feature of the ongoing negotiations in the English summer of 1903 was the parallel information coming formally to Lacey from Wardill in Melbourne and the informal comments coming to the *Daily Mail* from Sydney. The paper had appointed Frank Iredale, a former Australian Test cricketer and a professional journalist, as their correspondent and sometimes it seemed that Lacey obtained more information about the Australian position reading the *Daily Mail* than from his exchange of cables with Melbourne C.C.

By September Warner had his side (Spooner withdrew as late as 7 September) and the departure on the *Orontes* was set for 25 September from Tilbury. A crowd of some two thousand, including the President of MCC, saw seven of the team leave from St Pancras Station while the other seven players took the overland route to join the ship at Marseilles. Bishop Welldon also joined the ship, at Gibraltar, and would write of the 'happy relationships exist[ing] between Mr. Warner and his fellow-men'; of the match between the team and the ladies; and (as befitted the age in which the bishop wrote) of never 'wholly forget[ing] that we were Englishmen and Englishwomen representative of the greatest Empire under heaven'.

Warner himself, in a book to which reference will be made below, wrote of the fancy-dress ball, of stopping at Colombo (though not playing a match), of playing bridge and deck tournaments and the captain turning off the engines at Fremantle one minute after the estimated schedule.

And so to the cricket itself. MCC made substantial scores in the matches against South Australia, Victoria and New South Wales, though curiously they were behind on the first innings against

Queensland, by far the weakest state. Their 'excuse' was the long journey to Brisbane and the fact that they had left Hirst, Hayward and Tyldesley at Sydney. Nevertheless, MCC came to the First Test unbeaten. Australia's 285, with a century by Monty Noble, was followed by an England reply of 577. The centrepiece was an innings of 287 by Foster, on his Test debut. He shared in partnerships of 115 and 130 with Albert Relf and Rhodes for the ninth and tenth wickets. Foster's innings lasted for seven hours and included 38 boundaries. His score eclipsed the previous record of 201 set by Syd Gregory at Sydney in 1894. Albert Knight, of the touring party but not selected for the Test, wrote: 'one does not know how to convey an adequate idea of [his] wonderful innings: all around the wicket he made so many beautiful strokes.'

Victor Trumper matched Foster's performance, carrying his bat for 185 not out. It was an innings, said the *Melbourne Argus*, 'dazzling in its brilliance'. The same paper praised Rhodes for his second innings analysis of five for 94. Set 194, England struggled a little but came home by five wickets. *Wisden* declared 'a finer game had rarely been seen in Australia'. All that marred the game was the behaviour of the crowd over an umpire's decision on a run-out. 'People in England,' wrote Warner, 'can have no conception of the hissing and booing that went on.'

MCC then played a couple of matches against odds prior to the Test at Melbourne. In the Second Test, after a sound start including a half-century from Warner and 97 from Tyldesley, England slumped from 306 for five to 315 all out. Australia fared even worse, just avoiding the follow-on deficit of 200 runs. Only Trumper could master (in either Australian innings) the bowling of Rhodes who took fifteen wickets for 124 runs, besides having eight catches dropped. England won by 185 runs. It was generally accepted (and especially by the *Australasian*) that the weather had penalised Australia.

A Ballarat XVIII provided the opposition between the Second and Third Tests. MCC (who had a squad of fourteen) were struck by injuries and two visiting Englishmen helped them to field a side. Warner ('with a long-hop – a ball I not infrequently bowl') got his first (and only) wicket in Australia.

Australia outplayed England at every stage in the Third Test at Adelaide. Both Trumper and Gregory made centuries. Set 495 to win, England began with a partnership of 148, Warner making 79 and Hayward 67, but the target was never remotely possible and the Australians won by 216 runs. The match was played in a curiously quiet atmosphere, the players 'expressing their pleasure at such a contrast to the boisterous enthusiasm of Sydney and Melbourne'. Twenty-nine years later, the atmosphere at Adelaide would be very different as the sparks of the smouldering bodyline dispute leapt into flame with all the urgency and terror of the forest fires which could spring up in the nearby mountains.

Over a month separated the Third and Fourth Tests during which MCC visited Tasmania. The sea crossing was in a small vessel which rolled alarmingly and the players were billeted in overcrowded accommodation in a Hobart full of race goers – a bad start. Each of the two-day matches was drawn and the week ended with the players themselves at the races. Back on the Australian mainland came two overwhelming victories against Victoria and New South Wales. MCC were 50 behind on the first innings against Victoria, batting in difficult conditions following rain. The home team was then dismissed, on a sticky wicket, for 15 in three-quarters of an hour. Rhodes and Arnold shared the wickets. 'Few Australians,' commented Warner, 'have any idea of playing on a bad wicket.'

The match against New South Wales, at Sydney, was a curtain raiser for the forthcoming Test. A Man of the Match adjudicator, had there been such a thing in those times, would have had no difficulty in his decision. Bosanquet scored 54 and 114 and had a match analysis of eight for 96. A few days later England set up a winning score of 249 in the rain-affected Test match, which ran into a sixth day. The match was secured by the England bowlers, who dismissed Australia for 131 and 171 with Bosanquet taking six for 51 in the Australian second innings.

England therefore won 'the rubber', as *Wisden* prosaically put it. For Warner, the 'Ashes' had been regained and the prize 'for which we had striven so hard' had been won. That the back-to-back Fifth Test at Melbourne was lost by 218 runs (with the fickle weather this time in Australia's favour) seemed of little consequence. England's totals of 61 and 101 were low notes on which to end a triumphant series, compensated by a nine-wicket defeat of South Australia (and two half-centuries from Warner) in the final game.

Warner, on his return, published *How We Recovered the Ashes*. It was an impartial, thorough and analytical account of the whole tour in a well-illustrated book of 340 pages. The romantic in him had chosen a title which would set a pattern for a sequence of books, especially over the next 50 years, which would bear a similar title. Jack Hobbs wrote *Recovering the Ashes* after the 1911/12 tour and Monty Noble *The Fight for the Ashes* after the 1928/29 series, a title used by Warner himself in 1926, Hobbs in 1932/33 and Peter West in 1953 and 1956. Douglas Jardine chose *In Quest of the Ashes* as the title of his apologia for 1932/33, a book reissued in 2005. Yet Warner's adoption of the 'Ashes' from the famous *Sporting Times* mock obituary did not find favour with all the reviewers. 'Slang and only of very temporary significance,' said one and 'an undignified borrowing from the Yellow Press,' said another. But the book itself was praised as 'a bright and manly narrative genuinely worth writing'. At 18s 6d it was not cheap (though a paperback edition followed a year later). There was good value in what the *Sheffield Daily Telegraph* published for 3d – a 96-page booklet with scores, reports and illustrations compiled by the paper's sporting editor, James Stainton.

Some comment may be made on the manuscript accounts of the tour which remain – a century later – unpublished. Foster wrote a diary combining a narrative of the cricket with comments on the weather, the gate money and the hospitality. It is in the archives at Lord's. One of the professionals, Relf, provided another account in his own Diary which ends, somewhat abruptly, after he was not selected for the Third Test. It is in the archives of Sussex County Cricket Club at Hove. Of the two, Relf's is the more entertaining and serves as a reminder that among the professional cricketers of the day were men with the ability to write, even though their formal education might have ended well before the age of fourteen. Another professional, A. E. Knight, contributed some attractive descriptions of events apart from the cricket to the *Sheffield Daily Telegraph* booklet. In 1906 he wrote *The Complete Cricketer*. Finally, contemporaries might enjoy another account of the tour in Bosanquet's article for the 1905 *Wisden*, in which he had the highest praise for his captain. For Warner himself, the tour was a turning point (perhaps one of many) in his long life.

Warner had left for Australia as a comparatively unheralded young man. He returned a public figure, to marry Agnes Blyth in what the press called 'the wedding of the year'. His cricket would flourish in the Edwardian era and he would be asked (though not in 1907/08) to captain MCC in Australia again, in 1911/12. He was the man of whom Harry Altham would say: 'I do not believe there will be found anyone in [cricket's] long two centuries to whom a greater debt will be owed.'

A facsimile edition of P. F. Warner's How We Recovered the Ashes *was published in 2004 by Methuen in conjunction with MCC. There is an introduction by Gerald Howat and a preface by Marina Warner, Sir Pelham's granddaughter.*

20
Letters from Warner & Allen – 1932/33

It is now over seventy years since the departure, in 1932, of an MCC side to Australia for a tour forever to be identified with the bodyline bowling controversy. The literature is enormous, in terms of contemporary newspaper coverage, unpublished manuscript material and books. If the centre stage were held by Douglas Jardine, simply because his thinking and tactics were the *fons et origo* of all that took place, many others played star roles, in particular Harold Larwood and Bill Voce, the principal exponents of the leg-theory form of attack.

In my biography of 'Plum' Warner (1987) I devoted two chapters out of twelve to what amounted to seven months in the life of a man who died in his 90th year. Warner was manager of the tour and chairman of the selectors who had chosen Jardine as captain. Furthermore, as a journalist, his criticism of short-pitched bowling on the leg-side (as seen when Yorkshire played Surrey in August 1932) in the *Morning Post* would be thrown back in his face by the *Sydney Referee* in December of that year.

E. W. Swanton wrote his biography of 'Gubby' Allen in 1985 while his subject was still alive. He devoted a tenth of his book to the events of 1932/33. In an interesting two pages, Allen himself defined bodyline bowling and distinguished it from leg-theory. The latter 'means a packed leg-side field with the bowler aiming at the leg-stump with only an occasional "bouncer"'. To this acceptable pattern, bodyline added 'plenty of "bouncers", many of them on the line of the batsman'. Allen, an amateur cricketer and therefore less in bondage to his captain, had refused to be part of a tactic which (he wrote in 1985) was 'developed rather than planned in advance'.

Both Warner and Allen were deeply unhappy about the course of events. They both criticised Jardine's personality and lamented the impact of his tactics. This article draws on some of the letters which each wrote home – in Warner's case to his wife and in Allen's case principally to his father. The Warner letters remain in private possession, though I was able to draw on them when I wrote his biography. Those by Allen (twenty-four of them on 'bodyline') are now in the possession of the State Library of New South Wales, which bought them at an auction of Allen's cricket effects in 1993. I was able to see them before they went to Australia.

The tourists left England on 17 September and had been a month at sea when Allen wrote a letter to Warner's wife, Agnes. (One should mention the close relationship between the Warner and Allen families over the years.)

> 15 October – There have been no rows and everyone seems very happy but I am terrified of Douglas. For a well-read and well-educated man he is easily the stupidest I know and conceited as well. I am not saying I don't like him, as I do, but one can't help noticing his shortcomings.

Three days later the team landed at Freemantle. MCC had much the better of two drawn games at Perth and went east to record three victories, each by an innings, against South Australia, Victoria and New South Wales. Allen did not play in the final game and wrote two letters to his father, Sir Walter Allen.

> 22 November – Plum has cheered up a lot (he has been home-sick) but is still not his usual self. He worries over every sort of thing Jardine says or does.
> 24 November – Douglas changes his mind every five minutes. He seems too damn stupid but he is difficult and whines away if he doesn't have everything as he wants. We all try very hard with him

but things will be very difficult. I know, as time draws on, that someone will have the very hell of a row with him. It won't be me so don't worry. But sometimes I feel I should like to kill him and today is one of those days. I am afraid Plum has been feeling very homesick. Don't tell Agnes but he comes to my room sometimes and says how he would love to be back home in Sloane Street and is almost and, in fact, quite tearful.

A few days later, Warner wrote to Agnes:

29 November – D.R. Jardine is a very difficult fellow – such a queer nature – rather 'cruel' in some ways, and generally got his knife into someone for no reason at all. He is not easy or pleasant, really on the contrary but is very keen. Hates Australians and his special hate is now Bradman! Not an easy task to keep things nice and even but, so far, all right, but he is not the right fellow to be captain. Long ago, but for me, there would have been a row with the press. He was entirely wrong as he was very rude to the press for no reason at all. One cannot simply like him and I have tried very hard. He says cruel things of people and his language is poor at times, not often but he uses awful words on occasions in talking, e.g. of Bradman. He is very conceited, only He knows, and arrogant.

The press had, indeed, begun to take a closer interest in the course of events. Bill Woodfull, the Australian captain, was hit on the head by a ball from Larwood in the MCC match against 'An Australian XI' at Melbourne. England's aggressive tactics began to reverberate through the cricket world and, like the shots at Lexington in 1775, prefaced imperial conflict. The Australian papers coined the phrase 'body-line', hyphenated at first. To Jack Fingleton (who had made a century in the New South Wales game) the hyphen seemed irrelevant when you rubbed your bruises. As for Warner, he was deeply regretting his choice of captain. Sir Donald Bradman accorded me an interview in Adelaide in 1985 and remarked that the captaincy of a touring team 'needed the leadership and tact of an overseas diplomat'. Far from being a diplomat, Jardine was about to create a diplomatic crisis.

December, despite the press attacks on Warner, was deceptively calm. England won the First Test at Sydney, with Warner sufficiently relaxed at the end of the day's play to phone his son, John, at Eton and tell him that England needed to get one wicket and (as it proved) 1 run in the morning. The fact that the call had had to be booked and was seen as such an event (by both father and son) explains, in part, why the telephone was not used between Warner, as manager, and MCC in London. Two of the survivors of the tour told me, in the 1980s, that Warner should have phoned Lord's where the authorities were slow to take heed of the gathering storm.

Maurice Tate, not used in the Tests at all, joked that he was kept for Wagga Wagga and Tasmania, while Australia's win by 111 runs in the Second Test certainly suggested to those in England that there was no great crisis. Warner wrote to his wife early in January that he felt good 'off-the-field' work by himself had compensated for Jardine's attitude to the public and to the press. So he had persuaded himself. Ironically, the press directed their attacks as much against Warner as Jardine.

Allen had always stood his ground with Jardine and had refused to bowl 'bouncers like Larwood' (as sections of the press reported he had). As he wrote to his father:

> 7 January – That is ridiculous and I have never had more than four men on the leg-side on any occasion whereas Larwood has had eight and often seven. I have bowled fast at times out here and made the ball fly but never the leg-theory. I have refused to do it. In fact, before this Test started Jardine said I ought to do it which made me furious. I told him he could leave me out if he didn't like the way I bowled. I then went away and saw Plum and told him that if such a thing ever occurred again I should report the whole thing to Billy Findlay [MCC Secretary].

Allen returned to the conversation in his next letter home, written five days later, on the eve of the Third Test in Adelaide:

> 12 January – The newspapers and general public in this country, though they have all been exceedingly nice to me, are simply

dreadful. They never leave Douglas Jardine alone for a minute and they publish the most unfounded statements which are certainly libellous but, of course, one can do nothing about it. D.R.J. [Jardine] asks for it with his offensive manner and is then hurt when they say nasty things about him. I will tell you the story of what occurred on the morning of the Second Test. I didn't tell you last week as I thought you might worry. D.R.J. came up to me and said the following: 'I had a talk with the boys, Larwood and Voce, last night and they say it is quite absurd you not bowling 'bouncers'; they say it is only because you are keen on your popularity'. Well I burst and said if it had been a question only of popularity, I could have bowled 'bouncers' years ago. I concluded by saying if he didn't like the way I bowled he still had time to leave me out not only in this match but until he came to his senses; it would also give me time to complete a full statement of our conversation for the benefit of the MCC Committee. He said: 'Well I am afraid you will have to, or Larwood won't try'. I told him I had not intention of doing it but he had walked away by then and the matter was left. I bowled my ordinary way and only one more man on the off on purpose. Everyone is fed up with Douglas and there looks like being a fine row in the very near future especially if we lose this Test.

That conversation (recorded in both these two letters) had taken place during the Second Test at Melbourne. Allen, not playing in the match against a Victorian County XIII at Bendigo, had had time to write them at length. The second letter was finally dated the day before the Third Test. Two days later, on Saturday, 14 January, after England had been dismissed for 341, the Australian openers, Fingleton and Woodfull, went out to bat at 3 p.m. Woodfull was hit in Larwood's first over (by an orthodox ball) and, in the bowler's second over, to a packed leg-side field, had his bat knocked out of his hand. The denouement of the day's events has often been told embracing, as it did, Warner's visit to the Australian dressing-room and his dismissal by Woodfull. 'There are two teams out there: one is playing cricket, the other is not . . .'

The dialogue was manna to the press. Warner believed that Fingleton had leaked the conversation to the press, which the

Australians always denied. Sir Donald Bradman showed me where the scenario had taken place and (with his incredible memory) people's exact positions and he told me he thought that a dressing-room attendant had probably 'sold' the story to journalists. Who knows?

Between the Monday and the Thursday, the match took its course and England won by 338 runs; but what happened on the field was, in a sense, subservient to events off it. The Australian Board of Control sent off a cable, containing the emotive word 'unsportsmanlike'. Thus began the series of cables between the Board and MCC. Allen started a long letter home on this fourth day:

> 18 January – It has been a most unpleasant match as you will have gathered from the papers. There has been nothing but rows and barracking until I am fed up with anything to do with cricket. Plum is worried to death, and says the side may have to return at once to England, but that is rot. Premiers, Bishops and the Board of Control are all up in the air. I have not changed my mind in any way about the leg-theory and all the side is aware of the fact. I just hate it and will not do it. Douglas Jardine is loathed and between you and me, rightly more than any German who fought in any war. There is no getting away from it. Jardine is a perfect swine and I can think of no other word fit for mum to see which describes him well enough. Plum simply hates the sight of him and so does everyone else. I have never had a scene with him in public but I have had one or two on the quiet – of which not a soul knows – in fact we are thought to be good friends.

We may think Allen's sentence about the Germans has an absurd and almost childish note to it. But with memories of the Great War of 1914–18 (and Australia's part in the conflict) it was an effective analogy to suggest to his father. And, indeed, Jardine had used the same sort of analogy himself. Seeing Royal Australian Air Force planes flying over the new Sydney Harbour Bridge, he had remarked to Warner: 'I wish they were Japs and I wish they'd bomb that bridge into the harbour.' (So Warner had written to his wife, 19 November 1932.)

Allen had had a good match himself, taking eight wickets for 121 'without resource to intimidation' as a contemporary put it. He did not play in the late January match against New South Wales at Sydney and found time to write:

> 26 January – The leg-theory brawl seems to be blowing over slightly. I thought the MCC reply [to the Australian cable] was magnificent – so dignified after their common outburst. The whole thing has given Douglas a great fright and seems to have done him some good. He is less bumptious and seems to look on the leg-theory in a more gentlemanly light.

The players, in public, closed ranks in loyalty to their captain 'under whose leadership they hope[d] to achieve an honourable victory'. In private, differing views were held. Both Leslie Ames and Bob Wyatt told me, in 1984, they believed credit was due to Warner for bringing this about and saving the tour from disaster. Warner wrote from Sydney to Agnes:

> 27 January – I think the Board will withdraw the word 'unsportsmanlike' – they certainly ought to, and then things may be happier. I am hoping that this wretched row will die down. The Board's telegram was silly, tactless and rude.

There is an ambivalence about Warner's attitude to events which is inescapable. In his letters the loathing for Jardine as a person was always more strongly evinced than his disapproval of the tactics pursued. Between the end of the Third Test on 19 January and the start of the Fourth at Brisbane the crisis moved from the cricket field into the realm of politics and economics. This is not the place to deal with that in any detail and the interested reader may care to look at my biography on Warner (pp. 123–127). He wrote to Agnes on the eve of the Brisbane Test:

> 8 February – Nothing can compensate me for the moral and intellectual damage which I have suffered on this tour. D.R.J. is very trying and now a bundle of nerves. Job, Balaam's Ass and P.F.W. are the three most patient men that ever lived! D.R.J. is half-mad but the men are splendid and stick to me when I tell them that only the end

matters. Bear with him until we win (or lose) and then say what you like to him. Hammond says I have a wonderful nature and character. He is a great fellow both on and off the field. Obby [Allen] is a great help and such a good cricketer. But they are all good fellows and very loyal and patient but D.R.J. must not captain again. He is most ungracious, rude and suspects all. He really is a curious character and varies like a barometer. He is very efficient but inconsistent in his character and no leader. I ought to get a prize for Patience or Tact or good temper, if not a knighthood!! 75 per cent of the trouble is due to D.R.J.'s personality. We all think that D.R.J. has almost made me hate cricket. He makes it war. I do hope the Test will go happily. I rather dread it.

This letter is the fullest picture which Warner has provided of his opinion of Jardine. None of those I interviewed, some fifty years later, felt that his public relationship with Jardine was good despite that outward show of loyalty. One player remarked that any rapport between the two men ceased after Jardine had been rude to Warner on the ship going out. The letter throws light on Warner's relationship with the players as a whole. They found him warm, friendly, approachable and sympathetic. He did a great deal to break down amateur–professional social barriers, though it was naive of him of think that the professionals would say what they liked to Jardine after the Test series. Certainly, a bond was formed with Hammond who, with Allen as well, would be a future England captain appointed by Warner.

Bradman, however, never established much of a dialogue with Walter Hammond. Despite his considerable help to me when I was writing Hammond's biography, Bradman felt he would rather not accept my request to write a foreword. Sir Leonard Hutton, a great admirer, did so instead.

Warner's foreboding came to nothing and the Test at Brisbane passed without incident. England won by six wickets and so secured the Ashes. Voce had been unfit to play, Larwood found it too hot to bowl his best and the wicket was lifeless. Jardine showed leadership qualities of some sort in summoning Eddie Paynter from his hospital bed to make 83 runs and avert a possible collapse.

The team travelled from Brisbane to Sydney by ship and Allen wrote on board the SS *Orungal* to his father:

19 February – It is a great relief to us all that the series is decided and in our favour. I strained my left side rather badly. From then on I only bowled fairly well and everything went right. I am afraid I may not be fit enough to play in the Fifth Test but I hope I shall be as Douglas is very anxious that I should.

Despite all this, Allen had taken five wickets at Brisbane and he did play in the Fifth Test at Sydney, taking three wickets and making 48 runs – batting at number nine – which gave England a first-innings lead and, eventually, an eight-wicket win. Larwood, to a great reception from the crowd, made 98 but his injured toe eventually forced him off the field and out of Test match cricket forever.

In a formal sense the tour ended with platitudinous speeches at a dinner given by the New South Wales Government. Warner congratulated Jardine on the fighting spirit he had shown and he believed that the spirit of cricket and sportsmanship had not been lost. That jinx word 'sportsmanship' (or its kindred adjective, 'sportsmanlike') was also stressed by the New South Wales premier as if its repetition could belie the events of the series. Warner's final letter from Australia to Agnes goes over old ground:

2 March – D. R. Jardine is a trial. I never wish to see him again. His outlook and mentality are all wrong. Wyatt and Gubby say 'he is the man who made the game impossible'. I think I hate cricket now. It has been such a worry.

Allen's last letter home from Australia was much more up-beat:

14 March – I have simply loved it all and particularly Sydney. After all, I have seen it all in the very best possible manner with no work to do and not a care in the world.

These contrasting letters mark the difference between the two men, Warner, approaching sixty, had warm memories of his visit to

Australia in pre-1914 days as player and captain. That of 1932/33 had brought him nothing but trouble, sadness and conflict (something from which he always shrank in his public career). He visibly aged in those seven months. His relationship with the game, lovingly built up over fifty years, had to be laboriously and diligently reconstructed. Allen, younger, tougher and with Australian relations whose company he had enjoyed, had taken events in his stride. He had laid down his terms to Jardine, issuing his point-blank refusal to bowl as his captain wished. His letters were not as much as expression of frustrated anger (as were Warner's) as one's simply 'letting off steam' to a parent who wanted to be kept in touch.

Both Warner and Allen continued to present a united front of public loyalty to Jardine – Warner for the rest of his life. In his *Long Innings*, published nearly twenty years later in 1951, he wrote: 'let sleeping dogs lie and congratulate [Jardine] on his splendid captaincy of a great side' and 'if my life depended on the result of an England v. Australia match, I should select as captain of the team, D.R. Jardine.' He had said the same in his earlier book, *Gentlemen v. Players* (1950). Fifty years after the events of 1932/33, E.W. Swanton and I were allowed our respective access to these letters home – though Swanton used his discretion in writing during Allen's lifetime.

Warner's son, John, believed that Australians of an older generation remembered a great cricket leader more acutely than they did a hypocritical manager. All those associated with the 'bodyline' bowling tour – players and journalists – are now dead. For later generations of Australians the events of 1932/33 are consigned to the archives of cricket history. Yet they were, to some extent, a watershed. They heralded a dawn of a new world in which politics and sport would become inextricably associated, in which the imperial bonds unifying cricket would be weakened and in which the role of MCC would be diminished. Lord's could not continue to arbitrate over the cricket world, no more than Westminster could forever legislate for a declining Empire.

21
The First International 1844

A cricket match with claims to be the first ever international took place after the St George's Club of New York had resolved at a meeting in August 1844 that they would play 'any eleven players in Canada' on their own ground 'for any sum from $100 to $1,000'. The challenge appeared in the *New York Herald* with instructions to the *Toronto Patriot* and *Montreal Herald* to copy the invitation and send their 'bills to the secretary of St George's CC'.

Mr Philpotts of Toronto CC accepted the challenge while indicating it was not the custom of his club to play for wagers. Custom or not, terms were agreed and the *Toronto Patriot* reported that 'a spirited eleven started on Saturday night for New York to accept the challenge of St George's Club of that city for $1,000. We wish the Torontowegians every success.'

The journey by sea up the St Lawrence, across Lake Ontario and then by the new American railroad brought the Canadians to New York in time for play to start on Tuesday morning, 24 September 1844. Some five thousand people had gathered by 10 a.m., as instructed by the press, but it was 11.30 before a ball was bowled. 'Local' rules had to be discussed and umpires appointed. It was decided that 'running should continue, no matter where the ball was driven, until the judges were satisfied it was a lost ball,' while Mr Russell of Brooklyn and Mr Waller of Canada were elected 'umpires or judges'. The Canadians, as the *New York Herald* styled them, were dismissed in their first innings for 82, journalists grasping at what straws they could: 'Mr. Birch proved himself a most beautiful batter' (in making 5) and 'Mr. French's play elicited great applause' in getting 4 runs off one stroke. He was lucky to get his 'Mr' as he was the Toronto professional, renowned among the members of his club for cooking them chops after bowling to them in practice.

A correspondent was ecstatic about the Canadians in the field: 'Never was such bowling and fielding displayed – it was truly admirable – almost indescribable for excellence.' He reminded his readers to be on the ground for a 9.30 a.m. start with the odds in New York quoted at 6/4 on Canada.

Rain fell in torrents on the Wednesday and not until 3 p.m., after an hour's lunch interval, were the 'Americans' in the field. St George's, the hosts, had invited players from other clubs to strengthen their side, and contemporaries certainly saw the contest as an 'international' one. A first-wicket partnership lasting 37 minutes 'was admired by all on the ground, with every symptom of improvement as it proceeded'. However, two controversial decisions changed the face of things, 'Mr. Wright declared out by one of the judges, the ball striking his knee and being caught', and 'Mr. Tickner lbw although it was the general opinion that the ball struck his bat previous'. The Americans ended the day 61 for nine with play abandoned. The resumption on Thursday was delayed because 'the Canadian judge [Mr Waller] had to go to Philadelphia on business'. A gentleman from Boston (two home umpires!) was pressed into service and, with 3 more runs scored, the Americans were all out.

By mid-afternoon Canada, at the second attempt, had been dismissed for 63 and several players on both sides were suffering injuries. Mr Dudson was commended for his work at long-stop – 'not a single ball went by him' – while Mr Groom's 7 wides were excused 'by the somewhat high wind prevailing'.

The Americans, in betting around the ground, were favourites as they set out to get 82 runs. The opening pair both reached double figures and promised success 'against most beautiful bowling' and late in the innings Mr Wild, in making 8, achieved 'something more than his usual average'. However, despite the good start, the

Americans slumped to nine wickets down for 58; Mr Wheatcroft was nowhere to be found, though the press believed his presence would only have delayed the inevitable. Undeterred, the losers immediately challenged the Canadians to another match the next day for $2,000 but the offer was declined. The match was described as 'one of the most spirited of games ever played' in either country. Perhaps unwittingly, it began a sequence of matches which – with interruptions during the Civil War and from 1912 for some 40 years – has lasted ever since.

The New York Herald devoted over 60 inches of copy to its match report. Its reporter was clearly struggling with the slowness of play and a game only just beginning to achieve popularity in the United States and not yet challenged by baseball. The spectators probably included a twenty-year-old journalist called Henry Chadwick (unless the *Long Island Star* had sent him on some other assignment).

Chadwick's father had been editor of the *Statesman* and then the *Western Times*. The family had emigrated from Devon to the United States in 1837 when the boy was thirteen. Only his eldest brother had stayed in England to become, as Sir Edwin Chadwick (1800–90), a pioneer figure in public health reform. Following his father's profession, Henry was a journalist by the time he was nineteen. He popularised cricket reporting with his contributions to several papers, convincing editors of the sales value of a game attracting 5,000 supporters at major matches. He himself, as befitted the grandson of a friend of John Wesley, claimed for cricket the higher moral ground, with 'its love of order, discipline and fair play' in an American society cautiously welcoming sport as an antidote to work.

It was while returning from a cricket match with his new bride in 1848 that he first saw a baseball match – in the Elysian fields – and was convinced that this was the game for America 'as cricket is for England'. From then onwards, his loyalties were divided, although another eight years would pass before the press took up baseball and he began to report it.

He contributed two books – one on cricket and football, the other on baseball – to Mr. Beadle's dime handbooks for young people.

There were others on etiquette, letter writing, dancing, friendship and croquet and their sales ran into many thousands. The cricket pages gave the Laws, followed by a blatant plagiarism of Pycroft's *Cricket Field*. No copyright laws existed then, as Dickens, Thackeray and Trollope found to their chagrin. Then along came the advice on dress, umpiring and (rather surprisingly) betting.

After working as a correspondent during the American Civil War, Chadwick returned to sports reporting. Baseball prevailed but cricket was not neglected despite its distinct decline everywhere except in Philadelphia. Perhaps to give it some stimulus, he published the *American Cricket Manual* in 1873. It was partly instructional, supported by illustrations. This was his advice to wicketkeepers: 'In keeping wicket the keenest sight, steadiest nerve and the soundest judgement is required to be brought into play at a moment's notice, and yet a stout built man can play the position finely.'

The book reproduced the Laws, the scores of some important matches in the previous dozen years and a preface in which Chadwick attacked the blatant time wasting in cricket: '"Time is money" governs the American people.' Baseball was more economical in that direction. Baseball also attracted the 'odium' of gambling, against which (despite his comments on how to conduct cricket betting in the 'Dime' book) he campaigned all his life.

On his death in 1908, the American press understandably paid tribute to his contribution to baseball. He had written for over twenty papers and no one 'had done more to advance the game'. 'The Father of Baseball' in 1938 won the rare distinction, for a non-player, of election to the Hall of Fame. Yet it can be argued that cricket's popularity in America in the 1840s and 1850s owed much to his influence, providing a sufficient base for the game to survive the Civil War and, indeed, to flourish in Philadelphia.

22
Cricket and American Puritanism

Puritanism, as an identifiable movement, began in England in the 1560s about the same time as John Derrick played 'creckett' at Guildford. There is no connection between those two events, but between Puritanism and cricket in America there was an undoubted relationship, albeit hostile.

In the last resort, Puritanism was the *alter ego* of sixteenth- and seventeenth-century English society: to the Anglican, not to say Catholic, tendencies of the Church of England it provided a distinctly Protestant antidote; to the extravagance of the Elizabethans it brought sober realism; to those who would build an Empire it argued for patient labour rather than quick returns; to the authoritarian interventionism of the Stuart Kings it brought a separatist and independent response; and to the licence to play sport on Sundays which those same Kings encouraged, it offered and sustained a continuing enmity.

James I's *Book of Sports*, issued by Proclamation in 1618, arose from a petition from the 'servants, labourers, mechanics and other vulgar persons' among his Lancashire subjects complaining 'that they were debarred from all recreations on Sunday after divine service'. Fifteen years later Puritan shackles, in some clerical hands, were still denying opportunity for leisure activities to many a parishioner. Charles I reissued his father's book in stouter language: 'as for our good people's lawful recreation, our pleasure is that, after the end of Divine Service, our good people be not disturbed, letted or discouraged from any lawful recreation.' Archbishop Laud brought the stringency of the Court of High Commission to bear on those Puritan ministers who refused to read the second *Book of Sports* out in churches. Battlelines were joined: thousands of Puritans left England for America in the Great Emigration of the 1630s not just because they chose to be Sabbatarians on the issue of Sunday sport, but in protest against a royalism and an episcopacy they rejected. In the strength of their Puritan ideals of self-discipline and austerity and in the rigour with which they imposed their views, the leadership in New England had a profound moral and intellectual influence on American culture. In due course, cricket came under the flail of Puritan strictures.

Puritan attitudes were translated into actions by those who settled in the New World even before Charles I had reissued the *Book of Sports*. On Christmas Day 1621, William Bradford, the governor of Plymouth Colony in New England, found some of the settlers playing 'at stoolball and such like sports'. Bradford was put in a dilemma. Some men had already refused his request to work since they regarded Christmas Day as a holy day, yet by refusing to let them play he was giving it a religious significance which Puritan thinking rejected. In the end, the men neither worked nor played. Sabbatarianism was for Sundays and in the New England colonies, especially after the mass immigration of the 1630s, numerous laws were passed directed at those whose social activities violated its due observance. A leadership which had left an intolerant authoritarianism in England, or so it argued, proved equally intolerant in the colonies, especially on those whose sporting pursuits (Maypole dancing, for instance) smacked of an Anglican parochial tradition.

In the south, the Plantation colonies – Virginia, the Carolinas and Georgia – contained a more mixed society where planters, speculators and adventurers rubbed shoulders with those of genuine Puritan conviction. There the oldest colonial legislature in America, the Virginian House of Burgesses, forbade amusements on Sunday as one of its first measures. Elsewhere, in the Quaker colony of Pennsylvania, for some seventy years the assembly pursued a particularly hostile policy against those who indulged in 'needless vain sports and pastimes'.

Moderate Puritans directed their injunctions only against Sunday's activities, taking a broader, if somewhat ambivalent, view towards the use of leisure time in the rest of the week. Recreation was justified because, as one Puritan minister wrote, 'We need some respite and diversion, without which we dull our powers.' 'The end of all recreation,' wrote another, 'was to honour God.' Recreation was not at an end in itself. Nor, indeed, was it acceptable to all to those dour extremists within Puritan ranks whose evangelical influence in the mid-eighteenth century aroused the movement known as the Great Awakening, a religious revival which required its converts to reject all forms of recreational activity. George Whitefield, the English evangelist, told the governor and leaders of Maryland in 1739 that entertainments not only discovered a levity of mind, but were contrary to the whole tenor of the Gospel.

Those who had left England with a strong sense of religious persecution set out to create a society which separated itself from the social activities identified with the old country and from the sympathies and attitudes towards sport which the *Book of Sports* had espoused. The Puritans rejected traditional English sports primarily because they saw them as idolatrous rites and immoral occasions; hence the desire to obliterate them from memory and custom. While leaders and legislatures might call the tune, not all their followers were in harmony. The frequent repetition of anti-sport legislation in the New England colonies suggests continued defiance, and certainly in 1685 some brave spirits in Massachusetts played an inter-city football match. In the southern colonies, such as Virginia, Puritanism was a less sustained influence and scattered communities farming along the river banks found time to pursue the folk-games of their ancestors. A visiting preacher at Charleston was upset by the 'unparalleled wickedness of the people' who were playing, dancing and racing – which he sadly saw as 'their common practices and pursuits'. As the eighteenth century opened, none did so more enthusiastically than the Virginian gentleman William Byrd, on whom Puritan influences sat very lightly and who commands our attention if only for providing the first recorded evidence of cricket being played in the English American colonies.

William Byrd's father had established himself in the late seventeenth century as a planter in Virginia. In an economy based on slave labour he soon became wealthy through tobacco farming and land speculation. His son was sent to England to be educated at Felsted and Middle Temple, returning home in 1705 on his father's death to take over the estate at Westover, on the banks of the River James. This 'most polished and ornamental gentleman', as contemporaries observed, laid out a formal garden, collected a fine library of four thousand books, served as a member of the House of Burgesses and of the Council of State and travelled to England, from time to time, as Virginia's official agent.

From 1709 to 1712 William Byrd II recorded his daily activities in his secret diary, which gives us a glimpse of his approach to religion and to recreation, those uneasy Puritan bedfellows. But he was conscientious in his religious exercises and spent his Sundays quietly if not necessarily soberly, as these examples illustrate:

Sunday March 5:
I rose about 7 o'clock. I ate some milk for breakfast. About 11 o'clock we went to church, where Mr. Anderson gave us a good sermon. I ate boiled pork for dinner. In the afternoon we talked a little while and then took a walk about the plantation. We drank a bottle of wine and were merry for about an hour in the evening. I said my prayers and had good health, good thoughts, and good humor, thanks be to God Almighty.

Sunday March 12:
I rose at 8 o'clock and read the Psalms and some Greek. I said my prayers shortly and ate milk for breakfast. I took a little walk before dinner, when I ate fish. We had no company with us. In the afternoon we walked again about the pasture and then Mr. C-s and Mrs. Hamlin came to see us.

Sunday March 26:
I rose at 7 o'clock and read the Psalms and three chapters in the Greek Testament. I said my prayers and ate milk for breakfast. It

rained again almost all day, the wind at northeast. I read two sermons in Dr Tillotson. My wife was better. I ate boiled beef for dinner. In the afternoon Mr. Randolph and I walked to see Mr. Harrison and found him better. We stayed till the evening and then took our leave and returned home where we found all well, thank God. We sat and talked. I said my prayers and had good health, good thoughts, and good humor, thanks be to God Almighty.

Byrd and his friends played cricket at each other's homes regularly but never on a Sunday. By so doing he, as a member of the House of Burgesses, would have broken the laws set by the Legislature of which he was a member. Among typical entries in the spring of 1710 were the following:

Monday February 20:
I rose at 6 o'clock and read the Psalms and some Greek in Cassius. I said my prayers and ate milk for breakfast. We played at cricket and I sprained my backside. I ate bacon and fowl for dinner. In the afternoon we played at the same sport again but I could not run. When we came away I was forced to get on my horse by a chair. We found my wife not very well. In the evening we played at piquet.

Wednesday March 22:
I rose at 6 o'clock and read the Psalms and some Greek. About 2 o'clock we went to dinner and I ate bacon and fowl. In the afternoon played at cricket, four of a side, and Mr. Harrison among us, who looked exceedingly red a great while after it. About 10 o'clock we went to bed. I neglected to say my prayers but had good health, good thoughts, and good humor, thank God Almighty.

Monday March 27:
I rose at 6 o'clock and read a chapter in Hebrew and some Greek. About 10 o'clock Mr Blair, Mr. James Burwell and Major and Captain Harrison came to see us. After I had given them a glass of sack we played at cricket and after that at billiards till dinner. I ate boiled beef for my dinner. In the afternoon we played at billiards. Then we played at shooting with arrows till about 4 o'clock when we went all to Mr. Harrison's, whom we found better. Here we went to cricket again till dark; then we returned home where I [found] Jenny sick.

Byrd's diary is the record of a social group content with its prosperity, asking no moral questions about the slavery at the basis of the economy and, as the English visitor Andrew Burnaby observed later in the century, 'indolent, easy and good-natured; especially fond of society and most given to convivial pleasures'.

While only the extreme evangelicals – and their day came in the last ten years of Byrd's life – could have been upset by his cricketing activities, what raised spiritual hackles among Puritans as a whole was the gambling associated with all sports, whether indoors or out. Byrd himself laid only modest wagers, but his son, William Byrd III, would squander the family fortunes and commit suicide. Gambling among the gentry in the Southern colonies set them apart as a planter-aristocracy, identified with their English aristocratic kinsmen across the Atlantic, and their behaviour hardened Puritan convictions that sport, and associated gambling, ill-served the moral and spiritual fervour of a God-fearing, hard-working society in the New World.

William Byrd offers us an idyllic prelude to cricket in colonial America and a few years later another Englishman, William Stephens, introduced the game to the southernmost colony, Georgia, where 'townsmen, freeholders, inmates and servants were assembled in the principal square at cricket.' But it is to the bustle of mid-eighteenth-century New York that we turn for the first evidence of an eleven-a-side match, and scattered references in newspapers are evidence of occasional games being played there and in Maryland before the Revolution in 1776.

By the middle of the eighteenth century American Puritanism had established itself, certainly among political intellectuals, as a moral rather than a theological creed. Thomas Jefferson, one of the founding fathers of the Republic and a future president, was asked to suggest a list of books for a young gentleman (such as William Byrd) setting up home in Virginia. His list has few books on theology (apart from the Bible), and those he does recommend, in a proposed library of nearly four hundred, are principally philosophical works and, in several cases, ones of classical philosophy such as Xenophon's *Memoirs of Socrates* and Plato's *Republic*. Awareness of the classics led men such as Jefferson to examine what the ancient world had to offer to the infant Republic of the United States as it began its independent existence. Not least among the false assumptions made by the British was that which denigrated America's new leaders as lacking an understanding of political thought and the nature of government.

The ideals of the founding fathers pointed towards a Republic of virtue which, in the Greek sense of the word *arete*, meant the achievement of excellence, of fulfilment to the best of one's capacity. It was a doctrine which a Puritan society could easily accept because it implied that there was a moral obligation to strive and to achieve. But Plato also prescribed a path to such attainment which would include a predominantly physical education for young children. Play and sport were essential to the curriculum and, as the child gave way to the adult, communal games would remain as part of the psychological and physiological bases of citizenship in the ideal state.

In its neo-classical architecture – the familiar Palladian style of so many American buildings – the new Republic showed its allegiance to the classical world. Jefferson advocated Plato's physical exercise though he rejected the playing of games. Benjamin Franklin, who had brought from England a copy of the 1744 Laws of Cricket, perhaps regretted a rash purchase and was at one with the post-Revolution condemnation of games.

Samuel Adams expressed the feelings of the founding fathers best when he urged each of the new States to become a 'Christian Sparta'. Sparta, as Plato wrote, demanded that its citizens lead a hard and simple life. Adams's cousin, John, in a moment of euphoria urged that America's independence should be celebrated with games and sports 'from one end of this continent to the other from this time forward forever more' and brought cricket into the debate in 1788 when America was considering what to call its chief executive. Alluding to the New York club, he declared: 'There is a president of a cricket club'; and this, of course, was the title chosen.

'You cannot well imagine,' wrote an English visitor to Boston in 1780, 'what a land of health, plenty and contentment this is among all ranks.' American claims to economic deprivation at the hands of the English had to be matched against the evidence of prosperity and the protected markets which England guaranteed her colonies. There is no place here to debate the causes of the American Revolution, but it may be said that whatever had been achieved had been achieved by high endeavour. Puritanism in any generation represents the sharp end of labour. Not by idleness was an industrious society created. Benjamin Franklin – the laws of cricket in his luggage not withstanding – recalled with pride that his youth had not been spent 'in games or frolics of any kind'.

It was a tone set by the political leaders after Independence and it dictated terms to Americans for the next two generations. Both John Adams and Jefferson would live for exactly fifty years after the Declaration of Independence, fixing the mould for most of the characteristics of the citizens of the United States in their time – industriousness, a puritanical sense of obligation and, in Adams particularly, an Anglophobic attitude of mind. Jefferson believed ball games were effete and contributed nothing to manliness or fitness – the Platonic ideals he embraced. Both politicians and religious leaders encouraged the material expectations of the new America: 'the profound passion is the acquisition of riches,' said de Tocqueville, the French politician, who visited the US in 1831. Frances Trollope, mother of Anthony, in her critical volume *The Domestic Manners of the Americans* conceded how hard they worked, though the Cincinnati on which she commented would be an early cricketing city.

The overriding arguments against sport had been social and moral ones, holding that sport had no place in a society ploughing the furrows of a New World. A new nation, acutely conscious of its political philosophy and its independence could find ulterior reasons for rejecting cricket in particular. In political terms it was a game identified with an exclusive class, whether they be aristocrats who belonged to the newly-formed Marylebone Cricket Club (as John Adams observed when in London in 1787) or the men of substance who played in New York. To Jefferson, whose words on the equality of man found their way into the Declaration, this was anathema. Secondly, cricket was identified with the English and with those continuing, after the War ended in 1783, to come to America. It was, especially in New York, seen as the Englishman's game.

Cricket remained a rare and novelty sport until the 1840s. Only one match was reported in the *New York Times* between 1820 and 1840. Not only did an industrial society reject team games, so did a scattered rural one which attached more importance to individual endeavour – the mastery of horse and gun which Jefferson advocated – than to communal effort. Nor was the cause of cricket enhanced in Puritan eyes by its identification in New York with the gambling which had been the spur to its popularity in pre-Victorian England. To the Evangelicals, those Puritan extremists who stimulated another Great Awakening in the 1830s, cricket was even seen 'as one of the brightest on the primrose paths to the everlasting fire'.

But by 1840 a modern America had dawned. With increasing urbanisation, with the growth of cities such as New York, Chicago and Philadelphia and with continuing immigration from England (especially from northerners with a cricketing background), cricket clubs mushroomed. In the twenty years before the outbreak of the Civil War in 1861 some four hundred clubs sprang up throughout America, mainly based in the New York area, though many a pioneer went south and west armed with his bat to establish outposts of the game at Richmond, Cincinnati, Pittsburgh, New Orleans and San Francisco. An international between America and Canada in 1853 was, said the New York *Spirit*, the all-absorbing topic in sporting circles and spectators in their thousands crossed the Hudson River from New York in 1859 to see the first ever English Tourists (Parr's XI) play at New Jersey.

Only in Philadelphia did cricket become a game played very largely by genuine Americans. Elsewhere it was never more than a minority sport in nineteenth-century America. However, the very fact that it was accepted at all was helped by the changing mood of American Puritanism towards sport in the 1850s when, once again, the Greek view of physical fitness was espoused and now became linked to a new concept of muscular Christianity, as it embraced the pursuit of Christian ideals through manly endeavour on the sports field. Muscular Christianity found a receptive public in America among those who were ready to reject the negative attitudes of extreme Puritan thinking and who welcomed a change in the relationship between sport and morality. Manliness became the great criterion for Christianity: 'eliminate heroism from religion and it becomes effeminate,' wrote Josiah Strong.

The press in the 1850s became as enthusiastic about sport – especially cricket and baseball – as it had been derogatory in the 1830s. It was, said the *New York Tribune,* the 'duty of society' to promote relaxation in order to achieve a more orderly, committed, working nation less prone to crime and drink. From this it was but a short step to argue that sport created character. Henry Chadwick, the influential journalist and pioneer sports-writer, wrote that cricket extolled 'most of the cardinal virtues', teaching 'a love of order, discipline and fair play'. While generously encouraging cricket in his press reports in the New York papers, and writing *Beadle's Dime Book of Cricket* (1860), he hedged his bets (and sold another 50,000 copies) by simultaneously writing for his publisher Mr Beadle *The Dime Book on Baseball.* With the Civil War in 1861, cricket stopped in its tracks, not quite sufficiently entrenched in the American national consciousness to survive the challenge of baseball as the real 'native' game – as the periodical *Porter's Spirit* told its New York readers in 1857.

After the war ended, encouraged by both preachers and journalists America in 1865 embarked on a great wave of athleticism. Much of it was linked to the programmes of the newly formed Young Men's Christian Association. Cricket in colleges and schools was a beneficiary. The exploits of Tom Brown were widely read – as, indeed, was the American edition (1858) of Pycroft's *The Cricket Field,* with its exposition of the moral qualities of cricket alongside technical advice on how to play the game. At Harvard University, in 1858, 'A multitude from every class are playing at cricket in a manner that would excite the admiration, even if it shocked the taste, of Tom Brown and his fellows at Rugby.' Inter-collegiate cricket survived (just) until 1925, its main adherents being Harvard and Pennsylvania Universities together with Haverford College in

Philadelphia, whose unbroken loyalty to the game from 1834 to the present day deserves a chapter itself.

Sabbatarian attitudes could not be discounted – nor can they to this day – but most Puritans trimmed their sails to the prevailing wind and favoured the course American sport pursued into the twentieth century.

But it was baseball rather than cricket, in the post-bellum years, which enjoyed popular acclaim and a wider social platform. Those who held firm to the Puritan work ethic saw baseball as a game which made a minimal interference with working hours and comprised 'all the necessary elements for affording a pleasing and harmless excitement'. By contrast cricket, as the *New York Times* observed in 1876, forced Americans to make a choice between playing or business, because playing involved so many hours. The inference was that anyone who was American-born would know exactly where his duty lay: cricket was for English residents.

So it would be amongst an exclusive social class, making little effort 'to tailor the game to the limited leisure of the lower and middle classes' that cricket would flourish, nowhere more so than in Philadelphia whose Augustan Age reached its zenith in 1893. This was the year in which Philadelphia defeated the full Australian Test team by an innings and 68 runs, 'and joy knew no bounds'. *The American Cricketer,* whose motto was 'a goodly art, a wholesome kind of exercise', devoted 18,000 words of detailed eulogistic prose to its account ending: 'this was a victory so complete, so well-earned'. But pride beckoned and allowed the sustaining voice of Puritanism the last word in an epilogue to the match-report: 'O rising generation, it is still a game; a recreation to be subordinated to graver duties, and not a pursuit.'

23
Thomas Hughes' two Rugbys

Thomas Hughes, who died in 1869, was the author of *Tom Brown's Schooldays*, a semi-autobiographical account of his days at Rugby School under the famous reforming headmaster Thomas Arnold. The book, published in 1857, achieved immediate importance and Hughes' first biographers have argued that it deeply influenced the structure and philosophy of the English public schools in the second half of the nineteenth century.

Like the typical Victorian of the middle classes, which he was, Hughes crowded many activities into a busy life. He was a barrister who became a county court judge, a Christian Socialist who advocated the ideal of co-operative production and a radical reformer who sat in the House of Commons. But just as we cherish Samuel Pepys for his *Diary* rather than remember his work as the Admiralty civil servant, so Thomas Hughes claims the attention of posterity for his authorship of *Tom Brown's Schooldays*, written sixteen years after he had left Rugby.

The book concluded with a description of Tom's last match at Rugby against MCC. The fictional match is light on statistics but, in the end, the school needed 9 runs to win with two wickets left 'when the omnibus to take the Lord's men to the train pulls up at the side of the Close'. The match was therefore abandoned with MCC declared winners on the first innings. Tom had opened the batting, 'to give his men pluck,' and had 'scored twenty-five in beautiful style' and possibly a dozen more in the second innings.

From the earliest age, sport had been part and parcel of Thomas Hughes' life. He grew up in the Berkshire village of Uffington, where he played cricket with the local boys. He continued to do so at his 'private' school at Twyford, near Reading, and then went to Rugby at the same time as his elder brother George in 1834, when he was eleven. The cult of athleticism had not yet gripped schools such as Rugby. Sport was organised by the boys themselves rather than the masters – infrequently and for fun. To the end of his days Hughes was something of a paradox – welcoming athletic endeavour yet rejecting competitiveness. Sport at his Rugby might be cricket, football, steeple chasing or studying nature. A. P. Stanley, a famous contemporary, has left on record that he was not victimised for choosing not to play team games. Forty years after Hughes' time the frail young 'Plum' Warner was unfit in his first winter term to play football at Rugby and went for nature study walks with his housemaster's wife. No one mocked him for it, and not until the summer term would his prowess at cricket be known. Cricket therefore happened spasmodically, accepted with more enthusiasm by Hughes than by his headmaster, Thomas Arnold.

From 1831 onwards records survive of the matches organised among the boys, almost entirely internal affairs except for those against local clubs, MCC (after 1840) and the Old Rugbeians. It is difficult to evaluate how good a performer Hughes was. *Scores and Biographies* does not accord him a biographical entry, though the *Dictionary of National Biography* would say that he went up to Oxford with 'a great cricketing reputation'.

In 1840 the Rugby XI went by the newly opened Birmingham–London railway line to play MCC at Lord's. Hughes, for once batting late in the order, made second-top score (30) and 9 not out in the second innings. He was stumped by the Earl of Winterton, soon to be President of MCC. It was a time when the Lord's ground, according to its first historians, was 'at its roughest' and in appearance 'more like a field pure and simple'. To put the match in an historical context, Fuller Pilch and Alfred Mynn were playing for Kent on the same two days.

Twelve months later MCC came to Rugby. Hughes, now captain of the XI, opened the batting and made the top score of 29 – with a duck in the second innings. He got two wickets and a stumping and the game was 'given up on account of darkness' with Rugby needing 14 runs with the last pair together. Thomas Hughes – like Tom Brown – had played his last match for the school.

Hughes had never moved in the ranks of the Rugby 'intellectuals', boys who made up Arnold's inner core of outstanding pupils, but he was undoubtedly influenced by his high moral tone, social concern and liberal thought. Speaking at Rugby in 1892 he declared that Arnold had given to education 'a soul and a purpose which it had wanted since Queen Elizabeth's day'. As captain of cricket, Hughes opened the cricket field in summer evenings to boys from the town and himself arranged games for them. Cricket, as he wrote in *Tom Brown's Schooldays*, taught discipline, self-reliance and unselfishness, while captaincy required both firmness and gentleness. All these would be qualities he portrayed through his life as the 'tall, high-spirited, hearty, plain-spoken man' whom contemporaries recalled.

Despite making no claims to be a classical scholar, Hughes went up to Oriel, his father's old Oxford college, in January 1842, at a time when the college was conceding its intellectual pre-eminence to Balliol. Three-quarters of the fifty or so undergraduates in Hughes' time were sporting-minded, with a football XI able to beat colleges twice its size and a crew who were head of the river – Hughes rowed at no.2 in the college VIII. He played for the University against Cambridge at Lord's in his first year (though not subsequently), but his 15 not out in the second innings failed to save Oxford from a crushing defeat by 162 runs. It was, however, the second highest individual Oxford score in the match. Pycroft gives him credit simply for being selected: 'there was little chance for players who had not been at Eton, Winchester or Harrow.' Thomas Arnold died two days after the match, an event deeply mourned by the fictional Tom Brown whom one suspects was closer to his headmaster than Thomas Hughes ever became.

Hughes made one more appearance as a cricketer at his old school, turning out for the Old Rugbeians on an April day in 1844, left not out batting at six and with a wicket to his credit. Nearly fifty years later he gave an address at the school in which he admitted that in his Oxford days he had 'attended more to cricket and rowing' than to 'lectures on ethics and politics'. The intellectual fervour of Oxford of the 1840s passed him by, but he continued to forge the liberal ideas which dictated much of his life's work. In various guises, his concern would be for the 'underdog'. Sport played its part in this only in the sense that it could widen horizons and offer rest from toil. When he became one of the band of Christian Socialists centred around Charles Kingsley and F. D. Maurice, they welcomed him partly because of the cricketing links he brought with him. In 1854 he probably played for a Christian Socialists' XI against a factory team and he introduced the game to the Working Men's Institutes with which he was closely associated. When sport among working men came to assume a professional status in the 1880s with payment, self-interest and adulation to the fore, the ageing Hughes was far less happy with the course of events.

It is time to turn to Hughes' second Rugby. Thirteen years after the publication of *Tom Brown's Schooldays* he visited the United States – in the immediate aftermath of the Civil War – and conjured up the idea of a 'colony' to which England's 'second sons' might go. Schools such as Rugby had catered only for those who would inherit land and property or who would enter the professions. There were (he wrote) 'sadly increasing numbers of 'Will Wumbles' who found themselves stranded every year less and less fit to fight the battle of life'. He saw 'first-rate material going hopelessly to waste and drifting into weary, colourless, middle age'. There is some substance in the argument. The two great Education Commissions of the 1860s – the Clarendon and Taunton – had revealed the woeful irrelevance of what was being taught in the public and grammar schools to the real nineteenth-century world outside.

With financial help from both sides of the Atlantic, land was bought for such young men in Morgan County at the eastern end of Tennessee in the United States. A limited company was established

– the Board of Aid to Land Ownership – with title to 75,000 acres and options on five times as much. At both its London and New York offices (for Americans were to be attracted as well), advertisements invited prospective emigrants to settle.

Hughes went out himself, in the late summer of 1880, taking the train from Cincinnati to Sedgemoor, the nearest railhead, and covering the last seven miles in a light buggy with a mule wagon for his luggage. He was met at the station 'by four or five young Englishmen' and at the settlement itself 'by two young ladies'. On 5 October 1880 the 'colony' was officially named Rugby and formally opened. Within a year, it had some three hundred residents, a dozen buildings and its own newspaper, appropriately called *The Rugbeian* and sub-titled 'Shoulder to Shoulder'. Those who had gone to Rugby were certainly meant to put their shoulders to the wheel, and their hands to the plough. Land had to be cleared and industries developed. By 1884 – with hindsight, the high point of the enterprise – there was a sheep farm, a sawmill and a canning factory for tomatoes while the public buildings included an Anglican church, a library, an inn (for tourists) and a school, but the cricketing author of *Tom Brown* also visualised the need for recreation.

In his classic book, the XI on the morning of the match at Rugby against MCC had gone 'down in a body before breakfast for a plunge in the cold bath in the corner of the Close'. On his first morning at Rugby, Tennessee, Hughes had been awoken by 'the uprising of the boys in flannel shirts and trousers bound for one of the two rivers near by'. They were making the long but picturesque trek to the Gentlemen's Swimming Hole. *The Rugbeian* soon announced that it was 'horribly selfish for the male animal to engross it all. There is to be a Ladies' Bathing Place.'

Soon, Hughes was watching the opening doubles tennis match on the court of the newly formed Rugby Tennis Club. He noted 'an open space on the plans marked "cricket ground",' and it appeared on the map drawn up by the chief engineer Robert Walton.

Back home, critics of Hughes' experiment wrote that it was meant to be 'a colony of workers, not a pleasure picnic' and that too much time was spent on 'mixing tea and tennis'. The settlers were 'short on elbow grease and commonsense'. Excessive attention to sport was not the real reason why Hughes' 'colony' slipped into a long decline within a few years. The boarding school – appropriately called Arnold and founded on Arnoldian principles – failed to attract pupils from the start. The United States depression of the 1890s had an impact. Disastrous fires, epidemics, incompetent marketing, internal wrangles and conflicts in aims and organisation all made their collective contribution to tragedy and despair. By 1896, the year of Hughes' death, little remained of his high ideals.

Rugby, Tennessee was meant to offer fresh opportunities for the 'underdogs' – the 'second sons' of the English public school world. There would be a chance for so many of Hughes' convictions to bear fruit: co-operative endeavour, self-reliance, 'a spirit of hardiness and cordial fellowship'. But realism would triumph over idealism and, as the *Rugbeian* itself conceded, 'The Rugby colony is a failure.'

The Rugby Restoration Association, founded in 1966 and supported by the Tennessee National Trust, has made modern Rugby a vibrant community offering to its American visitors, and just occasionally to British ones, a tantalising glimpse of what has been called, incorrectly but romantically, the last British colony in America. For the genuine researcher, the archivist will reveal the miscellaneous papers and photographs which tell the tale of those pioneering settlers of the 1880s.

On his death in 1896, Thomas Hughes' obituaries either ignored or dismissed his search for his 'New Jerusalem', treating it as an aberration in an otherwise distinguished career. He may have failed to plant cricketers in nineteenth-century Tennessee; but on one of his many visits to Rugby he had stopped off at Haverford College in Philadelphia, watched the cricket, and conferred a moral benediction upon that Quaker institution whose greatest president, Isaac Sharpless, believed that cricket 'profoundly modified the sporting morals of the College'. Hughes would have welcomed that for his own ill-fated community.

24
Learie Constantine – the first West Indian star

Learie Constantine, Baron Constantine, was born in Trinidad in 1901. His mother and father were, respectively, the child and grandchild of slaves. He had a happy, if patriarchal, upbringing on their cocoa estate and he enjoyed an economic security that he would later compare favourably (but in private) with what he saw in the Lancashire of the 1930s. His father, who had toured England twice with the West Indies, secured him a clerkship in a firm of solicitors though it would eventually be as a barrister that he made his professional name in law. His first-class cricket debut was in 1922 for Trinidad against Barbados, the only time father and son played together at that level. He won selection, largely on his fielding, for the 1923 tour of England and later became employed by Trinidad Leaseholds Ltd, who gave him permission to tour again in 1928. It was a match on that tour, West Indies against Middlesex, that had long-term implications both for himself and for West Indian cricket. Constantine scored 86 in an hour, took seven for 57 and made a second-innings century, also in an hour, and brought the tourists victory by three wickets. The Australian Charles Macartney, who was watching, persuaded his own country to invite the West Indies to tour. Both Constantine and West Indies' cricket were assured a future. He joined Nelson, the Lancashire League Club, in

1929 and played for them for eight seasons, becoming one of the best-paid sportsmen in Britain and being well regarded in Nelson for his tact, his moral standing and his friendliness. He would ultimately receive the freedom of the borough.

His first-class cricket, almost entirely, was for West Indies in the Test matches of 1933 and 1939, and in eighteen appearances he averaged 19.24 with the bat and 30.10 with the ball. At the highest level he was a bowler rather than a batsman, achieving considerable pace, with a high and smooth action. His batting, better suited to the one-day game he played for Nelson, was aggressive, powerful, unorthodox and magnetic. But it was as a fielder than he shone. His close catching was feline in its anticipation and from the deep he would throw with disconcerting accuracy.

The outbreak of the Second World War saw him work for the Ministry of Labour as a welfare officer responsible for West Indians working in munitions factories in Liverpool and for race relations generally. This was matched by broadcasts for the BBC to the Caribbean and playing in charity matches, one game alone in 1943 raising nearly four thousand pounds.

'My future is obscure,' he said in a broadcast after the war, as he devoted the eight years between 1946 and 1954 to supporting himself through work for the BBC while qualifying as a barrister. He returned to Trinidad to his old employers, Trinidad Leaseholds Ltd. His stay with them was short-lived as he accepted political office as chairman of the People's National Movement Party, won a seat in the legislative council and became the Minister for Communications, Works and Utilities. He produced concrete results, though was less successful as a debater. He incurred some hostility by making invidious comparisons with political behaviour in Britain. He left politics with few regrets to become High Commissioner in London (1961) and was knighted the following year. Three years later he entered the Chambers of Sir Dingle Foot, a very junior counsel over the age of sixty. He was sent for by a judge and wondered what misdemeanour he had committed. 'My dear Sir Learie, what an honour to have you in my court,' was the unexpected greeting.

Broadcasting, at which he was a 'natural', continued to provide him with some employment, though he was less successful as a TV cricket commentator. He played his last cricket match in 1964 for the BBC, and four years later became a governor of the corporation. Meanwhile he also served on two newly created bodies: the Sports Council and the Race Relations Board. Constantine was elected Rector of St Andrews University in 1967, a life peerage followed in 1969, allegedly blocked in earlier years by the independent Trinidad. He died in 1971. He was posthumously awarded the Trinidad Cross, and there was a memorial service in Westminster Abbey. His reputation rests on his contribution to racial tolerance, his benevolent view of empire and Commonwealth and his personal qualities that ensured his acceptance within the British Establishment. In the end he was more English than Trinidadian, and he needed that wider platform. As a cricketer he paved the way – not least in the single performance against Middlesex in 1928 – for the great achievements of his fellow-countrymen in the middle and later years of the twentieth century.

25
Bermudan Hero

When Alma Hunt celebrated his 85th birthday in 1995, Randolph Horton, the island representative at both cricket and football and a former student of mine, said that 'the Champ' was to Bermuda as W. G. Grace was to England and Don Bradman to Australia. Everyone would call him 'the Champ', though few knew the origins of the nickname. It was an ironic accolade given him by his contemporaries when, as a boy, he made 'a pair'. He would become Bermuda's greatest cricketer.

Hunt first caught the interest of the wider cricket world in 1933 when he was selected – the first Bermudan ever – for the two trials in Trinidad for the West Indies side to go to England. Despite making the highest aggregate of runs in one match and taking eight for 36 overall he was not selected. No official reason was given, but the assumption was that he lacked experience and eligibility – Bermuda has never been seen as part of the Caribbean.

Later in 1933 he played in a memorable match for Somerset, Bermuda against Sir Julien Cahn's XI, an exciting and noisy occasion vividly described by one participant, E. W. Swanton, in his book *Sort of a Cricket Person*. The following year Hunt took his talents as an all-rounder to Scotland, where he became the first black professional to play for Aberdeenshire.

The parallels with his friend Learie Constantine, playing in the Lancashire League, were close. Both were pioneers as black professional cricketers in the United Kingdom; both achieved spectacular feats as all-rounders in seeking to achieve the double in what was only Saturday afternoon cricket. Hunt did so in 1935 with 1,190 runs and 108 wickets. Constantine came close with 1,000 runs and 98 wickets in 1933. Both could fill grounds and both saw themselves as entertainers. Hunt's favourite shot was the hook – 'my bread and butter shot' – and he shared Constantine's skill in taking wickets with his medium-fast bowling and his catching.

Among his successes for Aberdeenshire were 126 not out and nine for 43 against West Lothian in 1934 and 102 not out and six for 36 against Forfarshire a year later. His best feat of all, for the county, came just before the war in 1939. After taking seven for 11 to dismiss West Lothian for 48, he scored all 49 runs for victory himself in 25 minutes. 'We were in a bit of a hurry to catch an early train back to Aberdeen from Edinburgh,' he remarked.

Like Constantine, he played briefly after the war and then retired in 1947. The *Scottish Daily Record* wrote that he had earned a following no other Scottish professional had ever commanded. 'His right-mindedness, modesty and impeccable character on and off the field won him friendship wherever he went.' Norman Stevenson, the historian of Scottish cricket, called him 'a generous personality who played with a captivating and refreshing zest'.

Both Hunt and Constantine realised that they had to build a future outside cricket. Constantine eventually became a barrister (and much else besides). Hunt qualified as a teacher, doing some of his practice at Robert Gordon's College, Aberdeen and teaching in his native Bermuda in the close season. In 1944 he majored in Journalism and Recreation at Columbia University, New York and for the rest of his career he combined teaching and journalism. He was responsible for the development of Physical Education in Bermudan Schools and he spent several years setting up Bermuda's first Government Employment Office in the Department of Immigration and Labour.

His cricket in Bermuda was for his club, Somerset, for whom he played on eleven occasions in the annual two-day Cup match against St George's. The event is still a public holiday drawing crowds of up to 15,000 (a quarter of Bermuda's population) and represents the rivalry between two clubs at either end of the cluster of islands that make up Bermuda. In these matches Hunt made a half-century or more on eight consecutive occasions, performed a hat-trick and scored the first Cup century by a Somerset batsman. He captained, and later managed, Bermudan teams in the West Indies, Canada, the United Kingdom, Denmark and Holland. He was President of the Bermudan Cricket Board of Control (1966–84) and, subsequently, Life President. He was also Bermuda's representative on the ICC (1967–82) and campaigned for the establishment of the Associate Members' Tournament. Twice, in 1979 and in 1989, he was on a delegation to South Africa to investigate the progress towards integrated cricket. He coached the 1948 Bermudan Athletics team for the Olympics and he was a founder member of the Bermudan Football League.

He was not greatly distressed when, in the 1990s, Bermuda failed to qualify for the World Cup, believing they would be 'minnows'. Such an analogy might be applied to Hunt himself. He was, in cricketing terms, a big fish in both Bermudan and Scottish cricket. How he would have fared in the first-class game must largely be a matter of conjecture. He declined, in 1939, an invitation to join Glamorgan but always regretted that by the end of his career he had only played two matches officially dubbed 'first-class'.

When my wife and I met him in Bermuda in 1995 he was still as interested as ever in cricket and readily proffered his opinions. He was critical of the extent that overseas players dominated the English game, was against 'overs' cricket and strongly in favour of the traditional game of 'declarations'. He gave us lunch in his club, and later in the afternoon we took farewell of this fine and upright man, immaculately dressed and belying his years, in the company of his wife Elmira, a retired headmistress, graduate of Howard and London Universities, and a lady of great charm and capabilities. She had been the support to him that Gloria had been to Learie Constantine. And, like, Constantine, Alma Hunt had been a great ambassador for cricket. He died in 1999.

26
Hong Kong Cricket – the Colonial Chapter

'It is not an unusual sight to see strangely familiar hat bands and blazers – the IZ or the Free Foresters – [in Hong Kong] recalling memories of the leafy homeland, ties and personalities momentarily lost in the flotsam and jetsam of man's work and life in the Empire.' So wrote Ralph Haycock in *Imperial Cricket* in 1912. On leave in his 'leafy homeland' Haycock himself would appear for Somerset, and played his last match for the county against Surrey at Bath in May 1914. Less than six months later he was killed in France, one of the earliest 'cricket' casualties of the First World War. He gained the DSO before he fell. In a moving and evocative final paragraph he left his epitaph on Hong Kong cricket as he knew it:

> North of the ground is the harbour, masts flying the flags of every nation, the musical hum from the great Naval Dockyard, the scream of an occasional siren announcing the arrival or departure of the mails and to the west the everlasting hills, humped, rocky and bare and, as the afternoon wanes, the hot sun gilds the uttermost heights and then sinks swiftly, abruptly.

As determinedly as trade followed the flag, so went cricket in its wake. By 1840 traders and soldiers were playing the game in Hong Kong and in 1842 the Treaty of Nangking ceded it to Great Britain and opened five ports to British trade and residence. Nine years later, in 1851, the first of the colony's two great clubs was formed when the Hong Kong Cricket Club 'for civil professionals, the military and some trades people' came into existence. The *China Mail*, reporting in some detail the negotiations, hinted at some tension between those who saw the reclaimed land along the seafront by Chater Road as an area for general recreation and those who wanted it solely for cricket. It was to prove a lingering tension and, as late as the 1960s, came to a head when the Government decided not to renew the lease at Chater Road. What became a political issue of some magnitude led, in the end, to the Hong Kong Club moving to a site on the Wong Nai Chung Gap Road, with a Government grant towards the cost of turfing. All that, however, lay over a hundred years in the future. 'Messrs Bridges, Antrobus, Smith and Lane, Captain Lodder and Lieutenant Chadwick' were the Committee appointed, on the nomination of Mr. A. Shortrede, a founder of the *China Mail*, to launch the club.

In 1866 there began the long series of inter-port fixtures between Hong Kong and Shanghai – 800 miles and 54 steamship hours to the north. In the opening game Hong Kong won by an innings after making 430. Twelve months later, 'away' to Shanghai, it was again Hong Kong who won by an innings. The long voyage would, in 1892, bring the greatest single tragedy in cricket history. The Hong Kong side was returning from Shanghai in October on board the 2,900 ton SS *Bokhara* when the vessel ran into a typhoon. Monstrous waves smashed the lifeboats and flooded the engine room. Drifting helplessly, the ship floundered on Sand Island near Formosa (Taiwan) and sank within two minutes. It took a week for the news to reach Hong Kong that all but two of the cricketers had perished. Among those lost was John Dunn, the captain, who had made occasional appearances for Surrey and, only weeks earlier, had made the first century of the inter-port series in the previous match against Hong Kong. The fixture, which had always been played intermittently rather than regularly, went into abeyance after the tragedy, resuming in 1897 when both Shanghai and the Straits Settlements visited Hong Kong. A combined Hong Kong–Shanghai side lost by an innings to the Straits. With interruptions, mainly the two World Wars, the original inter-port series continued until 1948,

The author with Jack Parsons, another subject of a biography.

W.R. Hammond.

E.W. Swanton.

The author in Australia.

Jamestown, the 'cradle' of American cricket.

Above: Thomas Hughes' 'other' Rugby – the cricket ground 'discovered' by the author.

Below: Hong Kong pavilion.

Learie Constantine.

Western Kentucky University.

Radley College, Oxfordshire.

With David Money, the oldest wicketkeeper, when reporting at Bedford School.

Right: the author going out to bat in Kentucky on the Merion ground.

Below left: our daughter, Gillian.

Below centre: our elder son, David, in 1974.

Below right: Michael gets his Cambridge Blue, at Lord's, in 1977.

Our house in North Moreton.

The author as an editor, 1973.

The church and North Moreton House.

With David Rayvern Allen and my wife at Lord's.

With my son Michael on the Kent tour, 1997.

With Stephen Green, MCC Curator, at Lord's.

Moreton CC at home in 1973.

Moreton CC in Holland in 1987.

Moreton CC, 2002.

ending with twenty victories for Hong Kong and fifteen for Shanghai. Only on the very last visit did Hong Kong go by air. The horrors of 1892 were brought to mind again when the 1934 side, visiting Shanghai, arrived late because of a typhoon. While the Hong Kong Club provided the players in the early years, later others would be invited on merit, including those from the Kowloon Club.

Kowloon, Hong Kong's second club, was granted a site on the mainland in King's Park by the Governor in 1904. In the opening match, played as a league fixture, the Army Ordinance Corps were dismissed for 53, but Kowloon's batting let them down as they fell for 25. Participants in this early incarnation of league cricket included the Army, the Naval and Civil Service sides, Hong Kong University, the Police, the Parsees, the Eastern Extension Telegraph Company and the Craigengower Club. Cricketers were in abundance! The Hong Kong Club was a reluctant participant at the start, though it fielded both 'A' and 'B' XIs. But enthusiasm grew in the pre-war period, and Hong Kong won the First Division. Kowloon could only manage the title twice.

The First World War, as has so often been said, was a watershed in history. Its effect on cricket, as opposed to that upon society, was less marked – an argument as applicable to the English cricket scene as to that in Hong Kong. While military events in Europe had still their course to run, Hong Kong cricketers resumed their league programme in 1917. Both Hong Kong and Kowloon won a fair proportion of titles in the inter-war years. The memory of individual players and their achievements can be ephemeral to all except those closely involved with them. Nevertheless, there are some names in the first hundred or so years of Hong Kong's cricket history which deserve a passing mention. There was John Dunn, of the SS *Bokhara* disaster and, just after his generation, the brothers Richard and Harry Hancock. Immediately after the war P. Cobb and J. Stalker were two outstanding Kowloon players. The 1920s saw the performances of William Brace as an all-rounder, while Harry Owen-Hughes and Acky Bowker were prominent bowlers.

The two Pearces, father and son, made a notable contribution in the first half of the twentieth century. Tarn made his inter-port debut in 1903. His century, which won the 1923 match against Shanghai when all seemed lost, was memorable not least because the *Empress of Russia* delayed its departure to enable him to bat. *Wisden* called his son, Alec, 'an upstanding batsman with good style'. After leaving Charterhouse Alec played for Kent, putting on 194 with Leslie Ames against Northamptonshire in 1932 in one of his last matches before joining his father's business in Hong Kong. The two of them played together against Shanghai in 1935 in Tarn's last match. On leave in 1937, Alec again played for Kent. More impressively, in 1946 and after five years as a POW in a Japanese camp he made a century for the county against Northamptonshire. He played in the last inter-port match in 1948 and, in due course, became president of both the Hong Kong and Kent cricket clubs. The approach of war, in 1939, had an immediate effect on cricket in the colony. Service personnel and civilians both began to depart and the 1938–39 league programme was confined to three months in the early part of 1939. Sides dropped out of the League fixtures in 1940 and 1941 and on 8 December 1941 Japanese forces attacked Hong Kong. Great Britain declared war on Japan and by Christmas the colony was forced to capitulate, having earned – as Winston Churchill was to write – 'lasting honour . . . in the stubborn defence of the port and fortress'. The clubhouse at Kowloon was looted within days and the enemy used the ground for stabling horses and mules. One of the first matches to take place after the war was a friendly between the two major clubs, Hong Kong and Kowloon, on the sixth anniversary of the Japanese attack. They competed for the Hancock Shield and continued to do so until 1975 when there was no more space on the trophy for the names of the winners. League cricket resumed in 1948 with the Hong Kong entrants playing as Optimists, Alec Pearce captaining and batting effectively.

While domestic cricket continued to flourish, the development of air communications brought the colony closer to the rest of the world. The first major post-war visitors were the Australians in 1952. They included Keith Miller, with an unfulfilled ambition to hit a window in the Bank of China by the Chater Road ground. Ten years later came the first international touring party, nineteen of whom were Test cricketers. The side reads like a roll call of the best players from the 1960s who, in a world tour, travelled over 40,000 miles. To some extent, the multi-racial group was able to challenge the boundaries created by apartheid: West Indians played in southern Africa, though South Africans were not allowed to play in Pakistan or India. Hong Kong did nobly, losing by only 35 runs. Hard on their heels came E.W. Swanton's international XI. He has told of the emotional experience of returning to the Far East where he had been a POW. His side represented five Commonwealth countries and included such players as Richie Benaud, Sonny Ramadhin and the Nawab of Pataudi.

There were three matches in Hong Kong, with local bowlers Carl Myatt and Ian Lacy-Smith distinguishing themselves. Within a year (1964/65) Worcestershire played in Hong Kong before crossing the Pacific to Hollywood to complete the last lap of a world tour.

All this served as a prelude to the visit of MCC in 1966 on their return from their tour of Australia and New Zealand. Geoffrey Boycott used the occasion to make a century. Four years later he contributed an undefeated 79 at the conclusion of MCC's tour of Ceylon and the Far East. The MCC side to Australia and New Zealand in 1974/75 again visited Hong Kong, Keith Fletcher and Dennis Amiss each making a century. Soon afterwards, in 1977, MCC ceased to send fully representative sides overseas, and future Test sides, under the aegis of the Test and County Cricket Board, toured as 'England'.

This was the end, in a sense, of a short but exciting era in Hong Kong cricket. Future MCC sides would come as club teams, though with players of first-class status within their ranks. No tour under the auspices of TCCB visited Hong Kong during the twenty years (1977–97) of that body's existence.

The emphasis for the future changed. Hong Kong's proximity to Australia and to India continued to encourage visits from both. Hong Kong also became a venue for touring clubs in the new age of package holidays arranged especially for cricketers. The colony made its own first representative visit overseas in a 1976 tour of England: the highlight was a match at Lord's. An MCC XI, including former

England captains in Colin Cowdrey, Ted Dexter and Mike Smith, scored 220 for five, to which Hong Kong replied with a praiseworthy 199 for eight. Subsequent visits were paid to the United States, Canada and South America. Hong Kong cricketers of the 1990s participated in a round-robin tournament in Singapore involving Bangladesh, Malaysia and Singapore. In a sense, it was modern version of the historic inter-port fixtures against Shanghai. There had been triangular inter-port contests as early as 1904 and they were played spasmodically thereafter. In an inter-port fixture in 1982 the future England cricketer, Hong Kong-born Dermot Reeve, took eight for 93 against Singapore.

Hong Kong's entry that year (1982) into the Associate Members' Competition brought a new dimension into their cricket. They were competing against their peers, winning some and losing some and performing not unreasonably against sides such as Zimbabwe (who advanced to Test status in 1992) and Kenya. In 1994 they reached the quarter-finals. Individual players distinguished themselves: Reeve played as a nineteen-year old in the 1982 competition. His subsequent career took him to Sussex, Warwickshire, where he captained, and to three England Test caps. But Hong Kong could rightly claim him as one of their own, alongside Adam Hollioake of Surrey, who played junior cricket there when his family lived in Hong Kong.

A symbol of change had been the end of the Hong Kong Cricket Club's tenure of the Chater Road ground in 1975, the closing season marked by a match between an Australian Superstars' XI and the club. Hong Kong declared at 236 for nine, Peter Green making 95 before being one of Peter Philpott's five victims. The Australians replied with an opening century partnership between Jim Burke and Bob Simpson. With the dismissal of the openers, together with the wickets of Neil Harvey, Les Favell and Ian Craig, the colony's hopes rose. But Alan Davidson and Rodney Marsh saw the Superstars home by four wickets. It had been a fine performance and 'a fitting farewell to the Lord's of Asia,' said the *South China Morning Post*. A few days earlier, Lieutenant-General Sir Edwin Bramall made the last century in a League match on the ground. In due course, Field Marshal Lord

Bramall would become President of MCC and nominate Sir Denys Roberts as successor in that office. Over a period of a quarter of a century, Roberts himself would be a pivotal figure in Hong Kong as jurist, administrator and cricketer. The cricketers of Chater Road duly moved to their new ground at Wong Nai Chung Gap, but the change of tenure was symptomatic of a wider problem which would increasingly face Hong Kong cricket as a whole. Land was more and more at a premium; fewer grounds were available; municipal councils reclaimed facilities for sports with a wider representation of Chinese and the gradual withdrawal of British troops brought a further reduction in playing space. Nevertheless – in sharp contrast to the view held at the end of the 1980s – the future for Hong Kong cricket now seems optimistic. It is qualified by the extent to which Chinese, and especially the young, become involved. The 'historic' clubs like Hong Kong and Kowloon remain prominent, while there are more and more Asians playing. An all-Chinese team, the Dragons, performs well. Some forty different sides play regularly at weekends at secondary school level, despite the shortage of grounds, and the number of players is expanding rapidly with a Schools' Cricket Association organising competitions. Hundreds of youngsters of all ages take part in regular coaching and playing sessions and in periodic tournaments. In 1997 some two hundred Chinese children became involved for the first time.

All this has involved coaching and the Hong Kong Sports' Development Board, in conjunction with Institutes of Education, has been training teachers and students to produce Cantonese-speaking coaches. It has also involved funding, which has come from the Board and major sponsors such as Brierley Investments and Cathay Pacific Airways.

Just before the end of the colonial era Hong Kong took part in the 1997 ICC Trophy held in Malaysia. They beat the top-seeded Bermuda by three wickets and qualified for the quarter-finals, before being beaten by Bangladesh. This, the last 'international' cricket occasion before the handover of power, was followed in September 1997 by the first 'international' one under Chinese rule. It was business as usual as Hong Kong entertained cricketers from many of the Test countries in the annual Sixes Competition. Chinese sports administrators were guests at this occasion and Hong Kong officials had already visited Beijing.

Those involved in the ICC Development programme see cricket, wrote Ali Bacher of South Africa, as an 'especially suitable sport for China'. The executive director of the Hong Kong Cricket Association has written that Hong Kong 'is a serious contender within the game' and he foresees the day 'when the Hong Kong team is made up entirely of Chinese cricketers'. Ambitions are high and prospects good. Hong Kong may well accede to Test status before too many years go by.

Part III
Second Innings

III
Personal Essays

27
Radley College and Lord Williams's, Thame

My own school Glenalmond, Radley College in Oxfordshire and St Columba's, Dublin all have something in common, and might be said to form a loose confederation. Radley and Glenalmond were founded in 1847 and St Columba's four years earlier. Radley and St Columba's also share a founder in William Sewell. Similarity of aim united them: together with the great majority of public schools of the time they taught Christian principles. There were, however, different shades of Anglicanism. Radley, for example, was suspected of popish tendencies and certainly reflected the influence of the Oxford or Tractarian Movement. Glenalmond was closely identified with the Episcopal Church in Scotland, recently liberated from the penal laws which had severely restricted its activities ever since the Revolution of 1688 – an event which confirmed Presbyterianism as the official religion of Scotland.

Within these murky by-paths of theology, and equally oppressed by financial difficulties, Radley in Oxfordshire and Glenalmond in Perthshire sought to make their way under their first wardens, respectively the Reverend Robert Singleton and the Reverend Dr Charles Wordsworth. Singleton had already been Warden of St Columba's in Ireland and was now associated in what the official historian of Radley called 'The Second Attempt' at founding a school. Wordsworth would go on to become Bishop of St Andrews but with a greater claim, as we have seen, on the boys' affections as a player in the first Oxford and Cambridge cricket match.

To someone such as myself – a pupil at one and a master (or don) at the other – there were certain things that commanded a parallel examination. Each headmaster was called a warden, gowns were worn at both schools, the school day (comparing those of the 1940s and the 1970s) was strikingly similar and, of course, the Christian ethos was paramount. Having said this, many of these factors would be found in a large number of public schools. Those, such as University College, London, which were specifically secular in outlook, were very much the exception. Public schools, in short, were part of the great revival of religion in mid-Victorian society, with tentacles that stretched out to an empire in which many of their sons were destined to serve.

If Glenalmond, somewhat extravagantly, was sometimes called 'the Eton of the North', Radley took its place in the forefront of public schools in the south. In the 1970s it enjoyed, by general acclaim, an outstanding warden in Dennis Silk who would serve the College from 1968 to 1991. It almost became axiomatic, in the 1970s and 1980s, for a prospective headmaster of a public school to have taught at Radley under Silk.

If I did not entirely fit into the pattern of Radley's staff, the 'fault' was mine rather than Radley's. I was not ambitious to be a headmaster and I came to resent the fact that I never had time to put pen to paper (or, more specifically, to write a book) during my years there. We once had a staff meeting at 10 o'clock on Saturday night because no other time was available. Cricket played a major part in a school which had produced Ted Dexter in the past and would produce Andrew Strauss in the future. I recall, with pleasure, taking a successful colts side to the Oval for the finals of a tournament.

Staff cricket matches were pleasant domestic occasions, though it was entirely in keeping with Radley's ethos that the staff did not meet for a drink afterwards but retired to their studies to correct work. There was a rule that all work taken in had to be returned to the pupils within twenty-four hours. It encouraged one to modify one's testing.

There were domestic problems demanding my attention. Defying the analogy that lightning never strikes twice, we had two successive bad tenants at our house in North Moreton and their tenure was a permanent worry. The law, as it stood, favoured tenant rather than landlord. In the end, the only way I could regain access to my own house (on which no rent had been paid for two years) was by a technical 'eviction' from my Radley house, in which the warden was good enough to co-operate.

On the credit side, I gave Radley the scholarship they asked for and produced probably rather more Oxbridge successes than were really merited. On the debit side, I grudged the time given to cramming the weaker brethren towards the same goals.

My wife Anne was now an associate-specialist at the Fairmile Psychiatric Hospital and was making her way in a career which would ultimately lead to a consultancy; my children, meanwhile, had gone their separate ways. My elder son, David, who had taken a degree at Edinburgh at a very young age, went on to Magdalene College, Cambridge, as did his younger brother, Michael, two years later. David would subsequently have a distinguished career in the Forestry Commission, being chief conservator for Scotland before being attached successively to the United Nations in New York and as Head of Agriculture Policy in the Scottish Executive. He would marry Jean Buchanan-Smith and his four children would be Claire, Susanna, Fenella and Edward.

Occasionally Michael – a pupil at Abingdon School – would join in evening tutorials at Radley. Indeed, one boy who came to such occasions would, in years to come, be a valuable member of Moreton Cricket Club. This was Charles Batten, whose marriage would, in due course, make him a relation to my grandchildren. Michael was directly affected by our stay at Radley in another way. It was Guy Waller, the cricket master, who alerted me to the fact that he was good enough to get a Blue as a fast bowler. The incentive was enough to make him work hard and his reward was a Blue as a freshman. He played in the Cambridge XI of 1977 and 1980, missing one year through injury and another through loss of form. Thereafter his career lay in schoolmastering, but he continued to play cricket, winning selection for the England Young Cricketers' side and making appearances for the Quidnuncs as well as a local commitment to Moreton. He was once picked for Gloucestershire's 1st XI, but the match was rained off.

I had the melancholy experience of never actually seeing him take a wicket or get a run in first-class cricket – though he must have done so. His mother turned up for the University match of 1980 in time to see him injured which, effectively, brought his first-class career to an end. He was probably not strong enough to have made it as a professional, though he made a few appearances for Gloucestershire 2nd XI. However, his academic aspirations would lead him in other directions and he would be head of the history departments, successively, at Kingston Grammar School, University College, London and St Paul's. At St Paul's he also ran the school's cricket – unusual for someone holding a major academic appointment. Michael would marry Kathryn Crew and their children would be Georgina, John, Robert and William.

My daughter Gillian would leave St Helen's, Abingdon, go to an Oxford Secretarial College and be earning her living very early, before marrying and making her life in the United States, gradually moving westwards to southern California. She married Ian Bossenger and has two children: Thomas and Hannah.

When an offer came from the Principal of Lord Williams's, Thame, in Oxfordshire, of a senior pastoral appointment which involved responsibility for the very large number of probationary and student teachers which the school trained, I willingly accepted. The job was compatible with my previous experience at Culham College. It meant I could have the leisure to write while, I hoped, fulfilling my duties in what was an extremely large comprehensive school of over 2,500 pupils with a VIth form of 400 and with, at one point, the children of three heads of Oxford Colleges in the school. Dennis Silk, whom I asked over to lunch soon after going to Thame, made the wry remark: 'If all comprehensives were like Lord Williams's, there would be no need for schools like Radley!'

Lord Williams's had a distinguished lineage, called after its founder who was a public figure in the reign of Henry VIII. Lord Williams was a Justice of the Peace, a Sheriff in Oxfordshire and, for eleven years, Member of Parliament for the County. In due course he became treasurer of the Court of Augmentations, established to secure for the Crown a share of the revenues of the dissolved Monasteries and religious houses. Although he was never convicted of peculation, he undoubtedly did well out of his office and in due course – having been raised to the peerage by Elizabeth I and earning a princely salary of £1,000 a year as Lord President of the Marches of Wales – he was able to endow a Grammar School in Thame in the year 1559. Some have suggested he did so as a penance for having done so well out of the spoils of monastic wealth.

In the centuries which followed, Lord Williams's attracted some well-known pupils, especially during the seventeenth century when John Hampden attended. During those troubled times, Thame was seen as a safe haven, contrasting with Oxford a few miles away. But Hampden would die as a result of his wounds at Chalgrove, near Thame, not many years later. Like many another school in the early years of the nineteenth century it fell on hard times, but revived in the Victorian period just as schools such as Glenalmond and Radley were coming into being. Indeed, at one point in the second half of the nineteenth century it might have aspired to membership of the Headmasters' Conference, so acquiring public school status. But that was not to be, and in the late twentieth century Lord Williams's became a comprehensive school within the Oxfordshire local authority.

Part of the appeal to me had been the opportunity to run the cricket. Lord Williams's always had a strong cricket tradition. Between 1906 and 1911 it had won 48 out of 55 cricket matches, which suggests the teams could not find strong enough opposition. There was little co-operation between public schools and grammar schools nor, indeed, would there be fifty years on. When I joined the staff, however, Lord Williams's had broken into the closed shop of fixtures against public schools. This led me to approach MCC to suggest Lord Williams's became the first comprehensive school on their fixture list. My request was accepted – despite the fact that I did not then enjoy the influence at MCC which came later – and a match duly took place. It proved a low-scoring game and the last wicket-pair for Lord Williams's needed to make the highest partnership of the match to win. With proverbial nail-biting and umbrella-twisting, the target was achieved and Lord Williams's has played MCC ever since.

The principal of Lord Williams's School, Geoff Goodall, was a focal point in the success of the school's cricket. He was very much a 'hands on' man. When the chance came to get a new pavilion from an old site, it was he who was there with his spade. It was hardly his fault that it blew down in a freak storm on Christmas Eve. Nothing daunted, he saw it put up again. When I heard that Wellingborough School were parting with their old scorers' hut, he dispatched me (having *just* passed the appropriate test) with a minibus to bring it over in sections to assemble it. All was on a tight budget, but gradually we had secured everything we needed and got a very co-operative groundsman. One should pay a tribute to Goodall. He has been called the second founder of Lord Williams's School. He came as a young master from Uppingham to a small country grammar school. He saw it through the years of transition as it became one of the largest and most successful comprehensives in the country. When he felt his work there was done he became headmaster of Exeter School. He never thought, he once told me, he would have a son who would turn down an Oxford Fellowship. Howard Goodall has made his own national reputation as a musician and broadcaster.

One must also mention John Fulkes. He played a major part in Lord Williams's cricket. His early death, in 2005, was a profound event and produced a display of grief and affection towards a schoolmaster by some two thousand and more pupils which can scarcely ever have been equalled. His contribution to Oxfordshire cricket at every level was demonstrated in the huge representation of cricketers at his funeral and the town of Thame virtually came to a halt. That cricket still flourishes at the school is his legacy.

My years at Lord Williams's were extremely happy. A large part of my job was to take responsibility for the many student teachers who came to us from the Oxford Department of Education. As befits one of the largest schools in the country, we took a major role in the development of trainee teachers. I had my standards! I would meet the prospective students in Oxford and outline what I expected in terms of attitude and dress. The next morning they would come to Thame. One young man had completely ignored my directions on dress and informed me he did not agree with them. He was sent back to Oxford on the next bus and told to go elsewhere. We had some problems with one or two mature students, largely in their adjustment to dealing with youngsters, and I was able to bring my Culham experience to bear. I took the view, as I had done at Culham, that men and women over forty-five or so found the transition difficult.

The principal at Lord Williams's believed that all senior staff should take a share of teaching the lowest-ability groups. I had my third formers for three periods a week. One day they suggested going to see the old Grammar School. 'We can't get in,' I replied. 'Put on old clothes. We know a way.' Somewhat furtively (at least, I was the furtive one) we sneaked off after school on a dull November evening and found our way into the old sixteenth-century Grammar School in the town. There it was: hardly changed from the school that had done service for three centuries, with graffiti on the walls made respectable by its age. Time stood still and one could almost see those Tudor schoolboys diligently learning their lessons at the hands of the usher. A few weeks later the builders moved in and the building was 'developed'.

I may not have taught these youngsters much history in the technical sense, but they taught me some. In the years which followed I would see them in Thame working in the local shops and would always get a greeting. It was the flipside of the coin from teaching VIth formers at Radley. I have always been grateful that my teaching experience was so varied – not only in terms of the social range and abilities of pupils but also in terms of the subjects I have taught. Latin, English, Geography, Religious Education, Physical Education and Games have all claimed my attention from time to time. The year after I left Lord Williams's, I did some supply teaching and took an all-girl class in Home Economics. We finished up discussing how to bath the baby and they all voted it a great success.

Indeed, I never really left the school. I became archivist, with the perks of a fine office and the excuse to have a day out once a week or so for a further twenty years. I finally relinquished the post in the autumn of 2005. My role as archivist was linked loosely to my connections with another school. My daughter had, as I have mentioned, been a pupil at St Helen's and St Katharine's School, Abingdon. They approached me to write their centenary history, which was duly published in 2003. The book was demanding in that the time schedule was brief. There was plenty of archive material and, in its use, I was guided as to what one ought to preserve in the Lord Williams's collection. Again, I was led down the industrious paths of our ancestors who had founded schools with a Christian philosophy and St Helen's, in its origins, owed everything to the devotion and intent of Anglican sisters at Wantage at the end of the nineteenth century. A century and more later saw St Helen's in the very forefront of education, placed sixth in the National League Tables in 2005.

With my retirement from Lord Williams's I might have anticipated the end of my role in education, but my work in the archives and my history of St Helen's kept me in touch. Then, unexpectedly, another door would open.

28
An American University

'How about giving a lecture at Western?' was the casual invitation one day. I had retired from Lord Williams's and we had gone to visit our daughter in Kentucky. Why not, indeed? I talked to some undergraduates about English education and had lunch with some members of the faculty of the University of Western Kentucky.

It was a pleasant two hours and I thought no more of it. Two days later came a more formal invitation: 'Would you consider teaching a bye-term?' I was being invited to a visiting professorship of history for eleven weeks in the autumn (or Fall) of the following year: a bye-term was half of the full academic semester, which lasted for 22 weeks. We considered the pros and cons and they were mostly pros. It would mean seeing something of our daughter, it would be an adventure, I would not miss the cricket season back home and it would top up our pensions. There didn't seem any 'cons' at all. So it came about in the autumn (English-style) of 1990 I began what eventually turned out to be five bye-terms over six years. I taught variously a first-year class called Western Civilisation, a second-year class on the eighteenth century in Britain and a postgraduate class on the relations between Church and State in Tudor and Stuart England.

Western Civilisation was a compulsory course for all undergraduates whatever they were studying and, as far as I could gather, was mandatory in all American Universities. It might equally have been styled European History and my brief was to take the class, in fifty-five lectures, through the History of Western Europe from 1648 (the end of the Thirty Years' War) up to as far as I could get in the time. 1941 (not 1939) seemed a good, and possibly non-controversial, date at which to end. So far as 'controversy' was concerned, my head of department, Richard Troutman, only gave me one piece of advice: 'Don't mention Evolution.' I was hardly likely to unless I got myself involved in the great nineteenth-century debate at Oxford between Wilberforce and Huxley. 'Evolution,' Professor Troutman went on, ' is a tricky one here – a lot of people are fundamentalists.'

My class in Western Civilisation – one might style it colloquially 'Learning a little about a lot' – was made easier by the fact that at Edinburgh University first-year European History had not been dissimilar. The challenge was with the students who knew no history at all. I was slow to spot that my ablest, one year, was a medical student.

The class was big and I thought I had better assert myself at the start. 'We have a week to get used to each other's accents,' I announced. There was a young lady who persisted in talking. 'I haven't crossed the Atlantic to compete with you,' I said after one or two 'looks' and warnings. She burst into tears, rushed out and was never seen again. I learned that first-year students were sensitive plants.

The second-year class on the eighteenth century in Britain was my choice. It gave me a chance to present the conflict with America (about which students had learnt a lot at school) from the British angle. I think they enjoyed it.

I have been lucky always to teach at institutions which have been aesthetically attractive, and Western Kentucky was no exception. It has been described (allowing for a little bias) as unique in its lovely campus. The buildings, in the classical style and of white stone, command a vista of the rolling countryside of Kentucky. Inside the campus survives a trench used in the Civil War in which Kentucky, as a border state, was heavily divided in its allegiance.

I became deeply involved in the life of the University, attempting to play baseball, visiting other departments – especially that of Journalism – to see how they operated and taking my share in pastoral responsibilities for the students. Virtually all of them worked their way through University. I recall a girl whose work was gradually deteriorating and I asked her why. She replied that she now had to work in a shop for thirty hours a week. The solution, such as it was, was for her to take an entire term (or semester) off, work full time in her shop and resume her studies a term later. With the credit system, where an accumulation of points secured a degree, this was possible. My first-year class, for example, attracted eleven points if satisfactorily completed. And here another problem emerged. Failure by a professor to give that assurance could produce tears from women and near enough from men. It meant so much for them to pass their courses and within the quickest time. I am aware that I became more lenient as the years passed.

My appointment at Western required me to give some satisfactory evidence of research. Indeed, if I have a criticism, it was that some of my colleagues were not very good teachers and were far more interested in their research programmes. When I was asked what I might do, I suggested a history of cricket in the USA. It took some persuasion on my part; but eventually I was able to satisfy the Faculty that the subject might be pursued. Something of my research, though without the detail, appears in Part II of this book. I was able to explore the growth of cricket in the Eastern States, to pursue its special appeal to the citizens of Pennsylvania, to find out why it diminished in popularity in the Civil War (though not in Pennsylvania till the 1890s), to study its decline in the early twentieth century and to rejoice in its revival in the second half of that century. Some vignettes are worth recalling. My wife and I went to Virginia on the James River, where the owners of a Palladian eighteenth-century house were playing tennis at the spot where once William Byrd had 'played at cricket' and recorded his achievements – perhaps the earliest evidence for the game in America. Later, I played in a match in Philadelphia at the famous Merion ground where once thousands had watched an England team play at the turn of the twentieth century. I joined a modest group who included representatives of the British Council. The ground was marked out for tennis and cricket could only be played when the tennis players allowed.

On a Friday afternoon I asked my first-year class if they would do some research for me in the library. It would show them, I pointed out, the essential drudgery of research – perhaps, with hindsight, not a very encouraging introduction. I took them to the files of the *New York Times* and prompted them to take a year each and extract the references to cricket. It was worthwhile – only 1941 proved a blank year. But there was a codicil: my non-white students did not participate. There was nothing personal – we got on well – but they were not prepared to do me a favour. Race relations in Kentucky were still strained. I got myself into trouble when I asked a student group to look into their ancestry over the Thanksgiving Break. Many did so and produced some fascinating results. 'You realise we couldn't,' said one black student, 'we were not allowed, when slaves, to record anything about ourselves, not even our ages.'

The most exciting of my cricket pursuits was my visit to Rugby, Tennessee. There Thomas Hughes, of *Tom Brown's Schooldays* fame, had established what has been called the last British colony in America, discussed in Part II of this book, and on the map drawn up by his chief engineer, Robert Walton, there was an open space in the forest that was marked 'cricket ground'. The records, minimal indeed, show that on 9 May 1885 the pavilion had been painted 'by the prettily situated ground' and cricket was played on Saturday afternoons. I was determined to find Thomas Hughes' 'second' Rugby cricket ground and, armed with Walton's map, a compass and a stout stick I set out one Thanksgiving weekend. The going was hard and, deep in the forest, I almost abandoned my pursuit. My reward in the end was that rare commodity in modern life: total stillness and silence. And I suddenly found myself in a clearing which had once been the field in the 1880s where Hughes had taught his young men cricket. It was a far cry from the Close at Rugby.

Yet not everyone had given up the enterprise to stay in Tennessee. Later that same day I dined with a direct descendant of Robert Walton, the engineer who had mapped out the cricket ground for Hughes and who still lived in the family house. I don't think my colleagues at Western were very impressed with this as a contribution to original research on cricket in America. But I felt I had been part of a living bit of cricket history in the United States and, indeed, the visit to Rugby was a tale in itself.

Three aspects of Rugby, Tennessee remain in the memory: the Anglican church built in Carpenter (wood) Gothic Style; Hughes' library of 7,000 books as a rich repository of first-edition Victorian literature; and a collection of photographs which so graphically tell the story of those pioneering settlers of the nineteenth century. It was, indeed, romantically, though incorrectly, called the last British colony in America.

My seminars as a visiting professor at Western Kentucky University had been a rewarding experience. I was conscious that I was a guest and kept criticism to myself though, at this distance of time and space, I have to say that the marking of student work was more subjective than it ought to have been. Yet I had to be aware of the fact that the great majority of the students were first generation at the University, a similar great majority had never been out of Kentucky and a staggeringly large number of them would never do so. Even to the Faculty (or staff) this had some relevance. Something I thought was especially useful was a seminar I took once a week for my Faculty colleagues to ask me questions about British History which, from time to time, they themselves taught. I remember the surprise when I explained that Lord North (the villain of the piece in American history) sat in the House of Commons, and not the House of Lords. Whether my explanation was understood is another matter!

Apart from one instance when I taught in the Spring semester (and got back two matches late for the start of the cricket season at home), all my teaching was in the Fall semester. My students tried to teach me baseball and bowled generously 'soft' balls at me.

My wife and I lived in various rented accommodation. She took advantage of the opportunity to take a weaving class in the Art Department. Mature students might register as 'audio' students – they could 'hear' what was taught but need not do examinations.

Shortly after spending part of my retirement winters in Kentucky, I was invited to spend my retirement summers, in the

1990s, as a cricket journalist. I used to wonder, in October, if I knew enough history to teach at Western and, in May, if I knew enough about cricket to report on it. They were, collectively, an idyllic few years.

29
Journalist and Author

An invitation to write on cricket for the *Daily Telegraph* in my retirement exactly fitted in with my years in Kentucky. I came home from the States in the spring raring to go! It also fulfilled a youthful ambition of some forty years earlier. By the time I was an undergraduate, career prospects had to be taken seriously. Both my parents might be said to have dabbled in journalism, as we saw earlier, but each was adamant that I should not earn my living in the same field.

So I 'dabbled', as my parents had done, while an undergraduate. I had been nominated for the editorship of the University student publication, but my future wife, as we noticed already, brought the end to that ambition. None of my predecessors had completed his degree!

We move from the late 1940s to the early 1990s and a respectable career had been spent teaching at various levels – school, college and university. And then came that invitation from the *Daily Telegraph*. My brief was to report schools' and Under-19 cricket and my first match was nearly my last. Christopher Martin-Jenkins, to whose good offices I owed my appointment, told me to report Radley College against Wellington College. 'Get there for lunch,' he said. I did the odd forty miles south through Oxfordshire and Berkshire to arrive at Wellington only to find the 2nd XIs of the two schools performing. I knew I was a lowly incumbent, but surely the paper didn't really want to spread itself on a 2nd XI match. The awful truth struck home that I had gone to the wrong ground. I drove back again and then a few miles further to Radley College. I had been a master there and was welcomed, though there was some surprise at my turning up as a journalist and arriving about teatime to report an all-day game. A lot of people had their brains picked to assist my composition of something worthwhile.

Shortly afterwards came an Under-19 Test Match at Colchester. There I was joined by John Woodcock and Henry Blofeld. In years to come both would be colleagues on an MCC committee, but at that time they were god-like figures. They had years of experience in reporting cricket all over the world; this was my second or third game. Neither could have been nicer or kinder, though I have to say that each gave me totally different advice. But on one point they concurred. It was quite obvious to us in the press box that once when a ball had crossed the line the chasing fielder collected and returned it without signalling the boundary. He could not have failed to see it. 'Leave well alone,' they said, 'don't stir things up unless it happens again.'

One of the pleasures was reporting the annual Eton v. Harrow match. It was a mild travesty of what it had once been. Yet something of the glamour of past days remained, and female supporters supplied a colourful and assertive allegiance. But the match had become too defensive; and in the middle of 1990s *The Times* reporter and I decided to say so. My contribution to the *Telegraph* incurred a mild reprimand from E. W. Swanton for disturbing one of cricket's sacred cows. But, for whatever reason, it had the desired effect and the match became more positive in approach.

There was no rationale as to how much space one was given. In general I could 'command' 250 words for a school match, but the allocation of words for representative matches at school level and for Under-19 Test matches were quite unpredictable. One learned to estimate by how much cricket was happening elsewhere, what other sports were competing for space and what the weather was doing. I was urgently asked to raise 400 words to 800 words on one occasion, and never before 5 o'clock did one know how many words would have to be written.

All of us worked out our own salvation in this. My device was to get words on paper early on so that (in the blue biro) there were 200 done by lunch and another 200 by tea. It was after 5 o'clock when the real work began. I would cut ruthlessly, underlining in green what would survive – including the text of what happened in the closing session of the day. Finally, with the last over in sight, I would underline in red what was finally to be dictated to the copyists in Yorkshire. These ladies never ceased to amaze me with the speed at which they received copy on a whole host of subjects – a political crisis in Pakistan might precede a collapse at Lord's, to be followed by a drama critique.

Just occasionally, the game came down to the final over with four results still possible and I sometimes drafted (at least) three possible last paragraphs. Reporting was not for the faint-hearted in situations such as these or when the game was lingering on and a sub-editor was barking down the phone for copy.

So far as schools were concerned, I formulated very early what would be my approach. 'Para 1' would be something which had caught my attention: perhaps a portrait of a famous old boy or the score-sheet of some famous deed, the scene itself (schools are often blessed with lovely grounds) or the backcloth of a fine neo-Gothic building. Then 'para 2' would give the result of the game. One was told this must come near the beginning: the reader was not to be held in suspense. 'Para 3' would describe the morning and afternoon's play and 'para 4' (which might well be 'cut') offered some pertinent thoughts on the game as a whole. The formula suited me, and as often as not I stuck to it. But with the vagaries of different sub-editors entirely unaware of my intent, it could go astray. On one occasion I thought it right and proper to mention the name of David English, whose sponsorship efforts were well known and whose planning lay behind the particular game I was reporting. His name was deleted from my copy and, after one of my rare protests, I got the reply, 'Who's English? Never heard of him.'

One of the losses to schools' cricket has been the annual tournament which began in Oxford and ended at Lord's. Some forty-four boys would be chosen from Headmasters' Conference Schools (the public schools) and the English Schools' Cricket

Association. After three days' cricket at Oxford they were whittled down to fifteen who would play in three games at Lord's and all be guaranteed at least one appearance at headquarters. Some grand young cricketers were on display and I found myself constantly pursued by proud parents. 'Is my boy good enough to be a professional?' 'He got three 'A's at A level and —shire are interested in his cricket. Should he go to University first?'

Although the days of professional and amateur have long gone, some of these boys would opt for a short spell as a professional before taking up a different career. Others would retain a lifeline with cricket all their days by becoming a journalist or part of the television or broadcasting media. I did the job for ten exciting years in the 1990s, visiting over a hundred schools and seeing the current Test players (Michael Vaughan, Andrew Flintoff and Andrew Strauss *et al.*). I was aware of the increasing pressures which examinations and changes in curriculum made on schools and it was not uncommon to see several fourteen-year-olds in a 1st XI when the demands on time were acute. Heads also became less than enthusiastic about all-day games; but in those we may call 'the centres of excellence' standards, conditions and time allocated to cricket differed little from what it had always been. It is not those sorts of schools, with an elitist cricket tradition, that one worried about. My years of reporting, dove-tailing with my teaching in Kentucky, had been a pleasant way to begin one's retirement.

I had, as I have written elsewhere in this book, made my debut as a cricket author of books with my biography of Constantine. Some dozen years later came that of Len Hutton in 1988. My book was well-timed: it came out on the fiftieth anniversary of the '364' at the Oval in 1938 and the coincidence of day and date was too much to miss. We assembled at the Oval, the scoreboard recreated the scene and Sir Leonard posed for the press 'in the middle'. No fewer than thirty-four photographers and media men surrounded him. 'That's the big change,' commented Sir Len, 'We never had that number in my day: only a handful.' One interviewer asked him about the 'weaknesses of the modern breed of batsmen', but he was not a man to decry his successors. 'They've had a tough time of it against the

West Indians but I'm sure they will come good,' was his diplomatic reply. There was a (late) lunch given by the *Observer* that day and the publishers, Messrs Heinemann Kingswood, gave a reception that evening. There was also a documentary on BBC 2 and I was interviewed on the John Dunn show and by Valerie Singleton. The book reached the *Sunday Times'* bestsellers list, while Yorkshire Television had a commentary on the book which included contributions from Sir Garfield Sobers, Ray Lindwall, Clyde Walcott, Denis Compton, Cyril Washbrook, Fred Trueman and others – together with Sir Leonard and myself. The programme 'blurb' included the in-house instruction: 'It is important that people are warned well in advance and are stood by in time. This is no time for fun and games.' I hastened, at my peril, to make my way north and Hutton himself must have respected the indictment that it was not an opportunity 'for fun'. A '364' anniversary dinner was organised by Yorkshire and Pudsey Cricket Clubs and I went with Hutton to the occasion in the Queen's Hotel, Leeds. He was strangely nervous, doubting his welcome up north. He need not have worried, although the principal speaker went on till after midnight. I was next, with an audience wanting to get home. I had prepared something to say but confined myself to saying that my own 'innings' was brief after a long one. Hutton, due to bat at No. 3, did not speak at all. There was one more accolade before I was carried away by my basking in the reflected glory of the great man. Alan Hill wrote of me in the same breath as E. V. Lucas, Cardus, John Arlott and Jim Swanton: '[His] fervour and diligence provides a yardstick against which other biographers may be judged.' It was time to come down to earth. What better than playing a match for Moreton and making a duck!

My biographies of 'Plum' Warner and Jack Parsons followed later, and I find in my notes that I declined an invitation to write one on the West Indian cricket critic, C. L. R. James. I cannot now remember why, since I had met him and admired him. We had talked about our West Indian cricket connections and my admiration arose from one significant incident. 'I don't agree with what you have said about my relationship with Constantine,' he said, but followed the criticism with a most praiseworthy review of my book – 'not merely good but valuable'. Together with my earlier biography of Wally Hammond, those five biographies concluded my writing in that mode, and the books to which I later turned my attention in the 1980s and 1990s were *Village Cricket, Cricket Medley* and *Cricket's Second Golden Age*. The latter was the only book which I have written very much to the order of the publishers. It was sub-titled 'The Hammond–Bradman Years' and made a bold – and I think successful – attempt to cover the years from Hammond's debut in 1920 until Bradman's last appearance in 1949. To cover a wider market, the book looked at cricket in all the Test countries in those years. I wrote: 'Chronology and Theme never make a perfect marriage. I hope the reader will be reasonably satisfied with a reasonable solution.'

I was invited in the late 1990s to contribute to various publications. Oxford University Press asked me in 1997 to be an Associate Editor of their proposed *Oxford Dictionary of National Biography*. This finally appeared in 2004 comprising over 50,000 Notices. I supplied 70 of these, the majority of which were on cricketers. W. G. Grace commanded the longest entry. I also wrote on the Scottish eighteenth-century non-juring bishops, which gave me a pleasant two weeks working in the Scottish Record Office on the original manuscript documents while staying with my elder son, who was working at the Forestry Commission in Edinburgh at the time.

Oxford University Press also published the *Oxford Companion to Australian Cricket* to which I contributed some pieces. The same House produced *World Cricketers – a Biographical Dictionary*, in which I wrote the entries on all the English non-Test cricketers together with those cricketers of merit outside the Test-playing countries. The latter provided the 'excuse' to go from Kentucky to Bermuda one Thanksgiving to interview Alma Hunt and others. It also led to an amusing incident. 'Hullo Brian,' said someone in a shop. 'Hullo,' I replied and we had a brief conversation. Then he added, 'You *are* Brian, aren't you?' 'No,' I said, 'I'm Gerald.' 'Then why did you answer to Brian?' 'I wasn't thinking. It's my family nickname.' 'Then you have a double in Bermuda.' 'Tell him,' I said, 'to watch Bermudan TV tonight, I'm on it.'

These were the years when, in retirement, I was at my busiest as a journalist and writer and some of my contributions are found in Part II of this book. Three other works – nothing to do with cricket – also belong to these years: these were my *Culham College History* (to mark the College's closure in 1976), my *History of North Moreton* (to mark the Millennium) and *A History of the School of St Helen and St Katharine* (to mark the school's centenary in 2003). The 1980s and 1990s were also years in which I found myself guest speaker at a variety of cricketing occasions, such as the quaintly-named British Officers' Cricket Club of Philadelphia and at an MCC dinner hosted by my old Radley colleague and the then President of MCC, Dennis Silk. I was the first speaker in the series of on-going lectures on cricket history which MCC launched in the Long Room in 2004. I was also one of the honoured few to be invited to a dinner at Lord's to celebrate Jim Swanton's 90th birthday. It was not an unqualified success: the main course was quite uneatable. After an uneasy pause, the Archbishop of Canterbury announced that no one need feel compelled to attempt it. Overall, however, these years from the 1980s onwards were a busy and rewarding period. With the passing of the years, I find myself mildly amazed at the amount I did.

30
In the Press Box

7 a.m.: Leave home and make my way from Oxford, cross-country, to join the Ml. Not an easy run, though more traffic going south than north. Watch out for exit 24 and then simply follow signs which say 'Trent Bridge'. Arrive in plenty of time to greet my colleagues in the box for the next four days.

11 a.m.: For me, anyway, a slight beginning of term feeling: very much the new boy. My colleagues, wise men with years of experience, have a very much more philosophical approach to the game than I have. One had come, I suppose, very much down market to do this Under-19 Test between England and the West Indies; his last game had been a full international. The press box is superior to many. Trent Bridge, after all, hosts 'proper' Test Matches. Coffee and biscuits are available and there's plenty of room to move around. I'm ready to enjoy the play as Michael Vaughan and his partner, Matthew Dowman, go to the wicket.

12 noon: A fair crowd considering . . . considering it is an Under-19 Test. The 'lads' like to play these games on Test match grounds but the local publicity can be poor and the crowd disappointing.

Obviously, there has been good coverage for today's game and there is a sense of 'atmosphere'.

A wicket falls early and Vaughan is joined by Matthew Walker, a slightly rotund figure who will go on to do good things for Kent. He will make his contribution while Vaughan, very much in form at the moment, moves towards a half-century before lunch until thwarted by a shower of rain.

1.30 pm: We go in search of some lunch. I had been told that it was a good idea to chat to the odd spectator. You never knew what nuggets you might collect. Later, when the partnership between Vaughan and Walker reaches 134 there was a desultory round of applause. I learned that this was a new second-wicket record for Under-19 Test matches. 'Useful to have this booklet,' said one of my wise colleagues. 'I've got a spare copy: have it.' There was a camaraderie developing, endorsed by the next interruption for rain. We wrote and chatted and I scribbled: 'England are assuming a strong position. Vaughan, only giving the semblance of a chance at 86, is approaching his century and . . .'

5 p.m.: I remember a call to the sports desk of the *Daily Telegraph* at Canary Wharf, London, is due. 'Any idea of space for the Under-19 Test at Trent Bridge?' I asked. 'About 250 words,' was the reply as the loudspeaker told the crowd (and me) that Vaughan's century had contained fourteen boundaries. Soon both he and Walker were out and it was getting colder – obvious from the press box in the way West Indian fielders were sending for their sweaters and no doubt thinking of Port of Spain or Kingston. 'I could use that,' I thought as the composition of 250 words suddenly assumed some urgency. But of course I didn't: there wasn't the space and I settled for 'Vaughan's century contributed to the miseries of the fielding side whose shivering was evident.'

6 p.m.: 'You know who is here, don't you,' said a wise colleague. 'Mike Smith, Keith Fletcher and Mickey Stewart.' I noted this and added, 'which underlines the importance of Under-19 representative cricket.'

7 p.m.: A phone call to Yorkshire, where the 'copy' was co-ordinated, put my report through. It was time to go to the hotel for the night and have a beer. Just one more call required.

8 p.m.: 'Sports Desk? Gerald Howat, check-call, Under-19 Match . . .' There were no queries on my text but an apology from the office. 'Sorry, Gerald. We need another 40 words. Lots of cricket today interrupted by the rain and we have space to fill. Ten minutes?'

8.10 p.m.: Phone call to Sports Desk. Add to 'copy' on Under-19 Test: 'Vaughan brought his aggregate score against the West Indies in the series to 297 . . . To the West Indies' credit, their captain Ian Bradshaw, Ricky Christopher and Colin Stuart produced some well-controlled pace in the last hour.'

8.30 p.m.: Job done. Time for another beer and a meal. 'It would be nice to see young Chanderpaul make some runs tomorrow,' commented one of my wise colleagues. (He did: 203 not out, and, in due course, captained the senior West Indian side.)

31
English Village

This book has not burdened the reader with domestic chronology but we must go back some years, to my acceptance of a post at Culham College, to establish our tenure at North Moreton. The time had come to have our own place, after living in the various houses which my previous appointments had provided.

And so we came to own Old School House. It was constructed in the 1860s for the village schoolmaster John Barr, who had been an unusual appointment. Nearby, Culham College had begun to produce teachers and was the obvious source for North Moreton's National School teacher. But the parson, Albert Barff, had chosen to appoint a man totally unqualified who had served in the bar of the Bear Inn – where his father was landlord. Barff (and the similarity of names can cause confusion) would, in due course, leave North Moreton to be a headmaster of a cathedral choir school. No doubt, an inexperienced man at North Moreton would be more under his influence. John Barr raised thirteen children by two wives at North Moreton. Some eighty years later my younger son would teach at St Paul's in London. It challenges the girls' school, St Paul's Girls' School, as the leading school in the country. I had heard that John Barr's son had done the same and snobbishly rejected the thought. 'A village schoolmaster's son does not teach at St Paul's,' I thought. But social mobility, as so often, played its part and young Barr had, indeed, taught at St Paul's.

We made the house bigger, building on a study and another bedroom while an earlier generation had added a front room, a bathroom and a utility room. Imagination boggles at the two-up and two-down square block which must have served a growing household in the nineteenth century. But, like many a house in North Moreton, it had acquired a social mobility of its own.

I wrote the history of North Moreton to mark the millennium. It is one of many villages in historic Berkshire whose name ends with the suffix *ton*, derived from the Anglo-Saxon *tun* simply meaning a homestead. The Anglo-Saxon *mor* means a fen or moor. Thus North Moreton was the homestead on the moor and was first recorded as such in the year 944. Its boundaries, of ten hides, have not changed in the centuries that followed. It boasts an ancient church built with an outstanding chantry in the Decorated Gothic style, created by the Stapleton family in the thirteenth century. Four centuries later the village, due to its proximity to Oxford, Wallingford and Reading, was at the centre of events in the Civil War. In the seventeenth century allegations of witchcraft – *maleficium*, the intent to hurt people, animals or property – again put North Moreton centre-stage, with a bewitched girl taken before King James I himself. And so one passes through the centuries in which landowners, yeoman farmers and a rural peasantry make their brief passage through the ages. Indeed, the North Moreton I first knew in 1960 still equated its population with those three social groups. Forty years on it was a prosperous village on the commuter route to London with its quota of stockbrokers and lawyers. I was a witness to these changes and they were reflected in the social structure of the cricket club.

Moreton Cricket Club was over a century old when I first became a member, and the historian in me compels me to state that it was a club of farming folk with few pretensions. I became the secretary at once and would hold the office for twenty-nine years until I was elected president – and have been so for a further seventeen years. But the club over which I have the honour to preside is a very different one from that of 1960. Its membership largely reflects the middle-class and professional milieu; its standards are higher and its ambitions greater. We have toured the Netherlands on three occasions and an annual English tour is central to the fixture list. Two members of the club have, in recent years, won Blues at

Cambridge University. A grand pavilion has recently been completed and the presence of good schoolboys in the holidays who have played their cricket at the local public schools both adds to standards and illustrates the social pattern of the area.

One can exaggerate: two figures associated with the club in the 1960s were Derek Massy, the chairman, and Ian Crompton, the captain. Massy had been a pilot in the Royal Flying Corps and later, as a group captain, had commanded RAF Benson. Colonel Crompton was a colourful figure who, on his retirement, became town clerk of Wallingford.

An annual fixture was against the President's XI. Douglas Whinney, in the words of his successor Bud Finch, would 'bring down a wonderful sporting crowd from London. There would be lunch in the hall with the first strawberries of the year and the day ended with a party. But woe-betide any gatecrashers at that party in South Moreton Manor.'

Bud Finch, President himself in due course, was perhaps the last village 'character'. He had lived in the village since he was a small child – having 'emigrated' from South Moreton – and he was a farmer who greeted everyone warmly on their arrival in North Moreton. He had been treasurer of the cricket club as far back as 1919 and was its president at the time of his death. In a book of reminiscences, *Bud Finch Remembers*, he remarked: 'I've seen North Moreton over almost the whole of the twentieth century from the days of the scythe and the sickle to the combine; from a quiet little community to a village full of commuters.'

North Moreton, with its mediaeval church, its nonconformist chapel, its pub (once there were four) and its cricket club represented the pattern of many a village. The ecology of the village was affected by the 1970s by the nationwide outbreak of Dutch elm disease. Valiant efforts were made at some considerable financial cost to save the trees on the north side of the cricket ground, the Croft. The poet John Betjeman's description of North Moreton as an 'island of elms' had gone for ever, although oak, ash, walnut and maple were planted, which by the year 2006 had created a pleasing effect.

Some modest fame came to North Moreton when in 2005 for the

first time a villager born and bred was returned to the House of Commons, in the Conservative interest. This was Robert Wilson, who had also served as deputy leader of the party on Reading Borough Council. More pertinently (to some of us, at any rate) he had been a stalwart of the Cricket Club for many years, with a record of over 14,000 runs and holder of the club record of 897 wickets. Perhaps this is the place where I may slip in, with some modesty, that I made approaching nine hundred dismissals behind the stumps for Moreton until I retired in 2005.

North of the village lie prehistoric earthworks set around the Wittenham Clumps. That vantage-point commands a view of the Thames carving its river-valley; of Dorchester where St Birinus came in the seventh century; of Wallingford, a key mediaeval stronghold; of Didcot with its cooling towers projecting skywards as if the cathedrals of a technological age; of villages such as Little Wittenham clustered near the river. On a clear day the southern perspective points to low-lying land or *mor* and within it a little homestead or *tun*; a squat church tower is the only definable building and it symbolises almost a thousand years of history. From those Clumps are viewed the flat fields which North Moretonians have farmed from time out of mind. Even in the changing circumstances of the opening years of the twenty-first century there remained a vestigial connection with the land. The eye moves from surveying the broad acres of tilled fields to the ancient oaks marking the remains of the northern boundary of North Moreton. Those 1,100 acres, contained within boundaries that have not changed through the centuries, still represent something of a rural economy. The North Moreton of 2006 still offers to the ear the sounds of sheep bleating, of combines at harvest time and of tractors down the High Street. These, and much else, are evocative of a community whose eternal roots lay in the soil.

There I and my family have been content to pass nearly fifty years. We have done our bit. My wife has thrice been president of the Women's Institute and has served as chairman of the Parish Council. I have been, as I have shown, an office-bearer in the Cricket Club, a past organist of All Saints' and served on the Parochial

Church Council. Yet I should add a brief reference to one other activity. On the day after I ceased to be in full-time employment – the day, I suppose, I began to think of myself as a pensioner – I was cycling around rather aimlessly when I saw some ladies playing tennis at a club in nearby Wallingford.

With temerity – though it was hardly the temerity of youth as I was close to sixty – I asked if I could join. 'It is Wednesday,' they replied, as if that were an answer to my question. After a pause, there came the rather more informative comment that Wednesdays were for ladies. I must have looked crestfallen because a kindly lady said I might come next week. I came, and then the week after, and the month after; and I have stayed for twenty years. On that first Wednesday I was shown to be neither too good nor too bad, and soon my male monopoly was broken. Wallingford's Tennis Club, known as Portcullis, has over two hundred members and I felt honoured, in 2003, to be invited to become the president. It has always been a happy club and it has been a great joy to belong. It has provided yet another dimension in my retirement years and I can play tennis when the playing of cricket is just a memory.

I recall saying 'goodbye' to a visiting cricket team who had come from North America to play us. It was, indeed, a special occasion. They came to mark the centenary of the visit of a representative American side in 1896 – and played at Lord's. I thought, as I waved farewell and they set off for the New World, that I have enjoyed the goodly heritage of North Moreton, the epicentre of my Old World.

32
MCC 1

Let me explain. MCC 1 has been the convenient way I refer to my dealings and my paper work with the premier cricket club in the world, the Marylebone Cricket Club. In the next chapter, the reader will be introduced to MCC 2. Legions of books exist on *the* MCC (or more properly, MCC as the club likes to be styled) and I see a whole shelf-full as I write. MCC was founded in 1787 to meet the burgeoning demands of the middle classes in North London who were less inclined to drive down their cabs or horses to Hambledon where cricket had been played since the middle of the eighteenth century.

If I do not linger on Hambledon it is because it is not central to this chapter. I have dared, in Part II, to enter its historic portals and so encounter a minefield; or, at least, a cottage industry in which devotees honourably dispute the minutiae of its history.

MCC originated at a time of troubles in France and no less an historian than the late G. M. Trevelyan argued – only half tongue in cheek – that had the French nobility played cricket with their tenants a Revolution might have been avoided. But play cricket the English did; and on the day the Bastille fell the Earl of Winchilsea was bowled by the peasant, W. Bullen, for nought.

So MCC and Lord's prospered. I have shown elsewhere in this book how the club had the presence of mind to elect the young W. G. Grace but not the grace to make him a Committee member. By Grace's time, it was well-established as a club for aristocrats and as late as 1950 Sir Pelham Warner had to wait a very late turn to become President after a long list which consisted almost entirely of noblemen.

I became a member in the 1960s, proposed by M. M. Reese, an academic colleague who had played for MCC in his time and narrowly missed an Oxford Blue. Soon afterwards, I applied successfully for playing membership and I think my first match was against Reading School. The match-manager was that great Hampshire stalwart, Colin Ingleby-MacKenzie, and it was he who bade me have a gin and tonic before I batted. Ingleby-MacKenzie was a fine leader, a powerful personality and a colourful character who deservedly led Hampshire to the County Championship in 1961.

I had many happy matches for MCC, largely against the public schools. If the formula was a bit predictable, it certainly was not in a match against Oundle. The school won the toss and chose to bat. That broke the mould, for a start. Just before teatime they were still batting and our senior player, Essex's 'Tonker' Taylor came off the field. 'Not tea, yet,' he was told, 'maybe not, but we've had enough fielding.' Tea was taken and MCC failed to get 250 runs in the 45 overs remaining. The usual formula, whoever won the toss, was for MCC to bat and set the school a reasonable target. MCC play some four hundred of these matches a season and the object is to display (to use a later phrase) 'the spirit of cricket'.

Good dress was encouraged, bad manners were not. As everyone knows who has read a school story or two told by Thomas Hughes or John Finnemore, the MCC match was 'the thing' to which the school trooped down to watch and elderly masters wore fading blazers for the occasion with perhaps a College crest on them. Such matches might belong to a past age but they still are popular with the schools and they set standards. It is good that they are finding their way onto state school fixture-lists. The ground-preparation and catering for such matches is extensive, and I know from personal experience what an effort state schools make to ensure these aspects are as appealing as the cricket.

In due course, I became too old for such cricket and retired gracefully but on a high-point. As wicketkeeper I stumped the last two batsmen in successive balls, so ended my MCC playing career on a hat-trick. A presentation from my colleagues left a pleasant feeling and, indeed, taste. Soon after my playing-career for MCC ended I was invited by the MCC Committee, through the curator, to serve on the Arts and Library Committee. 'You have to be an expert in something to get in,' Stephen Green, the curator, remarked and then – after rather a lengthy pause – added, 'You've written a few books and know a bit about publishing. I think they'll have you.'

In the days of E. W. Swanton I confess to feeling somewhat *de trop*. He always seemed to have the answers off pat to the ones I knew but did not get out quick enough. I had to admire his mastery of so much at so great an age: he was in his nineties. When Swanton died in 2000 we felt his loss; but, somehow, we all felt liberated. Lesser mortals might now make their contribution.

Basically, Arts and Library is responsible for the care and maintenance of MCC's collection of portraits, pictures, photographs and archives. Its Curator should attend auctions, on behalf of MCC, and bid for appropriate acquisitions. It has an extensive library and has, in more recent years, established an MCC Cricket Library, marketing books of varying appeal. Some are facsimiles of rare first editions in the Library of which, say, 200 are sold. Others, of wider and more popular appeal, are original books with an appeal to a cricketing readership. There is also an extensive and ever-changing Museum for which Arts and Library is responsible.

While Arts and Library meets four times a year, two of its sub-groups have become my particular responsibility and in the chairmanship of each I succeeded Hubert Doggart, past President of MCC and former Test player. The loud laughter and good humour at our lunches between meetings still rings in my ears. Perhaps I have been a more phlegmatic chairman. The two groups are the Publishing Working Party and the Seasonal Publications Group. The PWP is responsible for the books and the SPG deals with more esoteric publications, including Christmas cards, the annual calendar and First-Day Covers. MCC today is nothing if not commercially minded: the revenue from SPG sales every year is considerable.

Among my colleagues on these two sub-committees, Jonathan Rice has been our most successful author, with *One Hundred Lord's*

Tests proving a real 'pot-boiler'. Graeme Wright, a former editor of *Wisden Cricketers' Almanack*, produced a splendid book on *Wisden at Lord's*, as did Duff Hart-Davis with *Pavilions of Splendour*. Two other interesting, but widely divergent, books were *Britcher's Scores and Biographies* and *A Breathless Hush*. The one was a reproduction of Britcher's eighteenth-century scorebooks and the other a verse anthology to which I contributed. David Rayvern Allen was responsible for both. Central to our work are the efforts of the curator Adam Chadwick, the historian Glenys Williams and the personal assistant Sally Goldfield. Nor should we forget Peter Tummons, the Managing Director of Methuen who has been the prime (but not the only) publisher of our books in the MCC Cricket Library. I have been proud to chair such an able, not to say erudite, group and MCC has appreciated their services.

MCC l, to revert to my personal title, *does* demand a lot of those who serve on its numerous committees, but it takes us to the heart of 'great matters' and I was perhaps most conscious of this when I sat on the MCC Membership Committee where we dealt with such issues as costs and charges, subscriptions, defaulting members and disciplinary matters against members. In a club of 22,000 a lot of responsibility had to be borne in the sheer election of members. The procedure is that a nominee has to be proposed and seconded and then endorsed by a member of an MCC Committee. I have only refused to endorse one member and Roger Knight, the Secretary and Chief Executive, accepted my reasons. Roger retired in 2006. He had played for three first-class counties and had served as a county captain. His background lay in schoolmastering; he was, briefly, headmaster of Worksop. One day we were discussing the complicated issue of authors' contracts: 'A far cry from our schoolmastering days,' I commented. We both felt we were now serving another world. From another world, too, came his successor Keith Bradshaw, the first Australian to be Chief Executive of MCC.

33
MCC 2

'I didn't know MCC had a meeting next Tuesday,' remarked Roger Knight, the Secretary and Chief Executive of MCCl, when he addressed the annual dinner of MCC2 a few years ago. I hastily looked at a notice which indicated the fact and I assured him that it referred to MCC2. 'There must be plenty of MCC2s around, when one thinks of it,' remarked someone – 'Milton and Moulsford, to take just two in Oxfordshire alone.' The joke was wearing thin.

The heroes of MCC2 – or Moreton Cricket Club – when I first knew it were Harry Marriott and Norman Lay. Marriott was a cheerful fellow who had allegedly once had a trial for Hampshire. He bowled reasonably fast with an inswinger which was effective and he would take seventy or eighty wickets a season. As a batsman, what he lacked in style he made up for in strength. One year, in the 1960s, he did the 'double' of 1,000 runs and 100 wickets. Norman Lay, a Yorkshire man and a somewhat dour figure for whom, in Len Hutton's famous phrase, 'you didn't play cricket for fun', was slightly slower and the more accurate of the two. He batted lower down. I was always scared of dropping a catch off him – which, inevitably, made it worse. Marriott did not worry! In a way that would not be acceptable to a later generation of players in village cricket, the two of them bowled almost unchanged. Marriott's batting was joined by that of Ken Gregory. If the former's trial for Hampshire was a legend, Gregory's was real enough, though neither of them came to anything. Gregory, I suspect, was too slow in the field and the gulf between county and village was far too wide.

The faded records show one weekend when Marriott made a century on Saturday and Sunday: a reminder that cricket was played regularly on both days. The social attractions of other events and the influence of wives and girlfriends have made that less likely to later generations, where Saturday *and* Sunday cricket is the exception rather than the rule.

There were plenty of clubs to play in the Thames Valley in the 1960s, from village sides to Oxford Colleges and three or four people would pile into each car to go to Oxford, in the north, and Reading, in the south, and the villages along the Thames. These were the days of single-wicket competitions and Moreton had one annually, though the entertainment palled for those who were dismissed in the first round and spent the rest of the afternoon fielding for others more successful.

Moreton has never played in a League. Fast as League cricket was growing, the club continued its long tradition of playing only 'Friendlies'. The only exceptions were occasional Cup matches such as the Cherry Court Cup and the Tappin Cup. It was said that the Cherry Court Cup had an interesting origin – given by a man who hoped he might be president but never was. With hindsight it seemed harsh. It was the one cup of genuine silver and at a recent valuation was worth nearly £1,000.

An interesting fixture from the 1970s was against Great Tew in North Oxfordshire. It was a pretty ground providing perhaps the best tea on the circuit and was an attractive village to explore, with strong Civil War associations. It was the last fixture of the season and I recall driving back (every other year) in the darkness listening to the Last Night of the Proms on the car radio. It was a nostalgic memory.

The 1970s saw the start of a thirty-year link with the club of the brothers Stimpson, Paul and Michael. Someone whose playing days went back to the 1950s and would still umpire in the 2000s was John Culley. He could hit the ball hard and had a strong arm in the field. An unusual 'newcomer' was Richard Spurling who had learned his cricket at Ridley College, Ontario and then lived and played in Bermuda. One who has worked tirelessly for the club is Nigel

Hessey. He has been the essential 'back-room boy' without whom any club flounders and he would contribute runs as well.

The changing economy of the Moretons has meant that the young have gone to live in the cheaper, urban setting of Didcot and sometimes are lost to Moreton cricket. The socio-economic aspects of a community are relevant to the fortunes of cricketers.

It was in the 1970s that the club began to tour. There has been an unbroken pattern of tours ever since 1977 with the club visiting East Anglia, Sussex, Kent and Shropshire. The club has sometimes undertaken a 1st XI and 2nd XI game on the same day. This has provided an opportunity for schoolboys to play in the 2nd XI and a much greater opportunity has come for youngsters in the Youth section which I started in the late 1960s.

In those days, primary schools still (up to a point) played cricket and our village youngsters would go with me to play such local schools as Long Wittenham and Cholsey. They had all the apparatus of major matches! Teams would be in 'whites' and all the protocols of the game would be observed. Several of the Moreton cricketers of the 2000s had been Moreton boys in the 1960s and 1970s. It was something I was responsible for over some forty years until 2005.

The list of names can go on. One is conscious, on the one hand, of those whom one leaves out and, on the other, of the savage truth that they mean nothing to a wider public. But this chapter is devoted to Moreton cricket and is an essential part of 'Cricket all my Life' so, without apology, I mention a few more Moreton names. John Harrison, in the later years of the twentieth century, was a talented batsman who made several centuries for us and was a noteworthy member of the village as Parochial Church Council treasurer and church organist. Greg Locke came to us from League cricket and was a good captain and batsman in the 1990s before being succeeded by Darren Clark (one of my youngsters of a generation earlier). Chris and Richard Macdonald were two redoubtable brothers, the former being one of several effective club captains and a match-winning all-rounder and the latter, incidentally, being awarded the CBE in the Queen's Honours List. All the way from High Wycombe, Richard Dawson came to make runs for us valiantly over many years; while on our own doorstep Trevor Denning was a useful player and a very good committee man. Kaz Miles earned our admiration for struggling successfully against ill health and producing some aggressive spells with both bat and ball. Tony and Sam Fletcher were a father-and-son combination; Tony proved an admirable treasurer, as had been his predecessor, Anthony Ryder. One also thinks of Nick Kane, Will Skottowe, Andy Southgate, William Thomas, John Gibbs and Ed Squires. And let there be a final thought for the Cross family whose contribution is manifold, not least in the creation of a new pavilion for which Jon Cross is the clerk of works.

We hear a lot about grassroots cricket and how money must be found for it, especially as the near absence of terrestrial coverage may deny a large number of the opportunity to watch major matches. Moreton Cricket Club is all about grassroots cricket and without it the sinews of the game would not survive. I may have spent too much time on it – I once played 57 matches for Moreton consecutively (for which belated apologies to my wife) – but it has been a source of great pleasure, given and received. May MCC2 flourish!

34
Talking on Cricket – Home and Away

'I was born in Glasgow but have hardly ever been back here,' I said conversationally to the driver who had met me at the station and was taking me to give my talk. 'Been here all my life: know Glasgow like the back of my hand,' was the reply in a fairly broad Scots accent. We drove on . . . and on. At last, my driver had to confess he was lost. He was very upset. I spotted a phone box and made a call. 'You're all right,' someone said, 'next on the right, then second on the left, then straight on for a hundred yards.' I arrived just at the time I was due to speak to the Glasgow Branch of the Cricket Society of Scotland. The advantages of arriving 'late' at cricket societies were twofold – one missed the well-intentioned but very large meal and avoided having to outline one's talk to the committee members over dinner before having to give it all over again to a larger audience. That was the standard formula for cricket societies: a meal then a talk (for at least an hour) and then the answering of questions. For fifteen years or so, from the 1980s onwards, I spoke to nearly all the thirty societies in the British Isles, sometimes two or three times over. Let me include extracts from some of the letters I received: from the Lancashire and Cheshire Society, 'No one has spoken to us so well at Old Trafford and held such a large audience'; from the Essex Cricket Society, 'By popular acclaim, top of the list for the last ten years'; from the Gloucestershire Cricket Lovers' Society, 'Everyone has been over the moon with your rendering'. So I must have done something right! The Cricket Societies invite players, administrators and writers to talk to them during the winter evenings and they represent deeply committed groups of devotees. They know their cricket and they will ask searching questions. In a sense, their members are the bedrock of support for the game because they will be at all the matches in the summer. It is fair to say they represent an older age group (for whom the need for baby-sitters of a winter's evening is a fading memory) and there will be a fair sprinkling of ladies in an audience. Geographically, their ranks are strongest in the north of England and I have spoken, on more than one occasion, to more than four hundred at Old Trafford. I suppose the smallest attendance was somewhere in the south where an official had got the date wrong . . . and I waited in vain for an audience!

One talked about (or, at least I did) the books one had written. The audience appreciated the background to a book and some of the sidelines. I once did three talks on three consecutive evenings; the third was not a success. I was probably too tired and my audience seemed strangely passive. In future, two consecutive 'performances' was my limit. I realised the burdens of those who perform in repertory companies and 'play' for a week. I am reminded of my childhood where my father was chaplain to both the Dundee and Perth Repertory Companies. We would see something of them 'off-stage' and realise they would be playing Play A, rehearsing Play B and learning the lines of Play C all in a single week. Talking to cricket societies was child's play by comparison. In December 2006 – long after I had retired from speaking – came a belated invitation to talk to the London branch of the Cricket Society on *this* book.

A particularly happy memory was being invited to speak at the centenary dinner of Forfarshire County Cricket Club in Dundee. I have mentioned my links with that club in Part I of this book. It was the only time I have flown to an engagement as the date was awkward. In my RAF days I once took half a day to fly in a Tiger Moth from Southampton to Edinburgh: this time was rather quicker, though I still had to get myself by train from Edinburgh to Dundee. I remember I was 'paired' with the old Derbyshire cricketer, A. V. Pope, who had been Forfarshire's professional in his later years.

I had a yearning for years to see Australia and I managed to create a programme in which I spoke to all the Australian cricket societies (except Brisbane) as well as lecture in history at two Australian Universities. The cricket societies (unlike their British equivalents) hold their meetings in season, so I was able to see some cricket as well. But the high point of that cherished visit was the interview which Sir Donald Bradman gave me at Adelaide. I knew I was privileged because he was a very private man and wary of journalists. At that point (1985) I was not yet a journalist – although, approaching sixty, soon would be. I honoured his confidence in me by not disclosing what he said to me. As we talked, a small boy ran up for his autograph and got it with a kindly word. This man, I remembered, had been a public figure for sixty years. He had been the folk hero of Australia in the 1930s and was an honoured and decorated elder statesman in the 1980s. He could go nowhere without being accosted and recognised. My trip to Australia had been something of a pilgrimage and my meeting with Bradman its climax. It had also been humbling. A lady in my audience in Melbourne had undertaken an 800-mile round trip to hear me, and 800 members sat expectantly in the pavilion. I spoke about Douglas Jardine and afterwards a Scotsman accused me of pandering to Australian taste. He was mollified when it turned out we had, coincidently, been at school together at Glenalmond. I was offered a lift back to my hotel by an elderly stranger to whom I remarked: 'What did you do for a living?' which brought the unexpected reply, 'Actually, I was Premier until they threw me out at the last election.' Let me add a last thought to my Australian adventure: I got nothing but courtesy from those I met in the two 'worlds' which I frequented – those of academic historians and cricket enthusiasts.

The C.C. Morris Library in Philadelphia, where I went to talk on cricket, is a treasure-trove of books and memorabilia, frequented by a dedicated group who cling to the traditions which the game once had and who foster its survival. I have spoken to that audience of cricket's disciples twice and played on their ground at Merion once.

One gets a sense of history, an evocation of the past and a reminder of the glory that once was. Cricket flourishes in that tiny corner of Pennsylvania. Modern technology has enabled Philadelphia's cricketers to keep in instant touch with the game worldwide.

Finally, I have talked on cricket (and, indeed, played) in Bangkok at the British Club where a small band of expatriates keep the game flourishing at the Royal Bangkok Sports Club. As I departed I remember a Sri Lankan journalist, Anton Perera, whose reporting in the Bangkok press did much to keep cricket alive, bidding me farewell as I drove away in the flooded streets in April: 'I see Gooch is in the runs already. It will rain now here till November.' Not the best advert for cricket in Bankok, I reflected.

With its rich heritage of literature, folklore and history, cricket perhaps attracts more speakers and audiences than any other game. I have enjoyed the opportunities I have been given both to talk and to listen.

35
Post Hoc

The President's Match at Moreton was always something special. In the 1950s our President, Douglas Whinney, had belonged to the firm of Ernst and Young. One would see their name all over the world and have momentary thoughts about the little Berkshire village. Boundary shifts moved it into Oxfordshire in 1974, which roughly coincided with the change of presidency at the club.

Douglas Whinney would bring a team from London, give us all lunch and tea in the village hall and drinks at his house, South Moreton Manor, in the evening. It was all very English. His successor, 'Bud' Finch, was a village worthy *par excellence.*

He had come to North Moreton in 1908 from South Moreton so regarded himself as a 'foreigner'; but no one could have commanded such affection as he in the Moretons and his death in 1990 marked the end of an era. Less extravagantly – for he was a village farmer rather than an entrepreneur – we celebrated the President's Match with a garden party known as the 'Finchmore' occasion. The suffix came from the chairman's surname – Passmore. He himself, Freddie Passmore, was briefly president until his death and I took over the office in 1991 – the first playing president ever and also the first, in due course, to be president of Wallingford (Portcullis) Tennis Club as well.

Socially, the event in my time meant getting a team together, arranging (for some years) a lunch, providing a tea and staging a village drinks' party in the evening. In the summer of 2005 events followed the well-worn path, though I felt rather tired and decided not to play myself: a young wicketkeeper was easily recruited. They say I was unusually subdued during the party and it may well be so.

That night, or rather very early on Monday morning, my wife rang National Health Service Direct and the system took over. Lights flashed and vehicles drew up and within an hour I was in the emergency ward of the Radcliffe Hospital in cardiac arrest.

It was my first major experience of the National Health Service and let me say at the outset how thoroughly impressive and professional it was. The staff showed immense dedication, courtesy and patience. The ward was mixed, of about a dozen people, and every effort was made to make that fact as acceptable as could be. Situations which might have caused embarrassment were handled with tact and commonsense.

Meals were attractively served from a wide choice. I saw no bugs, 'super' or otherwise. As for cricket, my stay coincided with the Third Test against Australia at Old Trafford. A genial Australian surgeon with a mild interest in cricket tolerated with good humour some of my gentle barracking; of course, he had the whip-hand over me as he performed an operation demanding great skill. 'What are you writing about?' asked a nurse twenty-four hours later. 'Cricket and my experiences here,' was my reply. Most of them knew of England's victory in the Second Test and how events were prospering for us in the third. On the very morning when I first fell ill, England had snatched that great success by a mere 2 runs.

Soon it was my turn to go from an Emergency Ward to a routine one and then home. Arrivals and Departures are the Rites of Passage in Hospital life. I suppose mixed wards might give an opportunity to that third Rite of Passage, a marriage, though one doubts there is much to kindle the spark of love in such brief acquaintanceships. To arrive is rather like going to school. One 'sniffs out' the 'opposition' and cautiously makes friends. Seniority is gained as others go. One's own departure provokes a mixture of reactions. One has lived in an enclosed and cocooned world for a few days. There is a hint of tears as one departs for home. The staff, like ladies who run a B&B, are cool and professional. We have been their charges for a few days and go on our way. But regard for their sheer devotion is a lingering memory. So back to North Moreton with something else, somewhat soberly, to add to life's tapestry of treasures. Whether or not I shall ever play cricket again remains to be seen. But tennis began for me again, at Wallingford, eight weeks later with a win in my first set!

Meanwhile, only three weeks after my return, I boarded the train for Paddington. The Thames Valley suddenly acquired an awakened appeal and I breathed a special atmosphere as I walked from the station to Lord's along the picturesque path by the Regent's Canal. The grass seemed greener. And at Lord's – greeted warmly my friends – I took the chair in the Committee Room. It was an even greater thrill than usual and here, perhaps, was a final fling at 'Cricket all my Life'.

Index

A
Adams, John 192–193
Adams, Samuel 191
Alington, Very Rev. C.A. 152
Allen, David Rayvern 159–161, 256
Allen, Sir George 109–110, 131–132, 171–180
Allen, Phoebe 98–99
Altham, H.S. 122
Ames, L.E.G. 132, 177
Archdale, Betty 9
Arlott, John 41, 122–123, 132–133, 160
Armstrong, Warwick 105
Arnold, Dr Thomas 83, 96, 197, 198, 199
Ashes 102, 104–105, 111, 141, 164–165, 169
   2005 series 101–102
   1905 series 102–105
Ashley-Cooper, F.S. 122
Australia 107–112, 164–169, 173, 263

B
Babb, Rev. Henry 47
Balaskas, Xenophon 133
Baldwin, Earl 112
Bangkok 264
Barnett, John 46–47
Barr, John 247
Barff, Rev. Albert 247
Barrie, Sir J.M. 100, 110
Batten, Charles 223
Beauclerk, Lord Frederick 60, 68
Bedser, Sir Alec 133
Beldham, William 58, 60, 62, 63
Bentley, Nicolas 52
Bermuda 207–209
Bligh, Edward 58, 62
Bligh, Ivo 164
Blofeld, Henry 147–148, 236
Blunden, Edmund 110
Bosanquet, B.J.T. 163-4
Bossenger, Gillian 41, 224, 228, 229
Boult, George 58
Bowes, W.E. 9, 140
Boycott, Geoffrey 215
Bradford, William 186
Bradman, Sir Donald 21, 107–112, 134, 173, 176, 263
Bradshaw, Keith 256
Bramall, Field Marshal Lord 216–217

Britcher, Samuel 65
Burley 61
Butler, Rev. H.M. 83
Byrd, William 187–190

C
Canada 181–184
Cardus, Sir Neville 110, 119, 120, 122, 132, 145, 151–157
Carew, Dudley 121
Chadwick, Adam 256
Chadwick, Henry 183–184, 194
Chanderpaul, Shivnarine 245
Chapman, A.P.F. 107, 109–111
Charles I 185–186
Churchill, Charles 60–61
Clark, Darren 259
Compton, D.C.S. 133
Conan Doyle, Sir Arthur 100, 110
Constantine, Lord 14, 31, 32, 35, 37, 123–124, 161, 203–205, 207–208, 209
Conway, Hugh 59
Cooke, Rev. Selwyn 12, 45
Cowdrey, Lord 216
Craig, I.D. 216
Crompton, Col. Ian 249
Culham College 45–51, 53–54, 224
Culley, John 258
Curtiss, Air Marshal John 26

D
Darling, Joe 102–103
Darnley, Earl of 58, 60
Dawson, Richard 259
Denning, Sqn Ldr Trevor 260
Dexter, E.R. 216, 222
Dickens, Charles 89–91
Doggart, Hubert 255

Duleepsinhji, K.S. 108, 109, 115
Dundee 6–9

E
Edinburgh University 14–21, 27, 28, 223, 230
Edrich, W.J. 133–134
Edwards, R.H.B. 43
England 62, 69–70, 107–112, 163–169, 173, 185, 266
English, Dr David 237
Epps, William 66
Essex 127–129
Eton College 62, 63–64

F
Fellows, Rev. Walter 86
Fender, P.G.H. 107–108
Finch, W.V. 249, 265
Fingleton, J.H. 175–176
First World War 111–112, 113, 176
Fitzgerald, R.A. 72
Fletcher, Sam 260
Fletcher, Tony 260
Foot, Dingle 204–205
Forfarshire 4–5, 262
Foster, R.E. 163–164, 167, 169
Frindall, William 149
Fry, C.B. 135, 163
Fulkes, John 226

G
Ganteaume, A.G. 31–32
George V 107, 111
Gillingham, Canon F.H. 123
Girvan 3–4
Glasgow 261
Glenalmond College 13–14, 221
Gloucestershire 72–73

Goldfield, Sally 256
Gomez, G.E. 32
Goodall, G.T. 226
Goodall, Howard 226
Grace, E.M. 69, 73
Grace, G.F. 94
Grace, Dr W.G. 12, 60, 69–76, 86, 94, 253
Graveney, T.W. 134, 150
Green, Stephen 148–149, 255
Gregory, Ken 257
Grieveson, R.E. 117, 133
Grimmett, C.V. 109

H
Hale, Edward 58
Hambledon 57–64, 66
Hammond, John 63
Hammond, W.R. 107, 109, 111, 119, 133–135, 141–145, 178
Hampden, John 225
Hampshire 61–64
Harris, Lord 94, 110, 124
Harrison, John 259
Hart, John 20, 24
Harvey, Douglas 30–31
Haycock, Ralph 211
Haygarth, Arthur 57, 66, 80
Headley, George 33
Hendren, E. 109
Herbert, A.P. 116
Hessey, Nigel 258–259
Hide, Molly 9
Hilton, F.K. 87
Hirst, Christopher 43
Hobbs, Sir J.B. 75, 108–109
Hong Kong 211–218
Hornibrook, P.M. 109
Horton, Randolph 207

Howat, Agatha 11–13, 235
Howat, Anne (née Murdoch) 13, 14, 17–18, 21, 24, 25, 27, 28–30, 53–54, 223, 224, 233, 235, 250, 266
Howat, David 39, 223
Howat, Gerald
  books 8, 12, 32, 33, 37, 41, 48, 49–54, 121, 131, 132, 139–146, 171, 177, 222, 224, 228, 238–241, 262
  childhood 3–15
  education 4, 7–8, 13–15, 17–21
  grandfather see Selwyn Cooke
  house at North Moreton 54, 223, 247, 250
  journalism 234, 235–238, 240–241, 243–245
  membership of MCC 226, 236, 254–256
  posting to Trinidad 28–37
  RAF 21–31, 42, 53
  speaking engagements 261–264
  teaching 40–44, 46, 47–48, 50–51, 53–54, 222–223, 224–228, 229–234, 236
  wife see Howat, Anne
Howat, Gillian see Bossenger, Gillian
Howat, Michael 41, 53, 132, 134, 223–224, 247
Howat, Very Rev. Rudolph 4, 6, 9, 10–12, 13, 29, 235
Hughes, Thomas 77, 86, 95–96, 197–202, 232–233
Hunt, Alma 207–209
Hutchison, Horace 97
Hutton, Sir Leonard 21, 28, 33–34, 116–117, 119, 120, 144–146, 238–239

I
Ikin, J.T. 134–135
Imperial (International) Cricket Conference (ICC) 114–115
Ingleby-MacKenzie, A.C.D. 254
Iredale, Frank 166

J
Jackson, Sir Stanley 102–104
James I 185
James, C.L.R. 120, 239–240
Jardine, D.R. 140, 171–180
Jefferson, Thomas 190–193
Jessop, G.L. 163

K
Kane, Nick 260
Kelly College, Tavistock 39–44, 45, 50
King, Edith 152, 156
Kingsley, Rev. Charles 83–84
Knight, A.E. 169
Knight, R.V.D. 256, 257

L
Lacey, Sir Francis 75, 165–166
Larwood, Harold 135, 173, 174, 175, 178, 179
Laver, Frank 104
Lay, Norman 257
Lennox, Colonel 62, 68
Lillywhite, James 69–70, 164
Lindwall, R.R. 239
Lloyd, Marie 143
Locke, Greg 259
Lord, Thomas 57, 62
Lord's 57, 60, 66, 72–76, 115, 117, 131, 139, 148, 174, 198, 241, 253, 267
Lord Williams's School 224–228
Lucas, E.V. 110
Lyttelton, Alfred 94

M
Macartney, C.A. 203–204
Macdonald, Chris 259
MacDonald, Ramsay 112
Macdonald, Richard 259
MacDonell, A.G. 122
MacLagan, Myrtle 9
MacLaren, A.C. 163
Maidenhead 63
Mann, Sir Horace 65–66, 68
Manning, Cardinal Henry 87
Markham, Captain 61
Marriott, Harry 257
Marshall, Howard 123
Martin-Jenkins, Christopher 235
Marylebone Cricket Club (MCC) 32, 57–62, 65, 71, 72–76, 96, 110, 112, 113, 114–115, 117, 131, 132, 136, 141, 144, 164, 167–168, 176, 180, 192, 199, 215, 225–226, 241, 253–256, 257
Massy, Derek 249
Mathers, Helen 96–97
McGilvray, Alan 124
Meredith, George 91–92
Middlesex 57–60, 63, 70
Miles, Kaz 260
Miller, K.R. 214
Millar, David 20
Montgomery, Bishop Henry 80–82, 84
Mott, Sue 148
Murdoch, Anne *see* Howat, Anne
Murdoch, W.L. 94

N
Napier, Rev. J.R. 87

Index

Nehru, Pandit 112
Noble, M.A. 86, 167, 169
North Moreton 247–251, 259, 264
   Moreton Cricket Club 248–250, 257–260, 265
Nottingham 60–61
Nyren, John 59, 66
Nyren, Richard 63

O
Orlebar, Rev. Augustus 86
Oundle School 254
Oval 70, 76
Oxford University Press 240

P
Pares, Richard 19–20
Parsons, Canon J.H. 118, 121
Passmore, Freddie 265
Pataudi, Nawab of 215
Paynter, E. 178
Peake, W. 86
Perera, Anton 264
Philadelphia 263–264
Phillips, James 165–166
Pickles, Canon Hugh 134, 149–150
Pilcher, Graham 4–6, 14
Pilcher, Rosamund 4–6,
Ponsford, W.H. 107
Pope, A.V. 262
Pullin, A.W. 121
Puritanism 185–195
Pycroft, Rev. James 77–80, 82, 95, 96

R
Radley College 53–54, 221–223, 235–236
Ramadhin, Sonny 31, 32
Rashleigh, Rev. W. 86

Reeve, Dermot 216
Relf, A.E. 169–170
Rhodes, Wilfred 117
Rice, Jonathan 255–256
Roberts, Sir Denys 217
Roberts, Randal 99
Robertson-Glasgow, R.C. 120
Robinson, Emmott 117
Rowan-Thomson, Cdr Graeme 25
Rugby, Tennessee 200–202, 232–233
Ryder, Anthony 260

S
St Columba's School 221
St Helen's and St Katharine's School 228
St Paul's School 247
Scott, C.P. 119, 152
Sealy, J. E. D. 32
Second World War 113, 123–124, 129
Seymour, Gerald 132
Silk, D.R.W. 222, 224
Sinfield, R.A. 135
Singleton, Rev. Robert 221–222
Smith, E.J. 136
Smith, M.J.K. 244
Snow, J.A. 46
South Africa 115, 142, 215
Spurling, Richard 258
Squires, Sir John 100
Stanley, A.P. 198
Stead, Jeff 30
Stewart, M.J. 244
Stimpson, Michael 258
Stimpson, Paul 258
Stollmeyer, J.B. 32
Stollmeyer, V.H. 32
Studd, Rev. C.T. 86

Surrey 63, 70
Sussex 63, 64–65
Sutcliffe, H. 108, 117, 118
Swanton, E.W. 110, 115, 122–123, 136, 159–161, 171, 180, 215, 236, 241, 255

T
Taswell, Wg Cdr Harry 25
Tate, Maurice 107, 111, 174
Taylor, A.J.P 51–52
Test cricket 74, 104, 115–116, 133-134, 163–170, 216
  1930 series 107–112
  1932-1933 series 171–180
  Under-19s 243–245
Thackeray, William 95
Thame, 225, 226, 227
Thanet, Earl of 60
de Tocqueville, Alexis 192
Trent Bridge 243
Trinidad 32–37, 42, 203
Trinidad Leaseholds Ltd (TLL) 31, 35, 42, 203, 204
Trollope, Anthony 93–95
Trollope, Frances 192
Trueman, F.S. 28
Tummons, Peter 256
Tyldesley, J.T. 104, 163, 167

U
University of Western Kentucky (Western) 229–233

V
Valentine, B.H. 32
Vaughan, Michael 243–245
Verity, Hedley 9
Victorian England 77–88, 89, 222
Vincent, Major R.B. 121

W
Waddy, Canon E.F. 86
Wakelam, H.B.T. 123, 124
Walcott, Clyde 24, 32, 33
Walker, Matthew 243–244
Wardill, Ben 165–166
Washbrook, C. 239
Warner, Marina 139–140
Warner, Sir Pelham 60, 70, 102, 104, 108, 110–111, 114, 120, 122, 123, 131, 132, 137, 139–141, 163–170, 171–180, 198, 253–254
Weekes, E. de C. 32, 33
Welldon, Bishop 166
Westall, Rupert 40–42, 46
West Indies 203–205, 243–245
Whinney, Douglas 249, 265
Whitefield, George 187
Wickham, E.C. 83
Williams, Dr Eric 32–33, 35
Williams, Glenys 256
Williams, Lord 225
Wilson, Robert 250
Winchilsea, Earl of 57–58, 61, 62–63, 66, 68
Winter, Rev. A.H. 86
Woodcock, John 136–137, 236
Woodfull, W.M. 173, 175
Woolley, F.E. 108–109, 119
Wordsworth, Bishop Charles 82, 221
Worrell, Sir Frank 32
Wright, F.W. 87
Wright, Graeme 256
Wyatt, R.E.S. 137, 177

Y
Yardley, N.W.D. 118